THE NEW CAMBRIDGE SHAKESPEARE

GENERAL EDITOR
Brian Gibbons, *University of Münster*

ASSOCIATE GENERAL EDITOR
A. R. Braunmuller, *University of California, Los Angeles*

From the publication of the first volumes in 1984 the General Editor of the New Cambridge Shakespeare was Philip Brockbank and the Associate General Editors were Brian Gibbons and Robin Hood. From 1990 to 1994 the General Editor was Brian Gibbons and the Associate General Editors were A. R. Braunmuller and Robin Hood.

TWELFTH NIGHT

From review of first edition
'The combination of careful scholarship emphasising the inspiration and excitement of the theatrical experience, with the freshly edited text, should make this one of the most useful new texts of *Twelfth Night*.'
Theatre Journal

For this updated edition of *Twelfth Night*, Penny Gay has written a wholly new Introduction to this well-loved Shakespearean comedy. She stresses the play's theatricality, its elaborate linguistic games and its complex use of Ovidian myths. She analyses the play's delicate balance between romance and realism and its exploration of gender, sexuality and identity. In examining the stage history, Professor Gay suggests that contemporary critical theory could have much to offer twenty-first-century directors and actors. An updated reading list completes the edition.

THE NEW CAMBRIDGE SHAKESPEARE

TWELFTH NIGHT OR WHAT YOU WILL

Edited by
ELIZABETH STORY DONNO

With an Introduction by
PENNY GAY
University of Sydney

CAMBRIDGE
UNIVERSITY PRESS

PUBLISHED BY THE PRESS SYNDICATE OF THE UNIVERSITY OF CAMBRIDGE
The Pitt Building, Trumpington Street, Cambridge, United Kingdom

CAMBRIDGE UNIVERSITY PRESS
The Edinburgh Building, Cambridge CB2 2RU, UK
40 West 20th Street, New York, NY 10011–4211, USA
477 Williamstown Road, Port Melbourne, VIC 3207, Australia
Ruiz de Alarcón 13, 28014 Madrid, Spain
Dock House, The Waterfront, Cape Town 8001, South Africa

http://www.cambridge.org

First published 1985
Reprinted 1998 (with revisions)
Eleventh printing 2003
Updated edition 2004

Printed in the United Kingdom at the University Press, Cambridge

Library of Congress catalogue card number: 84–28482

British Library cataloguing in publication data
Shakespeare, William
[Twelfth night]. Twelfth night or What you
will. — (The New Cambridge Shakespeare)
I. Title   II. Donno, Elizabeth Story
III. Twelfth night or What you will
822.3'3   PR2837

ISBN 0 521 82792 2 hardcover
ISBN 0 521 53514 X paperback

THE NEW CAMBRIDGE SHAKESPEARE

The *New Cambridge Shakespeare* succeeds *The New Shakespeare* which began publication in 1921 under the general editorship of Sir Arthur Quiller-Couch and John Dover Wilson, and was completed in the 1960s, with the assistance of G. I. Duthie, Alice Walker, Peter Ure and J. C. Maxwell. *The New Shakespeare* itself followed upon *The Cambridge Shakespeare*, 1863–6, edited by W. G. Clark, J. Glover and W. A. Wright.

The New Shakespeare won high esteem both for its scholarship and for its design, but shifts of critical taste and insight, recent Shakespearean research, and a changing sense of what is important in our understanding of the plays, have made it necessary to re-edit and redesign, not merely to revise, the series.

The *New Cambridge Shakespeare* aims to be of value to a new generation of playgoers and readers who wish to enjoy fuller access to Shakespeare's poetic and dramatic art. While offering ample academic guidance, it reflects current critical interests and is more attentive than some earlier editions have been to the realisation of the plays on the stage, and to their social and cultural settings. The text of each play has been freshly edited, with textual data made available to those users who wish to know why and how one published text differs from another. Although modernised, the edition conserves forms that appear to be expressive and characteristically Shakespearean, and it does not attempt to disguise the fact that the plays were written in a language other than that of our own time.

Illustrations are usually integrated into the critical and historical discussion of the play and include some reconstructions of early performances by C. Walter Hodges. Some editors have also made use of the advice and experience of Maurice Daniels, for many years a member of the Royal Shakespeare Company.

Each volume is addressed to the needs and problems of a particular text, and each therefore differs in style and emphasis from others in the series.

PHILIP BROCKBANK
General Editor

v

CONTENTS

ILLUSTRATIONS

PREFACE TO FIRST EDITION

The editor of a Shakespeare text who is responsive to traditions must at once acknowledge his indebtedness to other editors, beginning with the earliest and continuing down to the most recent. M. W. Black and M. A. Shaaber in *Shakespeare's Seventeenth-Century Editors* (1937) alerted me to early concern for the text, but I was very impressed by the care and attention that eighteenth-century editors, so frequently ill-treated in accounts of historical scholarship, gave to textual interpretation through their concern with pointing. I hope that the collation in this volume shows, in some measure, my respect for their efforts. Of more or less recent editions, the New Shakespeare volumes, G. L. Kittredge's fully annotated texts of sixteen of Shakespeare's plays and the many fine examples in the Arden series were of great value to me.

Any acknowledgement must extend to many fellow Shakespeareans for contributions either in published form or in conversation, and, for the latter, I am grateful most specifically to Hallett Smith and S. F. Johnson. Philip Brockbank, the General Editor of this series, and Robin Hood, the Associate General Editor most closely concerned with this volume, gave me much good advice and were unfailingly responsive to my queries. I also wish to acknowledge aid and assistance from my husband Daniel J. Donno, who invariably reacted sharply to a (non-Shakespearean) hysteron proteron or a Sir Tobyan wayward locution.

The Henry E. Huntington Library, where I did most of my research, afforded me not only its excellent collection of Shakespeare texts but also the help of its genial staff. To this institution I am also grateful for permission to reproduce some illustrations.

E.S.D.

Huntington Library, California   1985

PREFACE

In writing a new Introduction to the New Cambridge edition of *Twelfth Night*, I am honoured to follow in the footsteps of the fine Renaissance scholar Elizabeth Story Donno. I have been greatly assisted by advice from the General Editors, Brian Gibbons and A.R. Braunmuller, and from Cambridge University Press editor Sarah Stanton. I am delighted to acknowledge helpful conversations with colleagues in the English Department at the University of Sydney, particularly Liam Semler and Geoff Williams. My family – my husband, two daughters, and my mother – have been acute critical readers and theatre-goers, as well as offering unflagging support. I also particularly thank Ralph Alan Cohen and the company of Shenandoah Shakespeare for their hospitality and inspiring performances.

Penny Gay

2003

University of Sydney

ABBREVIATIONS AND CONVENTIONS

1. Shakespeare's plays

The abbreviated titles of Shakespeare's plays have been modified from those used in the *Harvard Concordance to Shakespeare*. All quotations and line references to plays other than *Twelfth Night*, unless otherwise specified, are to G. Blakemore Evans (ed.), *The Riverside Shakespeare*, 1974, on which the *Concordance* is based.

Ado	*Much Ado about Nothing*
Ant.	*Antony and Cleopatra*
AWW	*All's Well That Ends Well*
AYLI	*As You Like It*
Cor.	*Coriolanus*
Cym.	*Cymbeline*
Err.	*The Comedy of Errors*
Ham.	*Hamlet*
1H4	*The First Part of King Henry the Fourth*
2H4	*The Second Part of King Henry the Fourth*
H5	*King Henry the Fifth*
1H6	*The First Part of King Henry the Sixth*
2H6	*The Second Part of King Henry the Sixth*
3H6	*The Third Part of King Henry the Sixth*
H8	*King Henry the Eighth*
JC	*Julius Caesar*
John	*King John*
LLL	*Love's Labour's Lost*
Lear	*King Lear*
Mac.	*Macbeth*
MM	*Measure for Measure*
MND	*A Midsummer Night's Dream*
MV	*The Merchant of Venice*
Oth.	*Othello*
Per.	*Pericles*
R2	*King Richard the Second*
R3	*King Richard the Third*
Rom.	*Romeo and Juliet*
Shr.	*The Taming of the Shrew*
STM	*Sir Thomas More*
Temp.	*The Tempest*
TGV	*The Two Gentlemen of Verona*
Tim.	*Timon of Athens*
Tit.	*Titus Andronicus*
TN	*Twelfth Night*
TNK	*The Two Noble Kinsmen*

Tro.	*Troilus and Cressida*
Wiv.	*The Merry Wives of Windsor*
WT	*The Winter's Tale*

2. Editions and general references

Abbott	E. A. Abbott, *A Shakespearian Grammar*, 1901, first published 1869 (reference is to numbered paragraphs)
Alexander	*William Shakespeare: The Complete Works*, ed. Peter Alexander, 1951
Ard.	*Twelfth Night*, ed. J. M. Lothian and T. W. Craik, 1975 (Arden Shakespeare)
Cam.	*The Works of William Shakespeare*, ed. W. G. Clark, J. Glover and W. A. Wright, 1863–6 (Cambridge Shakespeare)
Capell	*Mr William Shakespeare his Comedies, Histories, and Tragedies*, ed. Edward Capell, IV [1768]
Collier	*The Works of William Shakespeare*, ed. John Payne Collier, 1842–4
Collier²	*The Plays of Shakespeare*, ed. John Payne Collier, 1853
conj.	conjecture
Dent	R. W. Dent, *Shakespeare's Proverbial Language: An Index*, 1981 (reference is to numbered proverbs)
Douai MS.	Douai MS. 7.87, Douai Public Library (contains transcripts of six plays by Shakespeare, including *Twelfth Night*. See G. Blakemore Evans, 'The Douai Manuscript – six Shakespearean transcripts (1694–95)', *PQ* 41 (1962), 158–72)
Dyce	*The Works of William Shakespeare*, ed. Alexander Dyce, 1857
Dyce²	*The Works of William Shakespeare*, ed. Alexander Dyce, 1891, first published 1864–7
ELH	*ELH: A Journal of English Literary History*
ELN	*English Language Notes*
ES	*English Studies*
F	*Mr William Shakespeares Comedies, Histories, & Tragedies*, 1623 (First Folio)
F2	*Mr William Shakespeares Comedies, Histories, & Tragedies*, 1632 (Second Folio)
F3	*Mr William Shakespeares Comedies, Histories, & Tragedies*, 1664 (Third Folio)
F4	*Mr William Shakespeares Comedies, Histories, & Tragedies*, 1685 (Fourth Folio)
Furness	*Twelfth Night, or What You Will*, ed. Horace Howard Furness, 1901 (New Variorum)
Halliwell	*The Works of William Shakespeare*, ed. James O. Halliwell, 1853–65
Hanmer	*The Works of Shakespear*, ed. Thomas Hanmer, 1743–4
Johnson	*The Plays of William Shakespear*, ed. Samuel Johnson, 1765
Kittredge	*Sixteen Plays of Shakespeare*, ed. George Lyman Kittredge, 1946, first published 1939
Kökeritz	Helge Kökeritz, *Shakespeare's Pronunciation*, 1953
Linthicum	M. Channing Linthicum, *Costume in the Drama of Shakespeare and his Contemporaries*, 1936

Luce	*Twelfth Night: or, What You Will*, ed. Morton Luce, rev. edn 1929, first published 1906 (Arden Shakespeare)
Mahood	*Twelfth Night*, ed. M. M. Mahood, 1968 (New Penguin Shakespeare)
Malone	*The Plays and Poems of William Shakespeare*, ed. Edmond Malone, 1790
MLN	*Modern Language Notes*
MP	*Modern Philology*
Nashe	Thomas Nashe, *Works*, ed. Ronald B. McKerrow, 5 vols., 1904–10, rev. F. P. Wilson, 1958
N&Q	*Notes and Queries*
NS	*Twelfth Night or What You Will*, ed. Arthur Quiller-Couch and John Dover Wilson, 1930, rev. edn 1949 (New Shakespeare)
ODEP	*Oxford Dictionary of English Proverbs*, ed. F. P. Wilson, 1970
OED	*Oxford English Dictionary*
Onions	C. T. Onions, *A Shakespeare Glossary*, 1949, first published 1911
PBSA	*Papers of the Bibliographical Society of America*
Pope	*The Works of Shakespear*, ed. Alexander Pope, 1723–5
PQ	*Philological Quarterly*
Rann	*The Dramatic Works of Shakespeare*, ed. Joseph Rann, 1786–[94]
RES	*Review of English Studies*
Rowe	*The Works of Mr William Shakespear*, ed. Nicholas Rowe, 1709
Rowe[3]	*The Works of Mr William Shakespear*, ed. Nicholas Rowe, 1714
SB	*Studies in Bibliography*
Schmidt	Alexander Schmidt, *Shakespeare-Lexicon*, 2 vols., 1962, first published 1874
SD	stage direction
Seng	Peter J. Seng, *The Vocal Songs in the Plays of Shakespeare: A Critical History*, 1967
SH	speech heading
Sisson	C. J. Sisson, *New Readings in Shakespeare*, 2 vols., 1956
SQ	*Shakespeare Quarterly*
SR	*A Transcript of the Registers of the Company of Stationers, 1554–1640*, ed. Edward Arber, 5 vols., 1875–94
S.St.	*Shakespeare Studies*
S.Sur.	*Shakespeare Survey*
Staunton	*The Plays of Shakespeare*, ed. Howard Staunton, 1866, first published 1858–60
STC	*A Short-Title Catalogue of Books Printed in England, Scotland, & Ireland, and of English Books Printed Abroad, 1475–1640*, compiled by A. W. Pollard and G. R. Redgrave, 1956, first published 1926; 2nd edn, rev. W. A. Jackson, F. S. Ferguson and Katherine F. Pantzer, 1976–
subst.	substantively
sugg.	suggestion
Theobald	*The Works of Shakespeare*, ed. Lewis Theobald, 1733
Tilley	M. P. Tilley, *A Dictionary of the Proverbs in England in the Sixteenth and Seventeenth Centuries*, 1950 (reference is to numbered proverbs)
TLS	*The Times Literary Supplement*
Tyrwhitt	Thomas Tyrwhitt, *Observations and Conjectures upon Some Passages of Shakespeare*, 1766
Upton	John Upton, *Critical Observations on Shakespeare*, 1746

Var. 1821	*The Plays and Poems of William Shakespeare,* ed. James Boswell, 1821 (3rd Variorum)
Walker, W. S.	W. S. Walker, *A Critical Examination of the Text of Shakespeare,* 3 vols., 1860
Warburton	*The Works of Shakespear,* ed. William Warburton, 1747

All references to the Bible are to the Geneva version, 1560. All references to classical texts are to the Loeb Library editions. Full references to other works cited in the Commentary in abbreviated form may be found in the Reading List at p. 169 below.

INTRODUCTION

Date and early performances

On 2 February 1602, the feast of Candlemas, a young lawyer of the Middle Temple called John Manningham wrote in his diary:

At our feast wee had a play called 'Twelve Night, or What You Will', much like the *Commedy of Errores*, or *Menechmi* in Plautus, but most like and neere to that in Italian called *Inganni*. A good practise in it to make the Steward beleeve his Lady Widdow was in love with him, by counterfeyting a letter as from his Lady in generall termes, telling him what she liked best in him, and prescribing his gesture in smiling, his aparaile, &c, and then when he came to practise making him beleeve they tooke him to be mad.[1]

A play suitable for the period of winter feasts between Christmas and Lent, *Twelfth Night* was also performed at court at Easter 1618 and Candlemas 1623. Twelfth Night itself is 6 January, the feast of the Epiphany, or the visit of the Three Kings to the Christ child. Leslie Hotson, in an extended piece of literary and historical detective work, argued that the play had its first performance before the Queen and an Italian visitor, Virginio Orsini, Duke of Bracciano, on Twelfth Night 1601.[2] Certainly the Lord Chamberlain's Men (Shakespeare's company) performed at court on that occasion, but although there are many details of the preparations, the actual play is frustratingly unnamed. We do know that, in keeping with the festive spirit of the occasion, the play chosen was to be one 'that shalbe best furnished with rich apparell, have greate variety and change of Musicke and daunces, and of a Subiect that may be most pleasing to her Maiestie'.[3] This is not a bad description of *Twelfth Night*, with its two 'great house' settings, its theme of romantic love, and its many musical interludes; and although it does not feature dances (as *Much Ado About Nothing* does), the extended joke on types of dance at the end of 1.3 might have amused the Queen, an enthusiastic dancer. Its three strong female characters, Viola, Olivia and Maria, who drive the plot, might also have appealed to the ageing 'Gloriana', Queen Elizabeth I. The clown's name, Feste, apparently Shakespeare's invention, also connects the play with festive occasions. And as E. S. Donno has remarked, the play's alternative title, 'What You Will' – that is, whatever you like – may 'evoke the mood of twelfth-night holiday: a time for sentiment, frivolity, pranks and misrule'.[4]

[1] John Manningham, *Diary*, quoted in Geoffrey Bullough, *Narrative and Dramatic Sources of Shakespeare, II: The Comedies, 1597–1603*, 1958, p. 269.
[2] J. L. Hotson, *The First Night of Twelfth Night*, 1954.
[3] Hotson, *The First Night*, p. 15, quoting the Lord Chamberlain's memorandum.
[4] Elizabeth Story Donno, Introduction to the New Cambridge edition of *Twelfth Night*, 1985, p. 4. She comments further that the repeated catch-phrase 'That's all one', 'adds to the air of lightheartedness and inconsequence proper to a comedy whose subtitle is What You Will.' (p. 5).

1

1   *Twelfth Night* as presented in Middle Temple Hall, London, on 2 February 1602, by C. Walter
     Hodges
a   Act 2, Scene 5: 'What employment have we here?'

Given the internal evidence that the play was probably written in 1600 or 1601,[1] a performance at court on Twelfth Night 1601 is not impossible. But there is nothing to sug-

[1] The two references to the 'sophy' or Shah of Persia (2.5.149 and 3.4.236) may reflect the contemporary
interest in Sir Anthony Sherley's accounts of his travels in Persia in 1599 (published 1600 and 1601). In
3.2.62–3 Maria refers to 'the new map with the augmentation of the Indies': this is probably Edward
Wright's *Hydrographiae Descriptio*, published 1599, one of the first to use rhumb-lines; it shows the East
Indies in greater detail than previously.

b Act 3, Scene 4: 'There's no remedy, sir.
He will fight with you for's oath sake.'

gest that this would have been the first night – nor that the performance that
Manningham saw the following year in the Middle Temple Hall was the premiere.[1] It is
safest to assume that the play had its first performance at the Globe in 1600 or 1601.
Manningham's memorandum shows that it was early adapted for temporary indoor
stages, and T. J. King established in 1971 that 'the play is well suited for performance in
front of an unlocalized screen with two doorways, such as those at the Middle Temple'.[2]

[1] Anthony Arlidge, *Shakespeare and the Prince of Love*, 2000.
[2] T. J. King, *Shakespearean Staging, 1599–1642*, 1971, p. 98. It is equally possible that the play was staged
   at the western (high table) end of the hall, as were those in Cambridge college halls in this period: see Alan
   H. Nelson, *Early Cambridge Theatres: College, University, and Town Stages, 1464–1720*, 1994. King's
   schema of the play's entrances and exits using only two doors (whether screen or high table end) is shown
   on pp. 99–115 of his book.

The play's sources

When Manningham wrote that *Twelfth Night* was 'most like . . . that in Italian called *Inganni*', he may have confused Nicolò Secchi's 1547 play of that title with *Gl'Ingannati* ('The Deceived') written and performed by the Academy of the Intronati in Siena in 1531 (published 1537, 1554). There is no known contemporary English translation of *Gl'Ingannati*,[1] but it is possible that some version of it was performed by one of the Italian companies that visited England in the second half of the sixteenth century, and that Manningham and Shakespeare saw it; or that Shakespeare read the play or the version made in French by Charles Estienne, *Les Abusés* (published 1543). In this play, rambling and dramatically simple though it is, there is a basic plot congruence with *Twelfth Night* in the story of the young girl who disguises herself as a page in order to be near the man she loves, finds herself wooing another on his behalf and in turn becomes the object of that woman's desire. There is a twin brother, who arrives after many years' adventures to look for his sister (and father), and is willingly seduced by the Olivia-figure. More significantly, there are at least four scenes that are strikingly close to scenes in Shakespeare: parallels to Orsino's and Viola's conversations in 1.4 and 2.4; another to Olivia's declaration of love to 'Cesario' in 3.1; and the threat of violence by Orsino to Viola in 5.1 when he believes his servant is unfaithful to him. However, the meeting between the twins in Shakespeare, 'One face, one voice, one habit, and two persons' (5.1.200), a climax which produces such wonder and delight onstage and in the theatre audience, is not in *Gl'Ingannati*: in that play the heroine Lelia changes back into her woman's clothes for the final dénouement.

Shakespeare's principal source for *Twelfth Night* was undoubtedly the prose narrative version of *Gl'Ingannati*, 'Apolonius and Silla', which formed part of Barnabe Riche's popular book published in 1581 (reprinted 1583, 1594), *Riche his Farewell to Military Profession*: 'conteining verie pleasaunt discourses fit for a peacable tyme. Gathered together for the onely delight of the courteous Gentlewomen bothe of England and Irelande, For whose onely pleasure they were collected together, And unto whom they are directed and dedicated.'[2] In fact the narrator frequently addresses remarks to his 'gentlewomen' auditors in the course of the story; this habit marks a major difference between the two texts' treatment of the romance narrative, particularly in their conception of the heroine.

Both Riche's story and Shakespeare's play centre on the adventures of a young woman who disguises herself as a boy in order to be close to her unknowing beloved, a powerful and self-absorbed duke. In both the heroine must woo the duke's aloof mistress – and in both the lady falls for the messenger rather than the absent suitor. Further, the heroine (Silla in Riche, Viola in *Twelfth Night*) has a brother (Silvio, equivalent to Sebastian in *Twelfth Night*) to whom she is virtually identical. (In Riche

---

[1] An edited translation can be found in Bullough, *Sources*, pp. 286–339. A more recent discussion of the play's complex genealogy can be found in Louise George Clubb, 'Italian stories on the stage', Alexander Leggatt (ed.), *The Cambridge Companion to Shakespearean Comedy*, 2002, pp. 38–42.

[2] Bullough, *Sources*, p. 344. Bullough reprints the whole tale, as does Ard.

the brother is already absent 'servyng in the warres' in Africa.) In due course he turns up, not knowing that his sister is in the same city and disguised as him, and he is quickly wooed and won by the lady (Julina/Olivia). After many misunderstandings and some grief, the truth emerges, and each of the siblings is happily paired off in marriage with the right partner.

The differences between these two narratives – one a story that was probably read aloud in a domestic context, the other a play designed for performance in a public theatre – might be characterised as embodying the different 'textures' of prose and poetry. Riche's tale is gossipy – hence his appeals to his 'gentlewomen' listeners: it has elements of sexual sensationalism such as can be found in gossip magazines today. In Riche's tale, the heroine's adventures begin on board ship when, after rebuffing an offer of marriage from the captain, she is threatened with rape (she is still at this point dressed as a girl, but one of lower class, and is accompanied by a faithful servant posing as her brother). The storm and shipwreck arrive just in time to save her from killing herself to save her honour. On gaining land she disguises herself in male clothing 'to prevent a number of injuries that might bee proffered to a woman that was lefte in her case'.[1] When her brother Silvio turns up and is 'entertained' by Julina, that one night – described in somewhat salacious detail – results in Julina's pregnancy. Silvio, unknowing, sets off on his travels again. And when the disguised Silla protests in the dénouement that 'he' is incapable of getting a woman with child, she proves her point by 'loosing his garmentes doune to his stomacke, and shew[ing] Julina his breastes and pretie teats'.[2] Silvio in due course hearing of his sister, now happily married, is 'striken with greate remorse to make Julina amendes, understanding her to bee a noble ladie and was lefte defamed to the worlde through his default'.[3]

Riche's story has a glamorous air of worldliness: sex and class are emphasised in a fairly straightforward way as motivators of people's behaviour. Shakespeare's play, so close to Riche in plot, has by contrast a poetic and anti-realistic air. 'Most wonderful!', as Olivia exclaims, on seeing the 'identical' twins finally on stage together (5.1.209). Importantly, Viola never removes her male clothing. At every point in the play where Viola's physical sex could clarify the situation, Shakespeare opts instead to emphasise through complex and suggestive poetry the infinite complications of both gender and sexuality.

Nicolò Secchi's Gl'Inganni (1547) also features 'identical' male/female twins, both dressed in male attire, the girl secretly in love with a noble youth, whose sister Portia is in turn in love with her, thinking her to be a boy, Ruberto. The brother and sister have previously rediscovered each other, so 'Ruberto' is able to persuade her brother to substitute for her in the bed of Portia; consequently, Portia has become pregnant. Bullough prints a selection of dialogue from this play which has similarities to the 'Patience on a monument' discussion between Viola and Orsino (2.4). As Bullough points out, 'Twelfth Night belongs to a tradition in which the Plautine twins become

[1] Ibid., p. 350.
[2] Ibid., p. 361.
[3] Ibid., p. 363.

differentiated in sex, thus affording a greater variety of intrigue' in both plays and prose stories.[1] There are, thus, several analogues to the play, but Riche's popular story (itself part of this tradition, and conveniently in English) is clearly the major source for Shakespeare's work.

Imaginary geography and stage space

The visual identity of the boy-girl twins is one of the signs that the play belongs to the genre of romance. The first ten minutes of the play chart a delicate course into this genre. The audience sees and hears a rich and noble young man, surrounded by attentive musicians and servants, uttering his own mellifluous variations on the clichés of Petrarchan love poetry:

> O when mine eyes did see Olivia first,
> Methought she purged the air of pestilence;
> That instant was I turned into a hart,
> And my desires like fell and cruel hounds
> E'er since pursue me.

(1.1.19–23)

> Away before me to sweet beds of flowers:
> Love-thoughts lie rich when canopied with bowers.

(1.1.40–1)

We could be anywhere in the artificial world of Renaissance romance. The next scene opens with an equally romantic image of a shipwrecked maiden, often appearing with long flowing hair and wearing the remains of a very feminine dress (as did Judi Dench in John Barton's 1969 RSC production). The scene's first words invoke the distant lands of classical romance:

VIOLA What country, friends, is this?
CAPTAIN This is Illyria, lady.

Illyria (though it may evoke *illusion* and *lyrical* to modern ears) is in fact the ancient name for that part of the eastern Adriatic coastal region north of the gulf of Corinth. It was, however, also noted for its pirates during the Renaissance (see note at 3.3.9–11), and Orsino accuses Antonio of being a 'notable' one (5.1.58). The Royal Shakespeare Company's 1987 production (director Bill Alexander) made a rare foray into realistic representation of this geo-political setting: the action took place in a recognisably Hellenic village square, all whitewashed houses; and Antony Sher's Malvolio was costumed as some kind of Orthodox church functionary, who had lost the respect of a decadent society.

Viola's response to the Captain's information is a decision to disguise herself, indicating an awareness of potential danger (like Riche's Silla); and she thus becomes an inhabitant of a liminal zone, an unplaceable figure. Cast up from a vaguely Italianate

[1] Ibid., p. 270.

2   Antony Sher as Malvolio, Jim Hooper as Fabian, Roger Allam as Sir Toby, Pippa Guard as Maria,
    Royal Shakespeare Company, 1987. Act 3, Scene 4: 'Which way is he, in the name of sanctity?'

'Messaline' on shore in Illyria,[1] abutting the Turkish empire, she elects to appear as
neither male nor female, a 'eunuch' – a sexual and therefore social neuter. When next
we see her, however, Viola is 'Cesario', a young male page within a European-style pattern of dependence on a great lord. Further, the 'town' which the characters traverse
is recognisably English – modelled on London, with its famous buildings, great houses,
gardens, orchards and 'south suburbs' where there is a good lodging-house, 'the
Elephant' (Shakespeare here flatters a local pub close to the Globe (see note at 3.3.39)).
Orsino's court is 'due west' of Olivia's house (3.1.119); it can be imagined as being near
the grand palaces of Westminster, Whitehall and St James. Standing on the stage of the
Globe theatre, Viola can say 'Then westward ho!' and knowingly invoke the cry of the
Thames watermen to be heard just outside the walls of the theatre. The theatre's stage
was oriented towards the north-east, so that Olivia and Viola might be imagined gesturing towards the stage-left door in the tiring-house wall during this exchange. These
local references might have created the shock of the familiar in the play's first audiences: where a 'romance' such as Riche's is by definition exotic, other-worldly, the theatre's transformation of the tale interweaves familiar English features with the exotic
dream-like atmosphere. The minor role of Antonio, Sebastian's loving friend (and

[1] Trevor Nunn's 1996 film somewhat confusingly locates the action in Sicily (Sebastian's guidebook is the
   fictional *Baedeker's Illyria from Randazzo to Mistretta*); the film was actually shot on location in Cornwall,
   where the weather is very different.

Shakespeare's invention) has the important function in the play of anchoring this realistic quality, with his talk of Sebastian's seeing this imaginary town – part London, part strange and distant – and spending money lent by Antonio on 'some toy / You have desire to purchase' (3.3.44–5).

The play's imagined world is represented by the semiotic use of stage space. The Globe had a deep and wide thrust stage, with its two doors of entrance in the tiring-house wall upstage; the same configuration could easily be re-created in Middle Temple Hall or the halls of royal palaces. A particularly important function of the two doors is to provide amusing (and sometimes confusing) near-misses for the encounters of the twins with each other or with those who are interested in them. This is a dramatic technique that Shakespeare had already energetically exploited in *The Comedy of Errors*, with its two sets of twins and its continual opportunities for farcical misidentification. In *Twelfth Night* a more serious (though still essentially comic) situation is explored, largely because the difference of gender identity in each twin produces different social behaviour, despite the fact that they look like one individual.

Tim Fitzpatrick has proposed a revision of T. J. King's theoretical staging of the play using the two doors, but with a more precisely delineated sense of this semiotic dramatic function. Alert to internal stage directions in the text, Fitzpatrick suggests the stage-left door always signifies 'outwards' from the current scene (e.g. towards the town), the stage-right door 'inwards' (e.g. into a house).[1] Olivia, for example, might regularly use the stage-right door: this would reflect her 'cloistered' status in her house – except for her exit with Sebastian and the Priest to the 'chantry by', a move outwards for her, physically and emotionally (4.3.24). In Act 5's appearance of both the twins on stage, this schema would place Viola downstage left, with Orsino upstage to her right (they have come from his house to visit Olivia). He would thus be shielding the view of her from Sebastian who would also enter from stage left, after the procession of wounded knights Toby and Andrew (who are led off to the surgeon 'inwards', stage right). Olivia would remain in her usual area, stage right throughout, so that she would be the first to see the alignment of the twins, Sebastian upstage, Viola downstage. During Orsino's and Olivia's exclamations Sebastian would come forward to stand downstage opposite Viola for their recognition dialogue, thus ending up close to Olivia just as Viola is to Orsino, in a symmetrical and symbolic pattern across the front of the stage. The play's romance plot is perfectly completed, though the play itself is not finished. (This is, of course, only one possible staging of this scene on the Elizabethan stage. Tim Carroll's production for the new Globe (London, 2002) used the two doors differently and produced more broad comedy during the final revelations: Viola hid behind a stage pillar when she first spotted Sebastian; Orsino addressed 'Your master quits you' (5.1.300) to the wrong twin, and was comically embarrassed at his mistake.)

---

[1] Tim Fitzpatrick, 'Stage management, dramaturgy and spatial semiotics in Shakespeare's dialogue', *Theatre Research International* 23, 1 (1999), 1–23.

Puritans and clowns

In 3.4.108–9 Shakespeare gives the minor character Fabian the line, 'If this were played upon a stage now, I could condemn it as an improbable fiction.' The audience's attention is deliberately drawn to the play itself and its artifice, although what Fabian is referring to is in fact the gulling of Malvolio in the sub-plot of the play. This story is not in the romance sources but is purely Shakespeare's invention, and it draws on elements of the Elizabethan world which he and his audience knew (hence Manningham's delight in the 'good practise' of tricking the steward). And as is customary in Shakespearean comedy, the dramatic themes of the main romance plot are reflected, played in different registers and ironically varied in the prose comedy and farce of the sub-plot.

Sir Toby Belch, for example: as a literal embodiment of the 'good life', that is, bodily pleasure, he represents an alternative idea of 'virtue' to the puritanism of Malvolio; he gives it a more generous epicurean meaning. At the end of his very first scene, encouraging Sir Andrew to dance, he cries, 'Is it a world to hide virtues in?' (1.3.107). When Malvolio reproves his roistering, Sir Toby replies indignantly, 'Dost thou think because thou art virtuous there shall be no more cakes and ale?' (2.3.97–9). Yet perhaps the play's most disturbing line is that of Malvolio's final exit: 'I'll be revenged on the whole pack of you!' (5.1.355). The repressive anti-life forces that Malvolio (in Italian, 'ill-will') embodies remain a real threat to the play's romantic optimism about 'golden time' (5.1.359), and remind us instead of the realities of the 'every day', in which there are periods when pleasure is denied. As Feste sententiously says, 'pleasure will be paid, one time or another' (2.4.68).

In Catholic European culture, the *topos* of Carnival versus Lent had been common for centuries.[1] Carnival, or Mardi Gras, was that period immediately preceding the forty days of self-denial of Lent, which in turn was relieved by Easter and the arrival of spring. Performances of *Twelfth Night* at Candlemas, 2 February, would remind the audience of the imminence of Lent. Sir Toby and his fellow-roisterers, with their creed of 'cakes and ale', symbolise a refusal of the self-denial required by this religious tradition. Sir Toby can also be seen as a Lord of Misrule,[2] the disruptive figure allowed temporary reign at feast-days, and he is therefore a problematic presence to one who is identified by Maria as 'a kind of puritan' (2.3.119).

Malvolio, Olivia's household steward, represents not only the anti-flesh asceticism of the allegorical figure of Lent, but also the very real spread of such attitudes at the time when increasing numbers of Elizabethans were critical of the imperfectly reformed Church of England, and were looking to establish a 'purer' religion and pol-

---

[1] For discussion of the critical theory of carnival, particularly as it applies to Shakespearean drama, see pp. 34–5 below.

[2] '[I]n the feaste of Christmas, there was in the kinges house, wheresoever hee was lodged, at the Feast of Christmas, a Lord of Misrule, or Maister of merry disports, and the like had yee in the house of every noble man, of honor, or good worshippe . . . These Lordes beginning their rule on Alhollon [All-Hallows] Eve, continued the same till . . . Candlemas day: In all which space there were fine and subtle disguisinges, Maskes and Mummeries . . .' John Stow, *A Survey of London*, reprinted from the text of 1603, ed. Charles Lethbridge Kingsford, 2 vols., 1908, vol. 1, p. 97.

3   Maerten van Cleve, Lent surprising revellers at a carnival meal

ity, cleansed of all the old Catholic practices. Within three decades of the first performance of *Twelfth Night* the Puritan party had made powerful inroads in Parliament;
Oliver Cromwell's English Revolution was the upshot, which culminated in the public beheading of the ritualist Anglican King Charles I in 1649. Ben Jonson satirises the
religious Puritan in the figure of Zeal-of-the-Land Busy in *Bartholomew Fair* (1614):
a hypocritical epicure who speaks a preacher's jargon, he does not have the psychological or social complexity of Malvolio, who is described as only 'sometimes . . . a kind
of puritan'(2.3.119). Maria goes on to qualify this epithet:

The devil a puritan that he is, or anything constantly but a time-pleaser, an affectioned ass, that
cons state without book and utters it by great swarths. The best persuaded of himself: so
crammed (as he thinks) with excellencies, that it is his grounds of faith that all that look on him
love him . . .

(2.3.124–8)

The attack on Malvolio is a familiar comic theme, the humiliation of a pompous ass
who thinks he is better than he is. For the time being only – and for pleasing relevance
to the play's first audience – is he represented by the word 'puritan'. In fact Malvolio
was played throughout the eighteenth and nineteenth centuries as a self-satisfied
'Castilian': Robert Bensley began with 'an air of Spanish loftiness' and metamorphosed into a manic Quixotic figure under the influence of his delusion. A century
later, Henry Irving was playing in the same visual style, but hinting at 'low birth', and
a sense of inferiority that culminated in a tragic humiliation. He exited from the letter

scene (2.5) 'not with a pompous swaggering strut, [but] . . . with his face buried in his hands, strangely moved, overwhelmed with his good fortune'.[1] Laurence Olivier, in Gielgud's 1955 production at the Shakespeare Memorial Theatre, was possibly the earliest to assume Puritan costume – and an obviously lower-class origin – in a more socially realistic Illyria.

The steward of a rich household was highest in status among the servants, eating at his own table in the hall. His obligations, as set down in a memorandum of 1595, were

in civil sort . . . [to] reprehend and correct the negligent and disordered persons, and reform them by his grave admonitions and vigilant eye over them, the riotous, the contentious, and quarrelous persons of any degree . . . the frequenters of tabling, carding, and dicing in corners and at untimely hours and seasons. . . .[2]

Clearly Malvolio is within his rights in reprimanding the revellers in the 'kitchen scene' (2.3). But there is also evidently a history of tension between Malvolio and Feste – who makes his living by begging tips from whomever he entertains with his wit or his music. Malvolio never finds him entertaining: almost his first speech is 'I marvel your ladyship takes delight in such a barren rascal' (1.5.67). These words will come back to haunt Malvolio when Feste invokes the whirligig of time to 'bring in his revenges' (5.1.354).

What is set up in this exchange in Feste and Malvolio's first scene is a professional battle for the attention and approval of the lady of the house. Will she follow a Malvolian regime of repression, as she has done since the death of her brother – reported in 1.1.26–32 ('like a cloistress she will veilèd walk') – and as we see her, attended by Malvolio, in her first appearance (1.5.26)? Or will she allow herself to respond to the potential in the wit displayed by Feste in the same scene, which encourages her to leave off her too protracted mourning by pointing out its irrationality (1.5.54–9)?

Significantly, Malvolio is absent from the stage when Olivia first meets 'Cesario' and decides to opt for the personal metamorphosis of romance ('Fate, show thy force; ourselves we do not owe', 1.5.265). It is arguable that Malvolio represents not only 'a kind of puritan', but the figure of the absent father or brother who would normally control the behaviour of the women of the household. Fortuitously, he is the most powerful male in a house nominally run by a young woman who has no husband, father or brother to take on the role of head of the household and holder of the purse-strings.[3] Malvolio's professional desire for control, evident in his ineffectual protests

---

[1] Gāmini Salgādo, *Eyewitnesses of Shakespeare*, 1975, pp. 204, 214, quoting Charles Lamb, 1823, and Edward Aveling, 1884.

[2] Anthony Browne, second Viscount Montague, *Booke of Orders and Rules*, Sussex Archaeological Collections, VII (1854), cited in M. St Clare Byrne, 'The social background', H. Granville-Barker and G. B. Harrison (eds.), *A Companion to Shakespeare Studies*, 1946, p. 204.

[3] For an overview of patriarchal ideology and its effect on the lives of women in the Elizabethan age, see Valerie Traub, 'Gender and sexuality in Shakespeare', in Margreta de Grazia and Stanley Wells (eds.), *The Cambridge Companion to Shakespeare*, 2001, particularly pp. 129–34. The plot of Shakespeare's early play *The Taming of the Shrew* is a notable example of this ideology at work, and the opposition to it in the different rebellions of both Katherine and Bianca.

4 Henry Irving as Malvolio, Ellen Terry as Viola, with supporting cast, London, 1884

in 2.3, reveals its personal investment in the letter scene. He believes *he* is the right mate for Olivia:

'Tis but fortune; all is fortune. Maria once told me she [i.e. Olivia, though he cannot name her] did affect me, and I have heard herself come thus near, that should she fancy, it should be one of my complexion. Besides, she uses me with a more exalted respect than any one else that follows her.

(2.5.20–3)

'Practising behaviour to his own shadow', falling for the forged letter and uttering unconscious obscenities ('these be her very c's, her u's, and her t's, and thus makes she her great P's', 2.5.72–3); then attempting to pronounce the meaningless 'M O A I' (an actor can turn this into a weird howl), Malvolio is turned through his 'self-love' (Olivia's word) into a type of the clown-figure that he so despises. Actors can take the opportunity to address the audience in this solo scene: Donald Sinden has provided a wonderfully detailed description of his techniques for performing it in John Barton's renowned 1969 production.[1] Speaking to his inferiors, the groundling audience, in a familiar way as a clown does, is something that the pompous Malvolio would never be seen doing; but he is metamorphosed by the apparent workings of 'Fortune'. When he comes on in yellow stockings and cross-gartered in 3.4, performing 'the lover', he is even more obviously and *visually* a clown, in a type of motley – complaining about his varicose veins, gesturing lewdly towards Olivia, humming snatches of popular (and indecent) song.

How close the Fool (or clown) is to the madman, the wandering outcast, is illustrated – shockingly – by the 'dark house' scene, 4.2. This scene has been played with overt cruelty in late twentieth-century productions (see Stage History, for the general tendency of post-World War II productions). For the Royal Shakespeare Company in 1987, Antony Sher's Malvolio was blindfolded and whipped, chained to a pole, like a bear being baited. The Bell Shakespeare Company (Australia, 1995) in a modern-dress production, had Malvolio in a metal dumper bin, with Feste viciously banging on the lid. Malvolio protests repeatedly that he is 'not mad' – or rather, 'I am as well in my wits, fool, as thou art.' 'Then', replies Feste, 'you are mad indeed, if you are no better in your wits than a fool' (4.2.73–6).

Feste is momentarily on top in this scene – but it could easily be him in there, confined and ill-treated as a 'vagabond', if he had not negotiated for himself a position in this play's world, moving between Olivia's house, where he is an 'allowed fool', part of the household (1.5.76), and Orsino's court, but living independently in the town. 'Foolery, sir, does walk about the orb like the sun; it shines everywhere' (3.1.32–3). Clowns in Shakespearean comedy are liminal figures – wanderers, observers, commentators, with a sceptical, even cynical perspective on the world of romance or myth. As Michael Bristol argues in *Carnival and Theater*, the clown 'traverses the boundary between a represented world and the here-and-now world he shares with

---

[1] Donald Sinden, 'Malvolio in *Twelfth Night*', *Players of Shakespeare 1*, ed. Philip Brockbank, 1985, pp. 41–66.

5   Cross-gartering in 1562. From John Heywood's *Workes*

the audience . . . In addition to his role within the narrative, he is also a chorus who stands outside it.'[1]

The opening of 3.1, Feste's conversation with Viola, is a moment in the exact middle of the play where the audience is alerted to an unexpected similarity between these two characters. Technically unnecessary to the plot, it is a thematically important discussion about fools, wordplay, and, finally, Viola's ambiguous identity (here Feste can, if he wishes, raise the dramatic tension by signalling – to Viola or to the audience – that he has guessed her secret). The exchange is smoothly witty on both sides, not unlike a two-person stand-up-comedy routine; the audience sees that the professional fool and the professional page who is not what he seems have much in common. The final soliloquy (Viola's second in the play), a confident address to the audience, has a self-reflexive quality, describing what not only the clown but also Viola has to do:

> This fellow is wise enough to play the fool,
> And to do that well craves a kind of wit;
> He must observe their mood on whom he jests,
> The quality of persons, and the time. . . .[2]

(3.1.50–4)

Having given up her true class and gender identity, she is playing a part which in the real world could be considered 'foolish'. She is reliant, like Feste, on her intelligence and wit and her performance of the subservient role of page.

Viola will come to a clear and unambiguous return to gender and social norms in the *anagnorisis* (the disclosure of the truth) which is played out so richly in 5.1. But this moment of revelation, as common in romance and comedy as in the tragedies with which it was orginally associated, does not solve everything, does not include all outsiders, and must be recognised as a fantasy by most of the audience. Feste, along with Malvolio, carries the class consciousness of the audience: the clown and his festive companions have engineered the humiliation of the puritanical steward of the aristocratic household. Malvolio's 'I'll be revenged on the whole pack of you!' includes the aristocrats who have colluded in his humiliation through being (unconsciously) the provokers of his ambition and self-delusion. There is no place for either the clown or the puritan in the world of romance, to which we must now turn in more detail.

Time, chance and the poetry of romance

Barnabe Riche's story is a romance, a tale of faraway places and extraordinary adventures, including a central love story. As we saw above, however, his familiar tone of address to his female readers or auditors deliberately drained the story of magic or any

---

[1] Michael Bristol, *Carnival and Theater: Plebeian Culture and the Structure of Authority in Renaissance England*, 1985, pp. 140–2. For an anthropological reading of the clown's (and Viola's) 'liminality' see Edward Berry, *Shakespeare's Comic Rites*, 1984, *passim*.

[2] Tom McAlindon (personal communication) points out that these lines are closely based on Thomas Hoby's translation of Castiglione, *The Courtier* (1561), Book 2 (ed. Virginia Cox, 1994), p. 159: 'he must be wise, and have great respect to the place, to the time and to the persons with whom he talketh, and not like a common Jester passe his boundes . . .' Viola compares her own role of courtier to the profession of the wise fool.

but the most threadbare morality. Shakespeare, in adapting this story, had by contrast
a large public stage, a mixed audience and the advantage of a finely honed poetic skill.

When Orsino in the opening scene invokes music as 'the food of love' (1.1.1) and
speaks of the sea in the same breath as 'fancy' and the 'fantastical' he establishes a self-
indulgent, almost hothouse atmosphere ('sweet beds of flowers') in which he performs, to an onstage audience of servants, his idea of the Petrarchan lover. Valentine's
evocation of Olivia implies that she is in a similar self-indulgent state. Yet he does tell
us that she has a genuine basis for her melancholy: 'A brother's dead love, which she
would keep fresh / And lasting, in her sad remembrance' (1.1.31–2). That figure of
the lost brother makes the first of the play's 'chimes' with the strongly contrasting
scene that follows,[1] in which we meet the literally shipwrecked Viola, whose speeches
starkly evoke her sense of *her* brother's loss. But both she and the Captain also speak
of 'chance', a word allied with 'fate' and 'fortune', and Viola eagerly seizes on the
Captain's hopeful image of a heroic survival for Sebastian – 'like Arion on the dolphin's back' (1.2.15; see note). If Orsino is an ineffectual Actaeon ('my desires like fell
and cruel hounds / E'er since pursue me', 1.1.22–3), Sebastian even in his absence
presents a more admirable and active image of masculinity; an image which is
confirmed when he finally arrives on stage. His sister is equally self-reliant, opting to
'serve this duke' in male disguise: 'What else may hap, to time I will commit.'[2]

Her confident reliance on 'time' is one of the keynotes of Viola's character.
Shakespeare hereby signals a belief in the genre of romance, where those who pursue
adventure in order to deliver themselves from perilous situations are more likely to
succeed than those who sit passively, 'like Patience on a monument, / Smiling at
grief', as Viola characterises her 'sister', her hidden self (2.4.110–11). It is this latter
note which has been often over-emphasised in readings of Viola's character; yet it is
really only in the company of Orsino that she speaks so poignantly. A more complex
moment is that in her first scene with Olivia, when Cesario is asked by Olivia what he
would do if he were in the same state as Orsino. The answer, 'Make me a willow cabin
at your gate . . .' may be read as an expression of Viola's own longing (the performer
often pauses on 'O-livia', as though she were about to say 'Orsino') , but its effect on
Olivia is electric. She is literally, at this moment in the play, called into love by the
power of Viola/Cesario's eloquence:

> Hallow your name to the reverberate hills,
> And make the babbling gossip of the air
> Cry out 'Olivia!' O you should not rest
> Between the elements of air and earth
> But you should pity me!

> (1.5.227–31)

---

[1] J. P. Kemble's production (Covent Garden, 1815) was possibly the first to reverse 1.1. and 1.2, presumably on the grounds that 1.2 can be played in front of a painted (coastal scene) drop-curtain, whereas 1.1
needs a full set. The practice has frequently been adopted since: modern directors justify it on the
grounds of giving prominence to Viola and her situation.

[2] 'As in other of Shakespeare's plays, there is a double-time scheme: the action requires three months for
its fulfilment, but two consecutive days serve for the sequence of scenes.' E. S. Donno, Introduction,
1985, p. 9, n. 2. Few audience members notice this discrepancy in performance.

PACIENTIA ·

FIRMA GRAVES ANIMO PERFERT
PACIENTIA CLADES ET MOLLIT
LONGA DVRA PERICLA·
MORA·
VII

6   Patience on a monument

'You might do much!' Olivia replies, acknowledging the charisma of this young emis-
sary of courtly love. And she, too, resigns herself to 'Fate': 'What is decreed must be;
and be this so' (1.5.266). On the Globe stage, as Olivia exits 'inwards' into her house
by one door, Sebastian and Antonio would enter at the other stage door, from 'elsewhere': thus, within moments of her exit we see the man she is actually destined for,
with his companion Antonio. But Antonio mistrusts fate, and sees it as 'malignant':
'My stars shine darkly over me' (2.1.2) is a line which the modern actor of Antonio is
as likely to read as an acknowledgement of sexual loneliness (his love for Sebastian will
be frustrated by Sebastian's marriage to Olivia) as of political alienation in Orsino's
fiefdom.

Antonio's brief soliloquy, in which he says that despite the danger he will follow
Sebastian, gives time for Sebastian to disappear from the stage before Antonio follows
him through the same door. The immediate entrance of Malvolio and Viola 'at several
[separate] doors' (2.2.0 SD) on a two-door stage offers the audience for the first time
an image of the puzzle of identity: is this Sebastian returning or is it his sister?
Malvolio's opening line – 'Were you not even now with the Countess Olivia?' (2.2.1)
– and Viola's affirmative response quickly clarify the situation, to allow the scene to
move on to a higher level of delight in the erotic confusion brought about by Viola's
male disguise. Viola's 'ring' soliloquy invites the audience to enjoy the riddles of fate
and identity with her:

> What will become of this? As I am man,
> My state is desperate for my master's love;
> As I am woman – now alas the day! –
> What thriftless sighs shall poor Olivia breathe?
> O time, thou must untangle this, not I;
> It is too hard a knot for me t'untie.

> (2.2.33–8)

We note again Viola's trust in 'time'. Metadramatically, this might be a gesture
towards the 'time' that the play itself will take. Certainly when Olivia hears the clock
chime at the exact middle of the play and comments that 'The clock upbraids me with
the waste of time' (3.1.115) in her romantic pursuit of Cesario, the audience might
subconsciously register that it is time for things to begin resolving themselves. (In
modern productions the interval is usually just before 3.1.) And in the long sequence
of 3.4, which begins with Malvolio's cross-gartered public display, goes on to Viola's
hilarious duel with Sir Andrew and concludes with Antonio's intervention and the
first indication to Viola that her brother might be alive, we sense the play moving
towards its dénouement. Viola's short soliloquy here prepares us for the clarifications
of Act 5, and reminds us of the position from which she started, a survivor of a shipwreck desperately trusting to 'chance': 'O if it prove, / Tempests are kind, and salt
waves fresh in love' (3.4.334–5).

Sebastian is much more in evidence by this point, missing Viola by only a few
seconds of stage time at the end of both 3.4 and 4.3. The comic confusions (based,
of course, on *chance* encounters) quickly bring Olivia and Sebastian together. And

although Sebastian momentarily doubts whether he is still sane, the audience knows that chance has brought about the right conjunction of persons. Sebastian's substantial soliloquy in 4.3 is a poetic assertion of this benign condition, in which an 'accident' – a shipwreck, say – can be transformed into a 'flood of fortune':

> This is the air, that is the glorious sun,
> This pearl she gave me, I do feel't and see't,
> And though 'tis wonder that enwraps me thus,
> Yet 'tis not madness.
> . . . this may be some error, but no madness,
> Yet doth this accident and flood of fortune
> So far exceed all instance, all discourse,
> That I am ready to distrust mine eyes . . .

(4.3.1–4, 10–13)

'Wonder' will be the keynote of the play's dénouement in the superbly orchestrated dramaturgy of 5.1. As the twins at last face each other, Olivia sees *two* 'Cesarios', and cries 'Most wonderful!' And the long moment of the twins' grave litany of mutual discovery is an actual enactment of wonder. Poetic images of the shipwreck which separated them recur as they re-create their family through shared memories (5.1.210–32). Orsino also invokes the 'wreck' which brought the siblings to Illyria's shores: for Orsino it is 'this most happy wreck' (5.1.250) since it brought him Viola. He can thus go on to speak, in the play's last speech, of 'golden time', the once-violent and jealous man echoing Viola's natural optimism in 2.2. Nevertheless the play's last verbal chimes take us back to the self-indulgent Orsino of 1.1, as he speaks (complacently?) of 'Orsino's mistress, and his fancy's queen'.

Myths and metamorphosis

Shakespeare shared the sixteenth century's enthusiasm for the Latin poet Ovid,[1] in particular his *Metamorphoses*, tales of the Greek gods' and mortals' transformations from human to animal, mineral, plant or heavenly form. Arthur Golding's translation of Ovid in 1565 was immensely popular, and undoubtedly known to Shakespeare (whether or not he had read the original Latin). The 'translation' of Bottom into an ass in *A Midsummer Night's Dream* via the agency of Puck, and the narrative poem *Venus and Adonis*, demonstrate Shakespeare's lively interest in the comic potential of the idea of metamorphosis from early in his career. In *Twelfth Night* Ovidian themes are used more subtly. Viola reminds us of the Ovidian *topos* when she calls herself a 'poor monster' (2.2.31) because she has disguised herself by changing gender, and this disguise has only complicated her love-life. Malvolio, thinking to transform himself into a gentleman and lover, appears as a strange, yellow-stockinged, cross-gartered, ever-smiling monster, and seems mad, 'possessed', as do many characters in Ovid who make the wrong choices in love.

[1] See Jonathan Bate, *Shakespeare and Ovid*, 1993, ch. 1, for an account of the popularity of Ovid's works in Elizabethan culture.

Narcissus

Despite Orsino's depiction of himself as an Actaeon in love with a frigid Diana/Olivia in 1.1, a more pertinent Ovidian model for Orsino is the figure of Narcissus.[1] In *Metamorphoses*, III, Shakespeare would have read the story of the beautiful young man who, because he rejected all other lovers, was fated to fall in love with his own reflection in a pool:

> as he drank, he chanced to spy the image of his face,
> The which he did immediately with fervent love embrace.
> He feeds a hope without cause why. For, like a foolish noddy,
> He thinks the shadow that he sees to be a lively body.
> Astraughted, like an image made of marble stone he lies,
> There gazing on his shadow still with fixèd staring eyes.
> . . . He is the party whom he woos, and suitor that doth woo;
> He is the flame that sets on fire, and thing that burneth too.[2]

That he wastes away and dies, unable to drag himself away from admiration of his own image, carries the clear moral that Narcissus's self-absorption is unhealthy. Like Malvolio (the other 'lover' of Olivia), Orsino is 'sick of self-love' (1.5.73). This is evident not only in his opening self-indulgent speeches, which include the comment that when Olivia does return his love it will have 'killed the flock of all affections else / That live in her', leaving 'one selfsame king' – himself; but also in his later claim to 'Cesario' that

> There is no woman's sides
> Can bide the beating of so strong a passion
> As love doth give my heart . . .
>
> (2.4.89–91)

Orsino's image of himself is best served by the fiction of a distant and unresponsive beloved, which enables him to continue affirming his own great sensitivity. Similarly, of Malvolio we are told at the beginning of 2.5 that 'He has been . . . practising behaviour to his own shadow this half hour' (actors playing this role have been known to come on preening with a hand-mirror), in order to build up his conviction that 'should she [Olivia] fancy it should be one of my complexion' (2.5.22). Viola, by contrast, in all her declarations of love for Orsino, puts her ego in second place ('After him I love / More than I love these eyes, more than my life', 5.1.123–4), and emphasises the reality of the adored other: her imaginary beloved is 'Of your complexion . . . About your years, my lord' (2.4.24–6).

When the twins are finally brought face to face, it is Orsino who strikingly comments on their likeness:[3]

---

[1] For an argument that Olivia is also a Narcissus figure, see A. B. Taylor, 'Shakespeare rewriting Ovid: Olivia's interview with Viola and the Narcissus myth', *Shakespeare Survey 50* (1997), pp. 81–9.

[2] Ovid's *Metamorphoses*, tr. Arthur Golding [1565], ed. Madeleine Forey, 2002, Book 3, lines 519–25, 536–7.

[3] Antonio also comments on the twins' likeness, but his overriding emotional impulse seems to be to discover 'Which is Sebastian?' (5.1.208): an example of the Platonic 'heart's delight' discussed below.

7 Narcissus

> One face, one voice, one habit, and two persons –
> A natural perspective, that is and is not!
>
> (5.1.200–1)

Orsino, here, speaks with double authority: as the person of highest rank and educa-
tion; and as one who has been brought face to face with an embodied myth, an image
of his own narcissism. His speeches from this point to the end of the play are mature

and gracious, which they certainly were not until this moment of *anagnorisis*: it's as though Orsino has grown up in the course of this one scene. The fact that he is an educated Renaissance nobleman suggests further that he is able to cast the twins' mutual rediscovery in terms of the Platonic conception of love spelt out in *The Symposium*, whereby human beings began as 'double' creatures (male and male, female and female, male and female) whom Zeus spitefully separated: now each separated person searches throughout life, longing for their other half. Not necessarily sexual, says Plato,

'Love' is just the name we give to the desire for and pursuit of wholeness . . . We human beings will never attain happiness unless we find perfect love, unless we each come across the love of our lives and thereby recover our original nature. In the context of this ideal, it necessarily follows that in our present circumstances the best thing is to get as close to the ideal as possible, and one can do this by finding the person who is his heart's delight.[1]

Shakespeare's twins' final meeting, fuelled by the longing that each expresses at moments throughout the play, presents an image of asexual Platonic wholeness. Viola's love for a noticeably imperfect Orsino provides her 'heart's delight'; but if we accept the cynical realism of Feste's final song, we might be inclined to judge such delight (perhaps) only temporary.

Echo

The 'old and antique' tune played throughout Orsino and Viola's tender scene in which so much is implied (2.4), helps to create a mood of pensive reflection. As Viola says, 'It gives a very echo to the seat / Where love is throned' (2.4.19–20) – that is, the heart, but the audience will recognise that Viola is covertly commenting on her own position as Echo to Orsino's enthroned Narcissus. In the myth, Echo is the nymph who wasted away for hopeless love of Narcissus, speaking only fragments of his words (as Viola does in her wooing visits to Olivia). Her first mention of 'echo' sets the mood for Viola's climactic speech in this scene:

> She pined in thought,
> And with a green and yellow melancholy
> She sat like Patience on a monument,
> Smiling at grief.
>
> (2.4.108–11)

This image of longing has already been aired, with a more urgent and active sense of desire, when Viola is wooing Olivia on Orsino's behalf. Away from Orsino, perhaps, she can speak more passionately of her love, even though it is still veiled and couched in hypothetical terms. Echo was never so proactive as this cabin-builder, writer, persistent singer:

> Make me a willow cabin at your gate,
> And call upon my soul within the house;

---

[1] Plato, *The Symposium*, tr. Robin Waterfield, 1994, pp. 29–30.

Write loyal cantons of contemnèd love,
And sing them loud even in the dead of night;
Hallow your name to the reverberate hills . . .

(1.5.223–7)

Twins

Viola is also implicated in a wider and more pervasive presence of the Narcissus myth associated with the play's interest in identity. Twins are a particular way of focusing this fascination: 'I my brother know / Yet living in my glass' (3.4.330–1). In classical literature, in the cosmic patterns of astrology (which includes the constellation of Gemini), in stories and dramatic romances, the motif of twinship provides a strong narrative element.[1]

Plautus's *Menaechmi*, used by Shakespeare in *The Comedy of Errors*, operates with a realistic identity confusion, one that most people have observed and experienced when twins are of the same sex; Shakespeare simply raises the stakes for farce by providing two pairs of identical twins.[2] It is, of course, biologically impossible for a girl and boy pair of twins to be 'identical'. Yet when a story takes this impossibility as the basis of its plot, we have entered the world of romance, a place where it is permissible to play with an idea and see where it leads the imagination. In the case of *Twelfth Night*, the idea presents a tantalising possibility. As Barnabe Riche remarks, 'the one of them was so like the other in countenaunce and favour that there was no man able to descerne the one from the other by their faces, savyng by their aparell, the one beyng a man, the other a woman'.[3] Is it only 'aparell', that is, the *performance* of gender, that differentiates the sexes in society? As has been suggested above, a profounder 'grief' to Viola than her unrequited love is the loss of her brother; a more passionate hope, that she might find him: 'Prove true, imagination, O prove true, / That I, dear brother, be now tane for you!' (3.4.326–7). It is in response to this loss that she dresses like him, so much so that she is indistinguishable from him:

> even such and so
> In favour was my brother, and he went
> Still in this fashion, colour, ornament,
> For him I imitate.

(3.4.331–4)

But her/his contradictory behaviour – and, in particular, Viola's admission in the abortive duel with Sir Andrew that she lacks the masculine ability to effectively wield

---

[1] Shakespeare himself was the father of boy-girl twins, Hamnet and Judith. Hamnet died in 1596; the father's and sister's sadness may well be reflected in Viola's intense sense of loss in 1.2. For the mythological and literary occurrence of different-sex twins, see Carolyn Heilbrun, *Towards a Recognition of Androgyny*, 1973, pp. 34–41.

[2] John M. Mercer points out that 'the twins' experiences in the two plays are . . . similar in a remarkable number of details, and the experiences of Sebastian in particular coincide with those in *The Comedy of Errors*'. 'Twin Relationships in Shakespeare', *The Upstart Crow*, 9 (1989), 24–39 (p. 27).

[3] Bullough, *Sources*, p. 352.

a sword (the symbol of the 'little thing', the penis, that she 'lacks', 3.4.255) – ensures that the audience remains aware of the essential *difference* of the sexes; a difference that will be properly re-established as the plot untangles.

Pausanias the Traveller, whose second-century *Description of Greece* was available in the sixteenth century both in the original Greek and in Latin and Italian translations, invokes the incest taboo in another version of the Narcissus story which co-incides with the intensity of feeling spoken of by Viola and Sebastian:

> Narkissos had a twin sister; they were exactly the same to look at with just the same hair-style and the same clothes, and they even used to go hunting together. Narkissos was in love with his sister, and when she died he used to visit the spring; he knew what he saw was his own reflection, but even so he found some relief in telling himself it was his sister's image.[1]

As in Ovid's version, the desire for the identical other leads to death. Willing separation, and the establishment of an emotional relationship with a different other (a 'heart's delight') is ultimately a healthier behavioural pattern, and this psychological wisdom is reflected in the final marriages of the romance: Sebastian and Viola, having remade their family, move on to include other, more adult relationships.

The complex sexual response that each twin evokes in other characters in the play perhaps finds a pre-echo in another Ovidian myth: that of Hermaphrodite and Salmacis. In this story, the beautiful fifteen-year-old son of Mercury and Venus (Hermes and Aphrodite), attracts on his travels the passionate erotic interest of the nymph Salmacis. In Francis Beaumont's witty version of the tale, published in 1602 (the year Manningham saw *Twelfth Night*), there is a close association made (which is not in Ovid) between this story and that of Narcissus. Salmacis' pool is the very same one that Narcissus gazed into. Hermaphrodite first sees himself reflected in Salmacis' eyes – 'How should I love thee, when I do espy / A far more beauteous nymph hid in thy eye?' She, practically, closes her eyes and continues her wooing. Here the comedy of a desiring and wooing woman is very close to Olivia's behaviour in 3.1:

> Then rose the water-Nymph from where she lay,
> As having wonne the glory of the day,
> And her light garments cast from off her skin.
> Hee's mine, she cry'd; and so leapt spritely in.
> . . . Betwixt those iv'ry arms she lockt him fast,
> Striving to get away, till at the last,
> Fondling, she sayd, why striv'st thou to be gone?
> Why shouldst thou so desire to be alone?[2]

But whereas Salmacis then prays the gods 'that never day may see / The separation twixt this boy and me', so that their bodies grow into one hermaphroditic person, Olivia, as befits her rank, says reluctantly that she 'will not have' the pageboy. A minute later she is once again declaring the force of her desire – 'Nor wit nor reason can

---

[1] Pausanias, *Guide to Greece*, vol. 1: Central Greece, tr. Peter Levi, 1971, p. 376 (Book IX, 'Boiotia').
[2] Francis Beaumont, *Salmacis and Hermaphroditus*, 1602, lines 865–8, 873–6 (Chadwyck-Healey *English Poetry Full-Text Database*).

my passion hide'. At this mid-way point in the play, such desire needs to begin finding its proper object: Sebastian enters, with Antonio, 65 lines after Olivia's passionate exit.

Gender, sexuality and the stage

The play thus flirts with the possibility of same-sex love, only, apparently, to eschew it in the 'real' social world of Orsino and Olivia, duke and countess. Each twin ends up in marriage with a member of the opposite sex, while having been in the course of the play engaged in erotic situations with a member of their own sex: 'Cesario' with Orsino, Sebastian with Antonio (Antonio's admission that he 'adores' Sebastian, 2.1.35, gives modern directors license to pursue a homoerotic subtext), and, on the stage where women's roles were played by boys, Olivia with Viola – perceived as either two girls, or two boys. Such conscious dramaturgical playing with the idea of gender seems a deliberate choice in this play:[1] it follows within a year or so of Shakespeare's *As You Like It*, which similarly enjoys displaying the entertaining and philosophical possibilities of a boy playing a girl playing a boy (then playing a girl wooing a man). Sebastian, who may be seen in the course of the play as moving from a close relationship with an older man who loves him passionately to an advantageous heterosexual marriage, insists even in the last scene on the fluidity of gender: 'You are betrothed both to a maid and man' he says to Olivia (5.1.247). He means literally that he is a virgin youth, but it is a reminder that on the stage at that moment are two apparently identical young men – both attractive to both women and men – one of whom is, in the 'improbable fiction', biologically female. In fact, in the world outside the dramatic fiction – the world of the Elizabethan actors and spectators – both are male. Thus at the same time as the plot is asserting the primacy of heterosexual difference as a basis for love, the stage image is re-asserting the power of the Platonic ideal of perfect male friendship as the best way to approach the Form of good.[2] Even though Antonio is left conspicuously alone as the play's final couplings are made, his alternative view of ideal love is represented visually by the play's refusal to let Viola don her 'woman's weeds' (5.1.257–9): she remains 'a man', Orsino's beloved companion.

   Few critical issues in Shakespearean comedy have been discussed more energetically in recent years than the question of what it meant to an Elizabethan audience to see boys playing the roles of women. For modern play-goers it is, of course, largely a dead issue (though see Stage History for some modern examples of cross-gender casting). Since the mid-seventeenth century the roles of Viola, Olivia and Maria have been claimed as their right by actresses who revel in the richness of Shakespeare's language and the potential for complex explorations of gender and sexuality, of love and human relationships, that the roles allow. Emma Fielding, for example, who played Viola in 1994 (RSC, director Ian Judge), reflects on 'She never told her love':

---

[1] See Barbara Hodgdon's perceptive analysis of these issues in *Twelfth Night* in Leggatt (ed.), *Cambridge Companion to Shakespearean Comedy*, pp. 179–81, 186–90.
[2] See Diotima's speech on the ascent to perfection, *The Symposium* (tr. Waterfield), pp. 41–56.

with a jolt Viola has to remember the history of who she really is . . . Her decision to conceal herself as a temporary measure to buy time and heal herself suddenly has no end for her. She has no escape. Still and serene, with no rancour or self-pity, she will continue to be in close proximity to the one person . . . who will cause her most pleasure and pain: Orsino.[1]

Zoë Wanamaker, Viola in John Caird's 1983 RSC production, writes of her character, 'she is always discovering things about life, and taking time off during the play to talk to her audience about them (now look at this person, isn't that interesting, isn't that wonderful, or odd), to share her sense of humour with them'. And this actress also imbues the relationship with Orsino with perhaps more than the text offers: 'Viola is let into his mind, his confidence, his imagination, in such a way that inevitably she falls in love with him, with this extraordinary, erudite human being.'[2]

But for those trying to fathom the place of *Twelfth Night* within the culture of its own time, the issue of 'boy actresses' must still be addressed. Elizabethan theatre and acting, obliged by strong cultural tradition to accept boys playing the roles of women, delighted in the conscious recognition of artificiality while at the same time praising the 'naturalness' of an effective performer. Michael Shapiro suggests that in the original performances of the play, these 'oscillations' between female and male identity 'became even more dazzling in the light of the spectators' dual consciousness of the boy actor producing all of these abrupt shifts. These multiple layers of identity and the swift movements from one to another produced a theatrical vibrancy.'[3] Shapiro further points to one of the particular pleasures that the play provides: the Elizabethan theatre's enclosed space is utilised to disrupt fixed notions of gender through a safe and pleasurable spectacle, the boy who plays the girl. Was it a homoerotic stage? That is, was the pleasure of the audience in watching the representation of heterosexual lovemaking in fact a much more subversive pleasure in watching a man and a boy make love? Probably not: the love of an educated Elizabethan man for a boy was rendered acceptable by the many literary models in Ovid, Plato and other classical texts. In fact, it was often seen as less dangerous than men's desire for women, whose sexuality was thought to be voracious, tending to effeminise or weaken even manly men.[4] And although puritans fulminated against the theatre in general,[5] the potential for homosexual behaviour was only one aspect of their larger phobia. It was basically 'the universal sexuality evoked by theatre, a lust not distinguished by the gender of its object'[6] which was unacceptable to puritans – especially in so far as it disrupted the specific definitions of gender and sexuality which are the bedrock of the conservative patriarchal system.

Other scholars argue that at some level boy actors playing women must simply have

[1] Emma Fielding, *Actors on Shakespeare: 'Twelfth Night'*, 2002, p. 42.
[2] Zoë Wanamaker, 'Viola in *Twelfth Night*', Russell Jackson and Robert Smallwood (eds.), *Players of Shakespeare 2*, 1988, pp. 89, 85.
[3] Michael Shapiro, *Gender in Play on the Shakespearean Stage*, 1996, p. 126.
[4] Stephen Orgel, *Impersonations: The Performance of Gender in Shakespeare's England*, 1996, p. 43.
[5] Most notably Philip Stubbes, *The Anatomy of Abuses in Anglia* (1583): 'Of stage plays, and interludes, with their wickedness' is excerpted in Smith (ed.) *Twelfth Night: Texts and Contexts*, pp. 345–53. See also Bruce R. Smith, *Homosexual Desire in Shakespeare's England: A Cultural Poetics*, 1991, pp. 147–8.
[6] Orgel, *Impersonations*, p. 28.

been accepted in performance as a convention.¹ Otherwise, there would have been little audience involvement with those aspects of the plays dependent on the representation of heterosexual desire. Jean Howard suggests that the whole purpose of the dramatic narrative in *Twelfth Night* 'is to release this woman from the prison of her masculine attire and return her to her proper and natural position as a wife . . . Despite her masculine attire and the confusion it causes in Illyria, Viola's is a properly feminine subjectivity.'² The plot, that is, privileges a heterosexual interpretation of the energy flow between adult male actor and adolescent boy-as-woman. Even so, this is perhaps somewhat to oversimplify the experience of the audience in the theatre, that liminal place where anything may happen. In performance, actors may offer, or audiences may interpret, any intimate moment between man and boy as imbued with homoerotic feeling.

Language³

A Shakespeare play is first and foremost words performed by actors, who bring into play the text's latent 'erotic friction',⁴ the energy and excitement of imaginative language. A large part of Viola's attraction as a heroine lies in her eloquence, whether it be the famous speeches on the willow cabin and Patience on a monument, or the wit evident in her prose exchanges with Maria, Olivia and Feste. Yet most striking, perhaps, is her soliloquising habit, in which she takes the audience into her confidence. Viola in fact is the only heroine up to this point in the Shakespearean canon who soliloquises and exhibits an awareness of the audience as *amused* listeners,⁵ that is, listeners who share a consciousness that they are present at a stage comedy (which has certain conventions). This is demonstrated by the register of her questions in the 'ring' soliloquy (2.2.14–38) – 'what means this lady?' 'How will this fadge?' – and her explanations – 'She loves me sure; the cunning of her passion / Invites me in this churlish messenger'; 'I am the man', followed by a wry spelling-out of the situation for the audience's benefit –

> What will become of this? As I am man,
> My state is desperate for my master's love;
> As I am woman – now alas the day! –
> What thriftless sighs shall poor Olivia breathe?

Viola transgresses her gender constraints (that is, that a woman should be silent and modest in public) and enters the territory of the clown by taking her 'poetical' blank

---

¹ Kathleen McLuskie, 'The act, the role, and the actor: boy actresses on the Elizabethan stage', *New Theatre Quarterly* 3 (1987), 120–30; Jean Howard, *The Stage and Social Struggle*, pp. 119–20. Smith agrees, citing 'the testimony of 16th- and 17th-century playgoers . . . to suggest that audiences simply accepted boys in women's clothes as a stage convention' (*Homosexual Desire*, p. 148).

² Howard, *Stage and Social Struggle*, p. 113.

³ Material addressed in this section is discussed at greater length in Penny Gay, '*Twelfth Night*: "the babbling gossip of the air"', in Richard Dutton and Jean Howard (eds.), *The Blackwell Companions to Shakespeare: The Comedies*, 2003, pp. 429–46.

⁴ Stephen Greenblatt, 'Fiction and friction', *Shakespearean Negotiations*, 1988, p. 90.

⁵ Rosalind's epilogue to *As You Like It*, in some ways comparable, takes place after the play is finished and the actor is moving out of character.

verse from the formal environment of Orsino's court and presenting it consciously and wittily as a performance (to Olivia, for example – 'I would be loath to cast away my speech: for besides that it is excellently well penned, I have taken great pains to con it,' 1.5.142–4). She thus undermines the cultural authority of such high-sounding language. In her doubleness – which is embodied as much in her wit and riddling as in her gender ambiguity – Viola constantly shifts between the representative figure of the pathos-producing romantic heroine in a fable, who 'never told her love', and the self-aware, self-delighting performer, chatting wittily to the audience (both on stage and in the auditorium) about 'her' situation within the plot.

This habit of verbal play and quick-wittedness stays with her until the final confrontations and resolutions of Act 5 require plain speaking from all (what could be more banal than 'My father had a mole upon his brow', 5.1.226?). Viola's last speech, a good ten minutes before the end of the play, is particularly prosaic, with just the faintest echo of the wordplay ('garments/suit') that has protected her hitherto, concealing what she is with riddle and double(t)-speak:

> The captain that did bring me first on shore
> Hath my maid's garments; he upon some action
> Is now in durance, at Malvolio's suit,
> A gentleman and follower of my lady's.

> (5.1.258–61)

Viola's eloquence while she is in the (relative) freedom of masculine disguise is at the centre of a play which constantly delights the audience with the rich expressiveness of the English language. *Twelfth Night* is full of puns and riddles, an appropriate characteristic for the audience of lawyers that heard it in 1602, but also for a general populace that by the end of the sixteenth century had developed a taste for linguistic extravagance.[1] Even Sir Andrew's questions, in his first scene (1.3), all revolve around his perplexity with the meaning of words and phrases: 'Is that the meaning of "accost"?' 'What's your metaphor?' 'But what's your jest?' He is still at it in 3.1, as Viola indulges in a spot of courtly euphuism: '"Odours", "pregnant", and "vouchsafed": I'll get 'em all three all ready' (3.1.76–7). Feste's tart comment on leaving Viola/Cesario at 3.1.48–9, 'Who you are, and what you would are out of my welkin – I might say "element", but the word is overworn', is a fitting conclusion to a scene that has played on the idea of 'words' and how they influence perception.

As well as the constant habit of punning – something that marks Shakespeare's work from the beginning – *Twelfth Night* displays two more instances of wordplay in greater abundance than in his other plays of this period: riddles and (near-)anagrams. Both are based on homophones (as are puns), an aural similarity that momentarily confuses the listener. Many readers of the play have noticed that Viola, Olivia, Malvolio are near-anagrams of each other. This is deliberate: the names are

[1] For a summary of the massive expansion of English vocabulary, and the concomitant development of handbooks of rhetoric and dictionaries in the second half of the sixteenth century, see Russ McDonald, *Shakespeare and the Arts of Language*, 2001, esp. pp. 10–29; for the uses Shakespeare made of this development, see Jane Donawerth, *Shakespeare and the Sixteenth-Century Study of Language*, 1984.

not thus in Shakespeare's sources. They are, we might say, an orthographic and aural reinforcement of the riddle of identity. If Viola and Sebastian are 'identical' (though not in behaviour), so, anagrammatically, are Olivia and Viola (almost); and Mal-volio, whose name also contains 'Viola', is in some sort of *malevolent* relation to these two.

Naming is a major issue in this play, both as regards plot and as one of the signs of its interest in identity, and although the names of the other two members of Viola's erotic triad are supplied (Orsino, Olivia) in 1.2, Viola herself is not named in the spoken script until the last scene of the play. By contrast, Sebastian's odd admission to Antonio in his first scene (2.1), that he has been going under the false name of Roderigo, suggests the shipwrecked male traveller's need for disguise in his inherently dangerous situation. Now that he is in Illyria, 'bound to the Count Orsino's court' and a re-entry into a stable social environment, he can safely resume his true identity, as the son of 'Sebastian of Messaline'.

Riddles

Riddling is a challenge to both onstage and theatre auditors, a variety of question that assumes the hearer is willing to play games with words, rather than use them for the sober purpose of gaining information. The very title *Twelfth Night, or What You Will*, is a riddle set by the elusive author, and not yet satisfactorily solved. Is it a metatheatrical joke involving a contemporary reference to John Marston's play *What You Will*?[1] Does it contain sexual punning of a kind that Will Shakespeare particularly delighted in, alluding to the multiple erotic entanglements of the play?[2] Much of a clown's stock-in-trade is riddles, as Maria and Feste remind us in their music-hall-style dialogue on his first appearance in 1.5. And riddling is the focus of two scenes at the centre of the play, 2.5 and 3.1.

The enigmatic letter that Maria throws in Malvolio's way centres on a riddle, of the classic rhymed variety:

> I may command where I adore,
> But silence, like a Lucrece knife,
> With bloodless stroke my heart doth gore;
> M.O.A.I. doth sway my life.

(2.5.88–91)

'A fustian riddle', as Fabian comments; it is less fine than it looks (or sounds), being deliberately misleading, or insoluble. But Malvolio cannot conceive of that, of words addressed to *him* without a sober meaning: '"M" – but then there is no consonancy in the sequel that suffers under probation. "A" should follow, but "O" does.' Malvolio

---

[1] Marston's *What You Will* was published in 1607 but probably performed in 1601 or 1602; its Induction contains lines describing the comedy to follow: 'even what you will, a slight toy, lightly composed, too swiftly finish'd, illplotted, worse written, I fear me worse acted, and indeed what you will' (Induction, lines 87–90.)

[2] See, e.g. Sonnet 135, 'Whoever hath her wish, thou hast thy will; / And will to boot, and will in over-plus . . .'

thinks that if he tries hard enough, he can *make* the 'alphabetical position portend' ('to crush this a little, it would bow to me, for every one of these letters are in my name'). But instead of this high intellectual endeavour, the commentary of the three observers in the box-tree emphasises the farcical ('I'll cudgel him and make him cry "O!"'), and the indecent potential of riddling ('thus makes she her great P's'). The scene becomes, on stage, an object-lesson in the proverb 'Pride goeth before a fall.' Malvolio's deliberate perversion ('crushing') of the riddle leads to an incorrect solution – or rather to the self-deceiving solution that the pranksters want: they know his vanity well enough to expect that he will misread 'M.O.A.I.'.[1]

Malvolio's humiliation is a self-contained narrative within the play; the plot against him uses the trick of riddling to bring about its ends in farce (the cross-gartered scene) and violence (the 'dark house'). The wider play is arguably interested in a more complex form of babble or riddle, embodied in the 'corrupter of words' Feste's aslant observations on the world, and in Viola's shifting gender. Unlike Malvolio, Viola is a *maker* of riddles; riddling is her particular 'habit', her conscious, teasing signalling of disguise. The role of the cheeky pageboy is a perfect cover:

OLIVIA What is your parentage?
VIOLA Above my fortunes, yet my state is well:
      I am a gentleman.

                                          (1.5.232–4)

VIOLA I am all the daughters of my father's house,
      And all the brothers, too.

                                      (2.4.116–17)

FESTE Now Jove, in his next commodity of hair, send thee a beard!
VIOLA By my troth, I'll tell thee, I am almost sick for one – though I
      would not have it grow on my chin.

                                      (3.1.38–40)

OLIVIA I prithee tell me what thou think'st of me.
VIOLA That you do think you are not what you are.
OLIVIA If I think so, I think the same of you.
VIOLA Then think you right: I am not what I am.

                                      (3.1.123–6)

VIOLA By innocence I swear, and by my youth,
      I have one heart, one bosom, and one truth,
      And that no woman has, nor never none
      Shall mistress be of it, save I alone.

                                      (3.1.142–5)

[1] Peter J. Smith's solution to Malvolio's riddle is among the most convincing of the many attempts, because it develops the theme of Malvolio's humiliation through the grotesque. Smith reads it as a contemporary reference to Sir John Harington's (notorious and much reprinted) *Metamorphosis Of A Iakes*, i.e. the treatise on the water-closet (1596). 'M.O.A.I. "What should that alphabetical position portend?" An answer to the metamorphic Malvolio', *Renaissance Quarterly* 51 (1998), 1199–224. Malvolio has had the contents of a chamber-pot emptied over him in the 'dark house' in some recent productions.

'What am I?' she might conclude, in classic riddler fashion: she could hardly be more emphatic, or more puzzling, about her identity. Viola/Cesario *needs* to speak of her doubleness.

In the play's last scene, there is a sixteen-line rhyming exchange, broken up ever more frenetically between Orsino, Viola and Olivia, which culminates in these lines:

> OLIVIA   Whither, my lord? Cesario, husband, stay!
> ORSINO   Husband?
> OLIVIA   Ay, husband. Can he that deny?
> ORSINO   Her husband, sirrah?
> VIOLA   No, my lord, not I.
>
> (5.1.132–4)

'Not I': it's as though 'Cesario' is trying for the last time to claim that 'he' is other than he appears. The comical succession of rhyming couplets reassures the audience that resolution of the puzzle is at hand (just as, throughout the play, couplets are an aural signal of the end of a scene). If 'not I', then who? A visual and aural answer to the riddle is supplied with Sebastian's manly and courteous entrance, claiming agency ('I'), in measured blank verse:

> I am sorry, madam, I have hurt your kinsman.
> But had it been the brother of my blood,
> I must have done no less with wit and safety.
>
> (5.1.193–5)

Riddles are no longer necessary; Viola finally gives straightforward answers to Sebastian's urgent questioning of her identity: 'What countryman? What name? What parentage?' (5.1.215)

Music

Twelfth Night begins and ends with music: it is the only play in the Shakespearean canon to do so explicitly. Altogether six of its eighteen scenes contain specific directions for music, including complete or partial songs and 'catches' or popular unaccompanied songs. 'We did keep time, sir, in our catches', Sir Toby wisecracks in response to Malvolio's indignant 'Is there no respect of place, persons, nor time in you?' as he interrupts the midnight revellers (2.3.79–80). As well as having a *time* signature, songs often use *rhyme*, which is then doubly reinforced by music. As a trope, music recurs continually in the play, most notably in the theme of echoes, 'the babbling gossip of the air' (1.5.228); rhyme itself is a kind of echo. The thematic words that recur, or echo, throughout the play, and the puns and wordplay which depend upon similar sounds to make their effect, all contribute to the play's extraordinary musicality.

'If music be the food of love, play on' (1.1.1). For Orsino, music is a theatrical effect that supports his performance as the unrequited lover; he commands it at his whim: 'Enough; no more. / 'Tis not so sweet now as it was before.' By 2.4, however, Orsino has moved from an indulgence in 'excess' to an appreciation of the Renaissance theory of music's celestial power,[1] commending Cesario's 'It gives a very echo to the seat / Where love is throned'; and commenting appreciatively himself on the psychological function of music in human society since time immemorial:

> Mark it, Cesario, it is old and plain;
> The spinsters and the knitters in the sun,
> And the free maids that weave their thread with bones,
> Do use to chant it; it is silly sooth,
> And dallies with the innocence of love
> Like the old age.

(2.4.41–6)

Thus it is that music adds a rich and melancholy atmosphere to the unspoken love scene between Orsino and Viola. Now Orsino has before him a tangible object for his love-fancies. He enquires obsessively about Cesario's love-life. As Feste performs the song, Orsino and Viola become listeners absorbed and enchanted by its mood: directors of the play usually ensure that the two move physically close to each other as it works its magic. Although there is no record of the tune of the song, 'old and antique' suggests one of the pre-harmonic modes which to late sixteenth-century ears would have sounded melancholy. The words, however, are another matter: exaggeratedly Petrarchan, with sad cypresses and black coffins and claims of being 'slain by a fair cruel maid'. The actor playing Feste can choose how far he emphasises the absurdity of this in his performance (we already know from 1.5.47ff that the clown does think such behaviour absurd – 'Good madonna, give me leave to prove you a fool.'). But even a heavily ironical performance is unlikely to break the mood that has been established between Orsino and Viola as they pursue their highly emotional discussion of constancy in love, and Viola tells her 'sister's' affecting story. This is, of course, her disguised declaration of her own hopeless love: 'on a monument', she too is a Petrarchan figure, powerless, in thrall to love. But she disengages herself from this self-pitying image to end the scene, resuming her young male persona: ' – and yet I know not. / Sir, shall I to this lady?' Many recent productions have had Orsino and Viola kiss at this point, irresistibly giving in to the highly charged atmosphere, before breaking off into their conventional public roles.

Feste's 'love song' in 2.3 has a similarly melancholy cast to its words, but the contemporary tune generally used for it (first published in an instrumental version by Thomas Morley in 1599) is a jolly piece in a major key which suits the lighter mood of the 'kitchen scene'. Nevertheless, ideas about love, death and time, and the message 'In delay there lies no plenty' are themes that chime with a prevalent mood of the play. And Feste's final song (to a tune that has now become traditional, though it was first printed in the late eighteenth century) is an extraordinary way to end the play. It pro-

---

[1] 'Music . . . hath a certain divine influence into the souls of men, whereby our cogitations and thought . . . are brought into a celestial acknowledging of their natures.' John Case, *The Praise of Music* (1586), cited in Smith (ed.), *Twelfth Night: Texts and Contexts*, p. 176. Cf. *The Merchant of Venice*, 5.1.75–94, in which Lorenzo offers a summary of Platonic ideas about music and the harmony of the spheres, concluding 'The man that hath no music in himself, / Nor is not moved with concord of sweet sounds, / Is fit for treasons, stratagems, and spoils.'

8   Judi Dench as Viola, Charles Thomas as Orsino, Royal Shakespeare Company 1969, Act 2, Scene 4

vides an epilogue that unsentimentally returns the audience to the real world of 'knaves and thieves' and unhappy marriages, where 'the rain it raineth every day'. It is also arguable that there is something depressingly limited in its cyclical repetition of tune and chorus; almost, perhaps, too much rhyme. The second and fourth lines of each verse (except the last) are identical: is this the comfortable iteration of everyday reality, or some sort of existential treadmill that we are being sent back to? Feste, as rhyming musician, is still the agent of 'the whirligig of time' which hereby brings in its revenges on the audience, who (like Malvolio) have briefly inhabited a fantasy world.

The fact that Viola does not sing in the play, despite her originally announced plan to present herself as 'an eunuch' to Orsino – 'for I can sing, / And speak to him in many sorts of music' (1.2.57–8) – has puzzled some scholars and encouraged them to theorise about an only partly revised text of 'foul papers' that provided the copy for the First Folio (see Textual analysis). Equally plausible is the suggestion that the change is simply part of Viola's characterisation: she has discarded her first plan for a more advantageous position as Orsino's young courtier. Or, if Robert Armin was the Feste in Shakespeare's company, perhaps it was more practical to capitalise on his musical abilities rather than those of a boy whose voice might break. Throughout the eighteenth and nineteenth centuries, however, Viola sang, and Feste's songs were cut in whole or in part.[1]

Critical fashions

C. L. Barber, in the seminal work *Shakespeare's Festive Comedy* (1959), observed that Shakespeare

> wrote at a moment when the educated part of society was modifying a ceremonial, ritualistic conception of human life to create a historical, psychological conception. His drama, indeed, was an important agency in this transformation: it provided a 'theater' where the failures of ceremony could be looked at in a place apart and understood as history; it provided new ways of representing relations between language and action so as to express personality.[2]

This has been a very powerful paradigm in critical approaches to *Twelfth Night* in the second half of the twentieth century, particularly as it is the play which names itself (and its clown) as festive; and in its 'kitchen scene' (2.3) has characters drinking, singing 'O'the twelfth day of December', and demanding from the puritanical Malvolio the right to enjoy 'cakes and ale'. Nevertheless it is important to look carefully at Barber's formulation: he is not talking about a simple opposition between the festive and the repressive. He speaks of the 'failures' of ritual, which might include the dis-

---

[1] See Laurie E. Osborne, *The Trick of Singularity: 'Twelfth Night' and the Performance Editions*, 1996, pp. 58–9, for changes in Feste's songs. For the singing Viola (and Olivia), see Stage history.

[2] C. L. Barber, *Shakespeare's Festive Comedy*, 1959, p. 15. More recent, strongly historicised discussions of 'carnival', engaging with the theory developed by Bakhtin in *Rabelais and his World* (English tr. 1968), are to be found in Michael Bristol, *Carnival and Theater: Plebeian Culture and the Structure of Authority in Renaissance England*, 1985, and François Laroque, *Shakespeare's Festive World: Elizabethan Seasonal Entertainment and the Professional Stage*, 1991.

tress felt by many spectators – including Sir Toby ('I would we were well rid of this knavery', 4.2.54) – over the excessively cruel 'dark house' treatment of Malvolio. The ritualistic casting-out of the scapegoat in this play will not be final: Malvolio threatens revenge. Further, the 'broken heads' of Sir Toby and Sir Andrew, needing a surgeon's attention (5.1.161–5) suggest a real world of dangerous drunken rioting, not a fantasy of harmless inebriated jollity. 'Games' and 'holiday magic' are, as Barber continues, complicated by the potential of 'personality' on the stage, its tendency to indulge in individual 'imagination' and 'expressive gestures'.

In the same way that reading the play as a simple instance of carnival festivity has been found inadequate, the notion that it is 'about' romantic love is limited. 'What *is* love?', as Feste's song pertinently asks. Late twentieth-century readings of the play in the light of new historicism, and gender, queer and performance theory, argue that it is not one thing – heterosexual, Petrarchan romance – but the apparently infinite variations of *eros*, physical and spiritual attraction between two people in any gender combination.[1] Stephen Greenblatt's new historicist essay 'Fiction and friction', for example, enables readers to enter by circuitous paths into the sixteenth century's thinking about gender and sexuality, and to see how that might be translated for public consumption into the play's explorations of the fictions of gender and its flirtatious and erotic 'dallying with words'.[2] Feminist critics have drawn attention to the different readings of the text that a focus on the female characters and their experience can bring.[3] In many ways this is the strongest and most influential strand of contemporary criticism, since it gives the woman-centred comedies the intellectual respectability that the male-centred tragedies and history plays have long enjoyed.

The psychoanalytic approach still has considerable adherents, however, especially among theatre directors, who (along with their actors) are looking for a reading that will allow them to construct plausible characters in order to tell the play's story. (My comments above on Orsino's narcissism tend inevitably in this direction, although based on a recognition of Elizabethan interest in Ovidian myths.) Examples of the continuing relevance of Jungian theory would include Peter Gill's 1974 production for the Royal Shakespeare Company; and Nicholas Hytner's 1998 New York Lincoln Center production, with its symbolic pools of water for shipwreck, reflection and ritual cleansing. Bob Crowley, the designer for Hytner's production, spoke of 'the narcissism of the characters, constantly looking at their own reflections. The idea of water being the first mirror, the twinning of things – all that has resonance.'[4] Underlying this approach is an attachment to Barber's notion of festive comedy, which in its turn is influenced by the anthropological idea that human society is dependent on ritual.

[1] Valerie Traub offers a particularly closely argued analysis of *Twelfth Night*'s homoerotic interests in *Desire and Anxiety: Circulations of Sexuality in Shakespearean Drama*, 1992, pp. 130–43.
[2] Greenblatt, *Shakespearean Negotiations*, p. 90.
[3] E.g. Lisa Jardine, *Still Harping on Daughters: Women and Drama in the Age of Shakespeare*, 1983, Jean Howard, *The Stage and Social Struggle in Early Modern England*, 1994, Cristina Malcolmson, '"What you will": social mobility and gender in *Twelfth Night*', and Dympna Callaghan, '"And all is semblative a woman's part": body politics and *Twelfth Night*', in R. S. White (ed.), *New Casebooks: 'Twelfth Night'*, 1996, pp. 160–93 and 129–59.
[4] *New York Times*, 28 July 1998.

Readings which utilise postmodernist psychoanalytic critical theory[1] may help both readers and theatre directors think laterally about how the play may be made to mean something less predictable than the romance of lost and found love, and the carnival attack on puritans, by looking at the marginal, the underside and unstated aspects of the text. Deconstructive and/or neo-formalist analyses of the play's linguistic games, its uses of rhetoric and recurrent metaphor, can assist in exploring these possibilities, and can also help actors and directors to get beyond traditional character analysis into, for example, the weird logic of a dream world that often seems to be operating in *Twelfth Night*.[2]

Stage history

For Manningham and the commentators who followed in the seventeenth century, the play's most important character was Malvolio.[3] Arguably this is because the play was first viewed and read in a time of social ferment which was to result in the English Revolution, based on an opposition between largely Puritan parliamentary forces and those loyal to the King. Since the play's revival in 1740–1 and the establishment of modern actresses as 'stars' (see below), the interest that the play engenders has shifted to its exploration of romantic love and desire, and it is read within the paradigm of romantic comedy, where the ending always envisages marriage. This essentially conservative model can, of course, be subverted by swinging the focus back to such resistant figures as Malvolio and Antonio, or to a 'queer' reading of the Orsino–Viola–Olivia erotic entanglement.

After the two performances of *Twelfth Night* noted at court in 1618 and 1623, there is no record of any performances until Samuel Pepys saw three revivals (1661, 1663, 1669) in London following the restoration of the monarchy and the reopening of the theatres. Pepys thought it 'a silly play, and not related at all to the name or day' (even though it was played on 6 January in 1663). John Downes, however, says the comedy 'had mighty Success by its well Performance'.[4] Nevertheless it was clearly not a hit in the Restoration period. Charles Burnaby's farrago, *Love Betray'd* (1703), which contains a rough echo of the plot and about fifty of Shakespeare's lines, unsurprisingly did not succeed after a couple of productions. It took another two generations until

---

[1] E.g. Laurie Osborne, 'Displacing and renaming love: a Lacanian reading', in *The Trick of Singularity*, pp. 137–173; Barbara Freedman, *Staging the Gaze: Postmodernism, Psychoanalysis, and Shakespearean Comedy*, 1991, ch. 7.

[2] E.g. Stephen Booth, *Precious Nonsense: The Gettysburg Address, Ben Jonson's Epitaphs on his Children, and 'Twelfth Night'*, 1998; Patricia Parker, 'Transfigurations: Shakespeare and rhetoric', in *Literary Fat Ladies: Rhetoric, Gender, Property*, 1987, pp. 67–96; Geoffrey H. Hartman, 'Shakespeare's poetical character in *Twelfth Night*', in *Shakespeare and the Question of Theory* (eds. Parker and Hartman), 1985, and frequently anthologised.

[3] '. . . lo, in a trice / The Cockpit galleries, boxes, all are full / To hear Malvolio, that cross-gartered gull', Leonard Digges, in Shakespeare's *Poems* (1640). T. W. Craik notes that 'in Charles I's copy of the 1632 Folio (at Buckingham Palace), the name Malvolio is written opposite the title in the list of contents'. Introduction, *Twelfth Night* (Ard.), pp. lxxix–lxxx.

[4] Both comments cited in G. C. D. Odell, *Shakespeare from Betterton to Irving*, 2 vols., 1966 [1920], vol. I, p. 38.

Shakespeare's play was revived in the 1740–1 season at Drury Lane. The roles of Viola and Olivia – exemplifying two favourite qualities of the mid-eighteenth century, wit and sensibility – soon became vehicles for star actresses of the eighteenth century such as Dora Jordan and Elizabeth Farren. Viola's pathos was even evoked beyond the play in a concert setting by Haydn of 'She never told her love' (*Canzonets*, 1795).

Actresses of *ingénue* roles were always expected to sing in eighteenth-century productions; thus we find Feste's songs being cut in favour of songs for Viola and Olivia. In 1820 there was a wholesale musicalisation of *Twelfth Night* under the direction of Frederick Reynolds at Covent Garden, 'the Overture and the whole of the Musick composed, and selected from Morley, Ford, Ravenscroft, Saville, Sir J. Stephenson, Winter, &c, and the Glees arranged by Mr. Bishop'. Most of the words of these songs were taken from other Shakespeare plays and the Sonnets; the whole masque of Juno and Ceres from *The Tempest* was included.[1] Leigh Hunt commented, 'Viola's [songs] are deep and tender; Olivia's, like her rank and pride, more vehement, gorgeous, and wilful; those of the others as wilful too, but light, festive, and seasonable.'[2]

By the late eighteenth century, various editions of the play with only minor variations from the Folio text, available in such series as Bell's British Theatre (1788), ensured that, as Jane Austen's Henry Crawford remarked, 'Shakespeare one gets acquainted with without knowing how. It is part of an Englishman's constitution. His thoughts and beauties are so spread abroad that one touches them every where, one is intimate with him by instinct.'[3] By the 1840s, with the growth of a Romantic and early Victorian interest in seeing the 'original' work of the greatest of English poets, audiences were experiencing the play more or less as first printed, though still with a good deal of interpolated music. *Twelfth Night* became a standard part of the theatrical repertoire from the mid-century onwards, always in elaborately 'historical' sets representing Elizabethan gardens, streets[4] and palaces, with some suggestion of the Aegean, for example, in Viola's Greek-style short skirt over breeches (see illustration 4). Herbert Beerbohm Tree directed a production in London in 1901 (he also played a much admired Malvolio) in which 'the garden of Olivia' extended 'terrace by terrace to the extreme back of the stage, with very real grass, real fountains, paths and descending steps . . . The actors were literally in an Italian garden.' As Odell reports of the production's 1913 revival, this meant that 'once put up, this scene could not easily be removed, and it was perforce used for many of the Shakespearian episodes for which it was absurdly inappropriate'.[5] But the expectations of theatre-goers were changing in response to a sense that Victorian materialism was old-fashioned and inappropriate to the modernist twentieth century, in which visual art was tending

---

[1] Odell, *Shakespeare*, II, p. 135.

[2] Ibid., II, p. 137, quoting Hunt's *The Examiner*, 12 November 1820.

[3] Jane Austen, *Mansfield Park*, 1814, ch. 34. Arguably Anne Elliot's great speech in defence of women's constancy, in Austen's *Persuasion*, ch. 23, is influenced by Viola's speeches in *Twelfth Night* 2.4.

[4] Of Irving's 1884 production at the Lyceum a critic noted, 'One of the scenes, the "Market Place,"[4.1] . . . is before the audience literally for only two or three minutes. It is painted with as much elaboration and finish as if it were to be the setting of all the action of a long play.' Salgādo, *Eyewitnesses of Shakespeare*, p. 211.

[5] Odell, *Shakespeare*, II, p. 455.

9   Elizabeth Farren as Olivia, with guitar, late eighteenth century

towards minimalism and a preference for symbolism over literal realism. The use of a single set, leading to a swifter performance, arose from the experiments of the Elizabethan Stage Society (William Poel's *Twelfth Night*, 1897 and 1903). Most notably, the design revolution of Gordon Craig and other artists, who brought on to the stage the bright colours and geometric shapes of early twentieth-century painting, completed the play's metamorphosis from exotic realism to a cooler, more abstract version of romance. Harley Granville-Barker's production at the Savoy in 1912 is an early example of the new approach:

Orsino's palace was nothing but a yellow and black curtain in triangular patterns . . . Olivia's garden was the only full stage set; formalized and overly symmetrical, it was a manifest critique of the lush illusion of Hawes Craven's set for Tree. No grassy steps here or pictures of topiary, only architectural components and hard geometrical shapes, an exercise in Cubist geometry. The box trees of the script were represented by two Futurist space needles . . .[1]

Despite this departure from tradition, in English-speaking countries in the twentieth century the approach to *Twelfth Night* remained fairly standardised. The setting rarely strayed from the period 1600–30. There was a sense, carried over from the nineteenth century, that the play had an atmosphere of melancholy – 'Youth's a stuff will not endure', 'She never told her love', were keynote phrases. Feste was an ageing clown, Viola tended to be petite and somewhat timid, Olivia a rather grand dignified lady in her thirties (or more). Changes began, slowly, after World War II, perhaps in response to the social changes brought about by that cataclysm: vastly increased mobility for women, and an uncomfortable recognition of where the exclusion of certain types of people from society might lead – whether that person is of the 'wrong' race (Olivier played Malvolio 'like a Jewish hairdresser' in 1955, 'with a lisp and an extraordinary accent'),[2] or of a 'deviant' sexual persuasion (there was increasing recognition of Antonio's importance in the play's emotional map). The sexual revolution of the 1960s and 1970s gradually liberated the play's image of desire from a simple representation of heterosexual romance. It is now quite common to see, for example, Sebastian and Antonio as a homosexual couple in 2.1; or Orsino kissing 'Cesario' at the end of 2.4. Sometimes Orsino's entire court will have the air of a gay bar. Olivia, similarly, might heartily kiss Viola/Cesario in 3.1, thus providing an element of lesbian flirtation. Olivia became definitively a skittish young woman in Geraldine McEwan's performance for Peter Hall in 1958, and the result – 'this pert puck-faced girl pouted, smirked, simpered and bit her lip as she pined for the disguised Viola'[3] – marked a turning point in depicting the play's dealings with sexual desire.

---

[1] Dennis Kennedy, *Looking at Shakespeare*, 1993, pp. 75–6.

[2] John Gielgud, *An Actor and his Time*, 1981, p. 143. Ronald Barker noted a combination of both Nazi pariah figures in his comment on Olivier's performance, 'a tight-lipped effeminate Shylock' (*Plays and Players*, June 1955). Of Walter Hudd's Malvolio in 1947 at the Shakespeare Memorial Theatre, a critic wrote, 'The scene behind the grill is too painful for comedy nowadays . . . we feel ourselves to be included in the condemnation, for did not we, too, laugh at his discomfiture in the garden?' (unidentified newspaper cutting, Shakespeare Centre Library). The tendency to see tragic potential in Malvolio goes back at least as far as Charles Lamb's essay 'On some of the old actors' (*Essays of Elia*, 1823); Irving's Malvolio, which was not liked by critics, was one early attempt to put this view into performance.

[3] Felix Barker, *Evening News*, 23 April 1958.

10   Lillah McCarthy as Viola, Granville-Barker's production, London 1912, designed by Norman Wilkinson

Viola, having spent most of the previous two centuries embodying a winsome femininity, emerged after World War II in England as a much stronger and more competent figure, quite at home in her boy's costume (even though Vivien Leigh, in Gielgud's famous 1955 production, got into a fashionable evening dress – 'woman's weeds', indeed! – for her curtain calls). Tall and elegant Diana Rigg brought the wit

and style of her role as 'Mrs Peel' in TV's *The Avengers* to Viola in 1966 for the Royal
Shakespeare Company, towering over the tiny Malvolio of Ian Holm. This production by Clifford Williams was also notable for the erotically tactile relationship
between Viola and and a sensuous Orsino (Alan Howard), a motif explored even more
explicitly in Peter Gill's 1974 RSC production, with its overt use of the Narcissus
myth: 'All are intoxicated with their own reflections, and the function of Viola and
Sebastian is to put them through an Ovidian obstacle course from which they learn to
turn away from the mirror and form real attachments.'[1] Jane Lapotaire's Viola
'accepts the double nature of her sexuality – yielding to Orsino's embraces as a page
boy, even wanting to satisfy Olivia as a woman . . . Olivia is clearly delighted at the
prospect of a ménage-à-quatre: doubleness adds piquancy to desire'.[2]

'Autumnal' Twelfth Nights

The practice of producing the play emphasising a specifically 'autumnal'[3] or fin-de-
siècle quality, seems to have begun with Peter Hall's 1958 Shakespeare Memorial
Theatre production, designed by Lila de Nobili as a romantic Caroline world to be
seen through a filter of gauze curtains. Its dominant figure was Max Adrian's ageing
Pierrot of a Feste. Fellow RSC director John Barton was clearly influenced by this a
decade later in 1969, in a production which toured the world and left its image for
many audiences as a benchmark. The sound of the sea was heard as a continual background to an almost bare, beautifully lit stage dominated by a tunnel-like 'long gallery'
running upstage. This poetic symbolism, suggesting an Alice-like dream world, was
combined with the historical specificity of Elizabethan costume. The emphasis was
thus on the actors rather than the concept: and, in the young Judi Dench, Barton cast
one of the great English actors of the twentieth century (see illustration 8). Deeply
touching in her moments of emotional vulnerability, yet sprightly and witty when
necessary (and particularly athletically hilarious in the duel scene), Dench's performance lives on for those who saw it as definitive – not because Viola cannot be played
any other way, but because Dench's art convinced the audience of the character's
complex reality. Donald Sinden's Malvolio, too, extremely funny in his bravura
scenes, brought a striking note of pathos both to the 'dark house' scene and to his final
exit. Stanley Wells summarises the overall effect of this production as 'a beauty of
communication, of sympathy, understanding, and compassion. It had a Chekhovian
quality . . .'[4]

Terry Hands' 'winter' production (RSC 1979) took the elegiac mood for *Twelfth
Night* even further, and set the play in its titular season, winter (a decision followed
by Kenneth Branagh's 1987 version, subsequently filmed for television, 1989). The
production was most notable for the empowering of a ragged, ill-looking Feste as a

[1] Irving Wardle, *The Times*, 23 August 1974.
[2] Peter Ansorge, *Plays and Players*, October 1974.
[3] Although, as E. S. Donno points out, the internal references in the play to the season suggest spring or
    summer for its action (Donno, Introduction, 1985, pp. 3–4).
[4] Stanley Wells, *Royal Shakespeare*, 1977, p. 62.

11   Geraldine McEwan as Olivia, Dorothy Tutin as Viola, Royal Shakespeare Company, 1958

sort of local deity. He was on stage all the time, watching – or occasionally (for example in the Sebastian scenes) with his back turned.[1] He was also to be seen throughout

---

[1] This focus on Feste was also a feature of a Bulgarian production of 1975: the clown was 'the play's creator ...[who] magically conjured up the tempest that would bring Viola to Illyria', and then remained on stage to observe the action: 'the whole work became his fairytale' (S. Leiter (ed.), *Shakespeare Around the Globe*, 1986, p. 771).

12   Cherie Lunghi as Viola, Geoffrey Hutchings as a watchful Feste, Norman Tyrrell as Fabian, John
McEnery as Sir Andrew, Willoughby Goddard as Sir Toby, Royal Shakespeare Company, 1979. Act
3, Scene 4: 'He named Sebastian'

the play occasionally planting daffodils in the still snowy ground of the bare woodland
setting.

By 1983 and John Caird's production for the RSC, the adjective 'autumnal' was
almost automatically applied to the play. This production took place in the shadow of
a huge, twisted, bare-branched tree; wind and rain permeated the play and overwhelmed any wit or resourcefulness Zoë Wanamaker's sad urchin Viola might have
tried to display. Trevor Nunn's 1996 film, using all the freedom of cinema to change
locations and create atmosphere through moodily lit shots, serves as a permanent
record of this English tendency to read the play as an intrinsically melancholy piece.
Nunn's unusual choice of period for the play, the late nineteenth century (which is of
course Chekhov's period), carries strong suggestions of the Empire coming to an end
– soldiers roam the streets of the seaside town; the luxury of the upper classes seems
claustrophobic, whether it is Olivia pacing her heavily draped rooms or Viola having
to show her masculinity by smoking cigars and playing billiards in similarly gloomy
surroundings. Ben Kingsley's Feste, who leaves the community (as does Nigel
Hawthorne's Malvolio) at the film's end, is a watcher, saturnine and cynical.

Sam Mendes's production for the Donmar Warehouse (2002), in repertoire with
Chekhov's *Uncle Vanya*, demonstrated yet again the fin-de-siècle or 'end of the old
order' feeling that can be located in the play if it is viewed through Chekhovian spec-
tacles. On the tiny Donmar stage, the production strove for psychological rather than

13 'Autumnal' set, designer Robin Don, Royal Shakespeare Company, 1983

visual realism: the most striking aspect of the design was a large empty picture-frame that was filled, as appropriate, with the absent character who was being described or imagined. Thus a certain postmodern self-consciousness made its presence felt in what was in many respects

a deeply conventional *Twelfth Night* for its time . . . The main effect of the twinning with *Vanya* . . . was a cast as alive to the social nuances of the Olivia household as they had learned to be to that of the Voynitskys. In inter-war costumes . . . these people, too, belonged to a social order on the wane.

Simon Russell Beale's 'closely observed' Malvolio 'managed to combine prissiness, profound earnestness and an underlying sense of insecurity,'[1] in a world that would soon have no place for such upper servants as himself.

It is not hard to read into such 'autumnal' evocations of Illyria the English artistic left's sense of hopelessness in the face of the triumphal march of Thatcherism and New Labour. And it may explain the relative failure of all Royal Shakespeare Company productions of the play in the 1990s: the state-subsidised theatre seemed no longer confident about making social comment, even obliquely. There was a succes-

[1] Michael Dobson, 'Shakespeare performances in England, 2002', *Shakespeare Survey 56* (2003), p. 261 (also previous quotation). This article includes a detailed description of Simon Russell Beale's comic and ultimately tragic Malvolio.

14 Anthony O'Donnell as Feste, Simon Russell Beale as the 'madly used' Malvolio, Donmar Warehouse 2002. Act 5, Scene 1: 'And thus the whirligig of time brings in his revenges.'

sion of vaguely fantastical and/or pseudo-Elizabethan productions, in which a 'different' look was wilful rather than organic. In 1991 Griff Rhys Jones directed a late Victorian *Twelfth Night* in the style of a Gilbert and Sullivan operetta; in 1994, Ian Judge gave the audience at Stratford a prettified reproduction of the Elizabethan streetscape just outside the theatre (this production was at least notable for Desmond Barrit's manic Welsh Malvolio); in 2001, Lindsay Posner went lushly Edwardian. Adrian Noble's pop-arty production in 1997 – with its cartoonish 1920s–1960s costumes and lurid green plastic box-hedge (looking, commented many critics, like a car-wash) – was a bizarre effort to move the play out of the comfortable tradition of period productions, but it substituted visual jokes for emotional or intellectual drive. Its saving grace was a powerful Malvolio from Philip Voss: 'he makes the character touching, even tragic. The tears of gratitude he sheds when he believes that Olivia loves him are a comic joy, as is his later, bumblebee-like appearance in preposterous yellow blazer, tartan socks and tennis shorts.'[1] This transformation was followed by bullying degradation in the 'dark house', a dog-kennel.

Non-traditional productions

At the end of the twentieth century it seemed that productions not in England, or not in English, were finding more varied meanings in the play. Continental European theatre, with a long history of experiment, is less reverential towards the Shakespearean text; the fact that it has to be translated no doubt contributes to this atmosphere of liberation, but it can also be argued that, in translating the play, what is produced is an adaptation, a modern version of the play, rather than an attempt to work within the parameters provided by Shakespeare's language. Eclectic, anti-historical costumes and sets emphasised psychological and even political possibilities that strongly reflected the cultural fashions of the time and place of the production.[2]

In Paris in 1982, for example, Ariane Mnouchkine offered *Twelfth Night* as an anti-realistic 'journey into the unconscious' which used Asian-style theatrical conventions and 'Indian and Persian visual images' and, in doing so, invoked an alienation effect that to some extent undermined the empathy-creating narrative of love.[3] By contrast,

[1] Charles Spencer, *Daily Telegraph*, 27 July 1997. There is an illuminating discussion of this production, in a comparison with the 'benchmark' Barton production of 1969, by Janice Wardle: '*Twelfth Night*: "One face, one voice, one habit, and two persons!"', in Deborah Cartmell and Michael Scott (eds.), *Talking Shakespeare*, 2001, pp. 105–22.

[2] An account of seventeen major productions from 1946 to 1983, with many details indicating varieties of style and interpretation, appears in *Shakespeare Around the Globe*, 1986, pp. 767–94. A survey of highly experimental German productions in the then GDR in the 1980s can be found in Maik Hamburger, 'A spate of *Twelfth Nights*: Illyria rediscovered?', in Werner Habicht, D. J. Palmer and Roger Pringle (eds.), *Images of Shakespeare*, 1988, pp. 236–44. Hamburger begins by commenting on the popularity of *Twelfth Night* in Germany, and the 'clichés that have . . . formed a kind of traditional crust around the play' (p. 236) since the early nineteenth-century Schlegel translation. See also Wilhelm Hortmann, 'Word into image: notes on the scenography of recent German productions', in Dennis Kennedy (ed.), *Foreign Shakespeare*, 1993, pp. 242–53.

[3] Adrian Kiernander 'Reading(,) theatre (,) techniques: responding to the influence of Asian theatre in the work of Ariane Mnouchkine', *Modern Drama* 35 (1992), 149–58 (p. 150). Dennis Kennedy comments on the 'great billowing pink cloth [that] swallowed the cast at the end' (*Looking at Shakespeare*, p. 288).

in Mnouchkine's sacred space, the Cartoucherie, in 2000, the travelling Troupe du Phénix gave a wonderfully engaging 'rough theatre' performance of *La Nuit des Rois* (*Twelfth Night*), with commedia *lazzi*, a watchful Feste always in evidence, constant irruptions of folk-style music and at the centre the circus magic of a pair of clown-like twins discovering each other again.

The radical English company Cheek by Jowl's 1986–7 production of *Twelfth Night* (director Declan Donnellan) was the first Shakespeare play performed in the RSC's Swan theatre at Stratford, and it revelled in the close contact with the audience provided by that space. An abstract minimalist set (featuring a hanging clock) accompanied costumes suggesting a decaying post-colonial outpost. The actors 'moved effortlessly from comic inventiveness to a sensitive apprehension of the pain and ambiguity at the heart of *Twelfth Night*'; in the final scene

the appearance of the identical twins provoked fear. Even when everything was sorted out, it was clear that the women had a tough task ahead – Orsino nearly went off with Sebastian, [the homosexual] Feste introduced himself to Antonio, and just for a few seconds everyone was frozen into immobility as a spotlit Malvolio swore revenge. This was updated Shakespeare at its best, using modern sensibilities to strip away pre-conceived notions about an all-too-familiar text.[1]

British director Neil Bartlett staged the play at Chicago's mainstream Goodman Theater as postmodern 'performance art' in 1991. The production was a determined effort to 'deconstruct the realistic acting of institutional Shakespeare within its own institutional space'.[2] All the actors were white women very transparently 'performing' their characters, except for the players of Viola, Sebastian and Feste, who were African-American males. Bartlett, fascinated by the 'doubles, twins and mirrors at the heart of *Twelfth Night*',

cast the play around a series of oppositions, not just that between men and women. Women dressed up as men played against and with women dressed up as women; but black [actors] also played against white, adolescent performers against mature performers, improvising comedians and singers against 'actors' . . . boundaries being crossed by cross-dressing were multiple.[3]

The radical dislocations of this interesting experiment were probably counterproductive for the usual audience at the Goodman Theater, just as they would have been at Stratford-upon-Avon. A less disconcerting 'alienation effect' can be gained by imaginative doubling, which foregrounds the performativity of the characters. With actors switching between characters in the course of a scene, even, at times, a single actor conducting a dialogue between two characters, the audience enjoys the presentational story-telling skills of the performers, which include, but are not limited by, naturalistic

[1] Review by C. C., *Cahiers Elisabethains* 32 (October 1987), 90. Orsino was patently disappointed that his beloved pageboy had turned out to be a girl: this 'len[t] his closing description of her as "his fancy's queen" a wishful, twentieth-century resonance', commented Duncan Wu (*Times Literary Supplement*, 23 January 1987).
[2] Keith Appler, 'Deconstructing the regional theater with "performance art" Shakespeare', *Theatre Topics*, (March 1995), 35–49.
[3] Neil Bartlett, 'Underneath our clothes', *American Theatre*, 9, 4 (July/August 1992), 44.

impersonations. A particularly effective doubling can be that of Feste and Malvolio, two 'clowns' – one who consciously works to produce laughter, the other unconscious of the comic effects he creates.

Neil Armfield's 1983 production for South Australia's Lighthouse company (subsequently filmed, 1985, with Gillian Jones doubling Viola and Sebastian) was pioneering in many respects. The single set, representing a Queensland beach resort, featured a large mirror-wall which constantly reflected both characters and audience. Kerry Walker was an androgynous humpbacked Feste, wary and faintly sinister in this holiday world. John Wood and Geoffrey Rush played Belch and Aguecheek as 'a drunken Ocker spiv and . . . a kind of caricatured car salesman on holiday'.[1] Two other Australian productions that demonstrated a consciously post-colonial reading followed on Armfield's holiday-island setting. In John Bell's production for the Bell Shakespeare Company (1995), Bell based his Malvolio on Conservative MP Enoch Powell ('a figure of fun in my university days'),[2] and added to that pillar of respectability the whiff of the Tory sex scandals of the 1980s and early 1990s: his cross-gartered appearance was in the fishnets and suspender-belt of the drag queen.

A World War II American Army base in Australia was the setting for the Railway Street Theatre Company's 2002 production in Sydney (director Mary-Anne Gifford), with a cast of seven actors and imaginative doubling (for example, Feste and Sir Toby). Orsino and his court were American soldiers living in idle luxury. Olivia, a lady of the local country establishment, began in a nurse's uniform (with veil) and changed to fashionable 1940s outfits. Most interesting for its political commentary, as with the Bell production, was Malvolio, a respectable farm-manager supporting the war effort in food production (and properly decrying time-wasting and inebriation). A bit starchy but quite likeable, Malvolio was defeated only by his lack of foreign 'class'. His yellow stockings outfit was a complete old-fashioned Elizabethan actor's costume, such as might have been seen in any Shakespeare production in Australia in the 1940s. Unconsciously embodying Australia's long-lasting cultural cringe towards England, Malvolio was obviously hoping to impress with this grandiose image.

These productions demonstrate that it is possible to read *Twelfth Night* politically, since its romance takes place in a realistic small community, where class and money matter. Finally, there has also been a resurgence of interest, a century after William Poel's Elizabethan Stage Society, in 'archaeological' performances, aided by the reconstructions of the Globe and other theatres. Two examples will suffice: the London Globe's all-male production in 2002, and Shenandoah Shakespeare's production, 2002–3, in the new Blackfriars Playhouse in Staunton, Virginia.

Tim Carroll's production for Shakespeare's Globe (London) purported to be a close reconstruction of an Elizabethan performance, in costumes and staging; it had a 'quatercentenary season' at Middle Temple Hall in January 2002. Despite this claim for historical authenticity, in an all-male cast the women's parts were played by adult men,

---

[1] Peter Ward, *The Australian*, 28 February 1983.
[2] John Bell, *The Time of My Life* (2002), pp. 241–2. This was 'the Empire writing back' with a vengeance, since Powell had been a very young and pompous Professor of Greek at Sydney University early in his career.

15   John Bell as Malvolio, 1995. The Bell Shakespeare Company

16 Act 5, Scene 1. Shenandoah Shakespeare at the Blackfriars Playhouse, Staunton, VA, 2003

not boys. The actors of Olivia (Mark Rylance) and Viola (Michael Brown) did demonstrate that femininity could be played as a performance without seeming 'camp' – each used a light voice and restrained walk and gestural style – but it could not be said that they created anything like the impression that the boys of 1601/2 would have done. Paul Chahidi played Maria as a middle-aged pantomime Dame. Specious historical claims aside, it was a revelation to see that the adult male 'twins' were literally indistinguishable in their identical costumes and wigs; to experience a moment of confusion when either Viola or Sebastian came on – which is it? And to experience the delighted wonder of all the other characters on stage when Viola and Sebastian are finally face to face, most convincingly 'One face, one voice, one habit, and two persons'!

Shenandoah Shakespeare's *Twelfth Night* (2002) in a reproduction of the sixteenth-century Blackfriars Playhouse (an intimate indoors venue used by Shakespeare's company after 1608), employed women for the female parts, but was otherwise performed in historical costume on a bare stage. The production highlighted comedy, even in romantic scenes such as 2.4: Orsino conducted and sang along with 'Come away, death', Viola having to lie on the floor to avoid his extravagant gestures. Feste (John Harrell) was a droll clown, improvising a mime with members of the audience at the beginning of 3.1, and able to make even the 'dark house' scene funny through his physical comedy (it helped that Malvolio was an invisible voice coming from the stage trap). Not only Viola's soliloquies, but Malvolio's letter scene and Olivia's asides were directed to the audience in the company's consciously presentational style; the audience shared the light provided by the electric chandeliers hanging from the theatre's

17 David Marks as Sir Toby, Sarah Marshall as Feste (replacing Fabian), James Sugg as Sir Andrew.
    Act 3, Scene 4. Folger Theatre, Washington DC, 2003

ceiling. The inclusiveness of the Blackfriars theatre and its company was underlined by the whole cast singing 'When that I was and–a little tiny boy' at the end, led by the charismatic clown. Antonio, played as a piratical and passionate Spaniard, seized the opportunity to escape through the audience.

Twelfth Night also had an outing at the Folger Theatre in Washington, DC, in early 2003 (director Aaron Posner). This intimate space, based on the architecture of an Elizabethan indoor theatre or great hall, was transformed into a 1970s mansion, with glass walls, grand balconies and stairs, and a music room for jazz and rock performances of the songs. While the 1970s might seem an unusual choice for a 'period' setting of the play, it infused it with youthful energy. Even those not young, like Sir Toby, wanted to appear hip. Viola and Sebastian, in identical gear of flared jeans, afghan coat, ponytail and beads, shared a confident, upfront approach to life, Viola in particular (Holly Twyford) being as witty and forward a 'youth' as any young man of the period. The comic highlight was the duel between Viola and Sir Andrew, played as a John Travolta-style dance-off between two less than brilliant dancers who knew what the moves *should* be. (Sebastian defeated Sir Andrew and Sir Toby simply by dancing with a ferocious and inventive energy that occasionally led to collisions.)

From America there also came, in 1998, John Madden's Academy Award-winning *Shakespeare in Love*, a film that combined historical re-creation of London in 1600 (including its theatres) with a witty script by Marc Norman and Tom Stoppard. The film uses many of the metatheatrical devices that are to be found in Shakespeare's

18   Act 3, Scene 4. Shenandoah Shakespeare at the Blackfriars Playhouse, Staunton, VA, 2003

Twelfth Night. The heroine, Viola de Lesseps (Gwyneth Paltrow) is an aristocratic young woman under the sway of her father (as in *Romeo and Juliet*); she disguises herself in boy's clothes to pursue her passion for the theatre. Shakespeare (Joseph Fiennes), who is suffering from writer's block, falls in love with her/him and they enjoy a brief passionate affair. After her masquerade is finally exposed and she is married off, she is shipwrecked on her way to the American settlement in the New World. As the film ends we see Shakespeare beginning to write the play that she has proposed to him. His writing is intercut with shots of Viola's shipwreck. Has Shakespeare only imagined this end to Viola's story? What is real? What is romance? 'What country, friends, is this?', he writes. It is, of course, the imaginary world – however different it and its inhabitants may look in various periods – that has been such a vital resource since *Twelfth Night* was first performed over 400 years ago. As Zoë Wanamaker writes, 'whichever way people try to direct it or to focus it . . . whatever you do as you dig and dig, and get deeper and deeper, the text remains for another attempt'.[1]

PENNY GAY

[1] Wanamaker, in *Players of Shakespeare 2*, p. 91.

NOTE ON THE TEXT

Twelfth Night was first published in the First Folio in 1623 where it is placed next to the last of the comedies, *The Winter's Tale*. It is a superior text, but for an account of some 'short-lived' trouble during the sequence of printing and for the nature of the copy, see Textual Analysis, pp. 163–6 below.

In this edition, acts and scenes correspond with the divisions in the Folio.[1] The somewhat anomalous clearing of the stage at 3.4.231 which, in accord with the law of re-entry, should mark a new scene but is instead immediately followed by the re-entry of Sir Toby and Sir Andrew, has been retained;[2] this allows for some business off-stage that is visible at least to Sir Toby and Sir Andrew (and perhaps to the audience through an open stage door), as is evident from Sir Toby's remark, 'Fabian can scarce hold him yonder.' Locations of scenes, traditional from eighteenth-century editions on, are given in the Commentary. Requisite entrances and exits not in the Folio have been inserted in square brackets, as have some few other stage directions and indications of 'asides'.

Because of the discrepancy in the rank of Orsino between what is given in the stage directions and in the text (pointed out at p. 165 below) and because of the general practice of referring to Shakespearean characters by name, all speech headings involving him (*Du.*) have been regularised to Orsino. On the same grounds, speech headings for the clown (*Clo.*) have been regularised to Feste, though he is named only once in the text.

The frequent contractions (*th'*, *o'th'*, etc.) have been retained in accord with the colloquial character of much of the dialogue; *h'as* (i.e. *he has*) has been retained as indicating the two words contracted and the variant *ha's* has been regularised; *an* meaning *if* has been regularised to *and* and *ta'en* to *tane*.

The punctuation in the Folio is not generally troublesome though there is a generous use of colons, and these have frequently been silently replaced by periods or by commas or dashes in the comic scenes; quotation marks have been inserted when required. When a final *-ed* is pronounced because of the requirement of metre, it is indicated by a *grave* accent; some few other differences from modern stress are indicated in the notes. Finally, the seventeenth-century practice of italicising proper names within the dialogue has been ignored.

In addition to substantive readings, the collation includes a number of punctuation changes, largely in the comic scenes, that have been introduced from the eighteenth century on; they serve to indicate how editors have gradually come to interpret the

---

[1] Furness gives Henry Irving's acting version with act and scene divisions, and it is still common for modern directors to transpose the first two scenes in Act 1.

[2] See C. M. Haines, 'The law of re-entry in Shakespeare', *RES* 1 (Oct. 1925), 449–51, where he notes sixteen occasions, excluding battle scenes, when the convention is disregarded.

text. The authority for the reading comes immediately after the square bracket, followed by the reading in F (the First Folio, the sole authority); other readings, if any, follow in chronological order.

The following abbreviations are used: *subst.* for *substantively,* followed by the name of the editor who introduced the change, usually of a stage direction or a mark of punctuation, and which is, in the main, adopted in this edition; *This edn* for a modification, again usually of a stage direction or mark of punctuation, that does not appear in earlier standard editions though it may be indicated as earlier having been *conjectured (conj.).* An asterisk preceding the lemma in the Commentary is used to call attention to a word or phrase that has been emended in the text.

Twelfth Night
or What You Will

LIST OF CHARACTERS

ORSINO, *Duke (or Count) of Illyria*
SEBASTIAN, *twin brother to Viola*
ANTONIO, *captain, a friend to Sebastian*
SEA CAPTAIN, *a friend to Viola*
VALENTINE ⎱
CURIO   ⎰ *gentlemen attending Orsino*
SIR TOBY BELCH, *a kinsman of Olivia's*
SIR ANDREW AGUECHEEK, *a companion of Sir Toby's*
MALVOLIO, *steward to Olivia*
FABIAN, *a gentleman of Olivia's household*
FESTE, *a jester in Olivia's household*

OLIVIA, *a countess*
VIOLA, *twin sister to Sebastian, later called Cesario*
MARIA, *a gentlewoman in Olivia's household*

PRIEST
Musicians, Lords, Sailors, Officers and other attendants
Scene: Illyria

Notes

The List of Characters is based mainly on that of Rowe, the first to appear in print, and on the Douai MS.

ORSINO For the variation between 'duke' and 'count' in F's stage directions and the text, see Textual Analysis, p. 165 below.

CURIO A frequent name for a courtier, from Latin *curia*, court.

VIOLA The first syllable receives the stress. For a discussion of the symbolism of the name, see Winfreid Schleiner, 'Orsino and Viola: are the names of serious characters in *Twelfth Night* meaningful?', *S.St.* 16 (1984), 135–41.

MARIA Olivia specifies that Maria is one of her gentlewomen at 1.5.135 and Malvolio confirms this at 1.5.136.

TWELFTH NIGHT OR WHAT YOU WILL

1.1 [*Music.*] *Enter* ORSINO, *Duke of Illyria,* CURIO, *and other Lords*

ORSINO If music be the food of love, play on;
    Give me excess of it, that surfeiting,
    The appetite may sicken and so die.
    That strain again, it had a dying fall;
    O it came o'er my ear like the sweet sound   5
    That breathes upon a bank of violets,
    Stealing and giving odour. Enough; no more.
    'Tis not so sweet now as it was before.
    O spirit of love, how quick and fresh art thou,
    That, notwithstanding thy capacity,   10

Title] Twelfe Night, Or what you will. F   Act 1, Scene 1   1.1] *Actus Primus, Scæna Prima.* F   0 SD *Music*] *Mahood;*
Musick attending. / Capell; *not in* F

Title: TWELFTH F's form 'twelfe' here (and
again at 2.3.73) for 'twelfth' appears nowhere else
in the canon though *Ham.* (Q2), thought to be set
from Shakespeare's autograph, has 'twelfe' for
'twelve'.

    WHAT YOU WILL For the sense of this catch-
phrase, see p. 1 above.

Act 1, Scene 1
    1.1 Acts and scenes divided as in F.
    Location A room in the duke's palace (Capell).
    0 SD *Duke of Illyria* Though consistently called
'duke' in stage directions and speech headings in
F, after 1.4 he is called 'count' in the text for the
rest of the play. See Textual Analysis, p. 165.
    0 SD *Illyria* On the eastern coast of the Adriatic.
    1 music...love Compare *Ant.* 2.5.1–2: 'music,
moody food / Of us that trade in love'. The
sentiments in 1–11 receive their own ironic
comment in Orsino's words to Viola, 2.4.91–7,
where it is women's love that is said to suffer
'surfeit, cloyment, and revolt'.
    4 That strain again Having specified a
'surfeit' of music, here Orsino demands that the
musicians (probably a household consort) stop and
repeat the musical phrase. Joseph Summers calls the
effect here, and in line 7 when the demand is
countered, 'a comic bit of stage business which is
rarely utilised in production' ('The masks of
Twelfth Night', p. 88).
    4 fall cadence.
    5–7 like the sweet sound...odour A substitu-
tion of the effect for the cause (a form of
metonymy); a rhetorically mannered style marks
Orsino's speech. For a comparable instance of this
figurative use, see *Comus* 555–7: 'At last a soft and
solemn-breathing sound / Rose like a stream of rich
distill'd Perfumes, / And stole upon the Air'
(Halliwell).
    9 quick and fresh alive and vigorous. For
'fresh', see *OED* sv *a* 10.
    10–14 That...minute i.e. the lover's sensibility
has the sea's capacity to take in everything, but
everything that enters, no matter how high its value,
quickly loses its worth. Orsino has taken in the
music which has now lost its significance for him,
leaving his love still 'quick and fresh'; compare his
words at 2.4.15–18.
    10 capacity ability to take in (and contain)
impressions (*OED* sv 4).

Receiveth as the sea. Nought enters there,
Of what validity and pitch soe'er,
But falls into abatement and low price
Even in a minute. So full of shapes is fancy,
That it alone is high fantastical.   15

CURIO Will you go hunt, my lord?
ORSINO   What, Curio?
CURIO The hart.
ORSINO Why so I do, the noblest that I have.
O when mine eyes did see Olivia first,
Methought she purged the air of pestilence;   20
That instant was I turned into a hart,
And my desires like fell and cruel hounds
E'er since pursue me.

Enter VALENTINE

How now, what news from her?
VALENTINE So please my lord, I might not be admitted,
But from her handmaid do return this answer: 25
The element itself, till seven years' heat,
Shall not behold her face at ample view;

---

23 SD] *As Dyce; follows* her? *in* F

11 **Receiveth** For another of the frequent instances of a third-person singular used with a second-person antecedent (Abbott 247), see *AYLI* 3.5.52–3: ''Tis such fools as you [foolish shepherd] / That makes the world full of ill-favor'd children.'

11 **there** With the immediate antecedent 'sea', the statement here and in the next two lines characterises what happens to objects in the 'never-surfeited sea' (*Temp.* 3.3.55). Many, however, take 'there' to refer to the 'capacity' of love, which of course it does by the analogy.

12 **validity and pitch** i.e. high value. This use of two nouns in place of a noun and an adjective (hendiadys) is another example of Orsino's rhetorical manner; 'pitch' (from falconry, describing the highest point of a flight) is frequently metaphorical, as in *Ham.* (Q2) 1740 (3.1.85): 'enterprises of great pitch and moment'.

14–15 **So...fantastical** So full of imagined forms is love ('fancy') that (like the sea) it is the most capricious of all things. 'Fantastical' in Shakespeare is generally derogatory, though it can simply mean 'imaginary'. Compare *LLL* 5.2.762–3,

where love is said to be 'Form'd by the eye and therefore like the eye, / Full of straying shapes, of habits, and of forms', and *MND* 5.1.3–22.

17–18 **hart...I have** Punning on hart/heart, the latter being his 'noblest' part.

20 **purged...pestilence** Though Olivia purged the air, Orsino caught the plague of love; she is thus both remedy and cause. Compare her similar response in 1.5.250: 'Even so quickly may one catch the plague?'

22–3 **desires...pursue me** Like the hunter Actaeon who, having seen Diana bathing, was turned into a stag and pursued by his own hounds (Ovid, *Metamorphoses* III, 138 ff.). Orsino is thus both hunter and quarry. The identification of erotic desires with pursuing hounds was common. See Daniel's *Delia* (1592), Sonnet 5, for an elaboration of the conceit.

22 **fell** fierce.

26 **element** sky.

26 **heat** i.e. the heat of seven summers (an example of synecdoche, taking the part for the whole).

But like a cloistress she will veilèd walk,
And water once a day her chamber round
With eye-offending brine; all this to season　　　　30
A brother's dead love, which she would keep fresh
And lasting, in her sad remembrance.
ORSINO O she that hath a heart of that fine frame
To pay this debt of love but to a brother,
How will she love, when the rich golden shaft　　　35
Hath killed the flock of all affections else
That live in her; when liver, brain, and heart,
These sovereign thrones, are all supplied and filled
Her sweet perfections with one selfsame king!
Away before me to sweet beds of flowers:　　　　40
Love-thoughts lie rich when canopied with bowers.

Exeunt

1.2 *Enter* VIOLA, *a* CAPTAIN, *and Sailors*

VIOLA What country, friends, is this?
CAPTAIN This is Illyria, lady.
VIOLA And what should I do in Illyria?
My brother, he is in Elysium.
Perchance he is not drowned: what think you, sailors?　　　5

---

39 selfsame] F2; selfe F　Act 1, Scene 2　1.2] *Scena Secunda.* F

28 cloistress A nun cloistered in her chamber.
30 season preserve with brine. This play on 'season' and 'brine' is used in Shakespeare either for a rhetorical or a comic effect, as in *The Rape of Lucrece* 796: 'Seasoning the earth with show'rs of silver brine', and *Rom.* 2.3.69–70: 'Jesu Maria, what a deal of brine / Hath wash'd thy sallow cheeks for Rosaline!' Other instances are in *A Lover's Complaint* 17–18 and *AWW* 1.1.48–9.
32 remembrance An obsolete form, pronounced as four syllables.
33 that fine frame Compare *AWW* 4.2.4: 'In your fine frame hath love no quality?'
35 golden shaft Cupid's 'best arrow' (*MND* 1.1.170) induced love, the one tipped with lead, hatred (Ovid, *Metamorphoses* 1, 468–71).
36 affections else other feelings.
37–8 liver...thrones The liver was the throne of the passions, the brain of reason, and the heart of emotion.
38 filled (hath) satisfied. Paralleling 'Hath killed' at 36. See *OED* sv v 10, 17.

39 *selfsame An intensive. F's omission of 'same' is corrected in subsequent folios both for metre and clarity of meaning. Shakespeare uses the form 'selfsame' most frequently. Kökeritz observes that in everyday speech '-ion' was normally a monosyllable (p. 293).
40–1 Away...bowers Orsino's directive to his attendants allows him to express the final sentiment of the couplet as they are leaving the stage. For its significance in relation to the projected season of the play's action and the metaphorical nature of its title, see p. 41, n 3 above.

Act 1, Scene 2
Location The sea coast (Capell)
4 Elysium Equivalent to heaven as the abode of the blessed; the similarity of initial sound with 'Illyria' points up the difference in locales that Viola wishes to emphasise.
5–7 Perchance Viola uses the term to mean 'perhaps', the Captain uses it to mean 'by chance', and Viola then plays upon both senses.

CAPTAIN It is perchance that you yourself were saved.

VIOLA O my poor brother! And so perchance may he be.

CAPTAIN True, madam, and to comfort you with chance,
  Assure yourself, after our ship did split,
  When you, and those poor number saved with you,   10
  Hung on our driving boat, I saw your brother
  Most provident in peril, bind himself
  (Courage and hope both teaching him the practice)
  To a strong mast that lived upon the sea;
  Where like Arion on the dolphin's back   15
  I saw him hold acquaintance with the waves
  So long as I could see.

VIOLA For saying so, there's gold.
  Mine own escape unfoldeth to my hope,
  Whereto thy speech serves for authority,   20
  The like of him. Know'st thou this country?

CAPTAIN Ay, madam, well, for I was bred and born
  Not three hours' travel from this very place.

VIOLA Who governs here?

CAPTAIN A noble duke in nature as in name.   25

VIOLA What is his name?

CAPTAIN Orsino.

VIOLA Orsino! I have heard my father name him.
  He was a bachelor then.

CAPTAIN And so is now, or was so very late;   30
  For but a month ago I went from hence,
  And then 'twas fresh in murmur (as you know
  What great ones do, the less will prattle of)
  That he did seek the love of fair Olivia.

VIOLA What's she?   35

---

15 Arion] *Pope;* Orion F

8 **chance** possibility of good fortune.

11 **driving** drifting. A nautical term.

14 **lived** floated. Another nautical term.

15 ***Arion*** After leaping into the sea to escape some murderous sailors, Arion climbed on the back of a dolphin; both paying his fare and charming the waves by the music of his lyre, he was brought to shore in safety (Ovid, *Fasti* II, 93–118). Herodotus (I, 24) also tells the story.

19–20 **Mine…authority** My escape gives me hope for his to which your words give sanction.

22 **bred and born** This looks like an inversion of sequence (the figure hysteron proteron), but 'bred' meaning 'begotten' is frequent in Shakespeare, as in *The Rape of Lucrece* 1188: 'So of shame's ashes shall my fame be bred.'

32 **murmur** rumour.

33 **the less** those of inferior degree.

35 **What's she** i.e. of what quality or rank (Abbott 254).

CAPTAIN A virtuous maid, the daughter of a count
That died some twelvemonth since, then leaving her
In the protection of his son, her brother,
Who shortly also died; for whose dear love
(They say) she hath abjured the sight   40
And company of men.

VIOLA   O that I served that lady,
And might not be delivered to the world
Till I had made mine own occasion mellow
What my estate is!

CAPTAIN   That were hard to compass,
Because she will admit no kind of suit,   45
No, not the duke's.

VIOLA There is a fair behaviour in thee, captain,
And though that nature with a beauteous wall
Doth oft close in pollution, yet of thee
I well believe thou hast a mind that suits   50
With this thy fair and outward character.
I prithee (and I'll pay thee bounteously)
Conceal me what I am, and be my aid
For such disguise as haply shall become
The form of my intent. I'll serve this duke.   55
Thou shalt present me as an eunuch to him –
It may be worth thy pains – for I can sing,
And speak to him in many sorts of music
That will allow me very worth his service.

40–1 sight / And company] F; company / And sight *Hanmer*   50 well] *Conj. Walker;* will F

40–1 **sight...company** The F reading is
satisfactory though most editors, ignoring the
logical sequence but thinking the versification
improved, follow Hanmer's transposition 'company
/ And sight'. There is in this period and earlier in
Shakespeare a pervasive insecurity of verse form
with a tendency to move into prose.

42–4 **delivered...is** i.e. I wish that my position
(estate) should not become known until the time is
ripe. Compare *LLL* 4.2.69–70: 'delivered upon the
mellowing of occasion'.

44 **compass** bring about.

46 **not** not even.

48–51 **And though...character** The possible
disjunction between the outward character (appearance) and inner nature of an individual is

commented on again at 3.4.317–19 and at 5.1.120.
It is a frequent motif in the *Sonnets*.

50 *****well** Walker conjectured an e:i confusion
as occasioning the reading 'will' in F. There is a
similar confusion in *Lear* 1.4.1: Q1 and Q2 read 'If
but as well I other accents borrow' where F reads
'will'.

53 **am** i.e. conceal that I am a woman. For the
redundant object ('me'), see Abbott 414.

54 **become** suit.

56 **eunuch** *castrato*, male soprano. In fact, Viola
disguises herself as a page. Since this first idea is not
picked up, some argue for a revision of the text; see
p. 34 above.

59 **allow me . . . service** prove me worthy to
serve him.

What else may hap, to time I will commit,   60
Only shape thou thy silence to my wit.
CAPTAIN Be you his eunuch, and your mute I'll be;
When my tongue blabs, then let mine eyes not see.
VIOLA I thank thee. Lead me on.

Exeunt

1.3 *Enter* SIR TOBY [BELCH] *and* MARIA

SIR TOBY What a plague means my niece to take the death of her
brother thus? I am sure care's an enemy to life.
MARIA By my troth, Sir Toby, you must come in earlier o'nights. Your
cousin, my lady, takes great exceptions to your ill hours.
SIR TOBY Why, let her except, before excepted.   5
MARIA Ay, but you must confine yourself within the modest limits of
order.
SIR TOBY Confine? I'll confine myself no finer than I am: these clothes
are good enough to drink in, and so be these boots too; and they
be not, let them hang themselves in their own straps.   10
MARIA That quaffing and drinking will undo you: I heard my lady talk
of it yesterday and of a foolish knight that you brought in one night
here to be her wooer.
SIR TOBY Who, Sir Andrew Aguecheek?
MARIA Ay, he.   15
SIR TOBY He's as tall a man as any's in Illyria.

Act 1, Scene 3   1.3] *Scæna Tertia.* F   0 SD BELCH] *Malone; not in* F   3 o'] *Capell;* a F

61 wit invention. As in *Oth.* 4.1.189–90: 'Of so
high and plenteous wit and invention!'
62 mute A dumb (i.e. silent) servant, as at the
Turkish court. Suggested by 'eunuch'. In *H5*
1.2.232, a 'Turkish mute' is said to have a
'tongueless mouth'.

Act 1, Scene 3
Location Olivia's house (Rowe).
3 By my troth By my pledged faith. A mild
oath.
4 cousin There are seventeen references to
Olivia as Sir Toby's 'niece', six references to either
of them as 'cousin'; this latter term was widely used
to denote an imprecise degree of kinship.
5 except...excepted with the exceptions that
have already been named. From the Latin *exceptis
excipiendis,* a legal phrase which Sir Toby uses to

deride Olivia's having already taken 'exception', in
Maria's words (4), to his earlier deportment.
6 modest moderate.
8 confine...finer (1) 'I will accept no further
constraints', (2) 'I refuse to dress more finely.' Sir
Toby plays upon chimes of sound and sense
between 'confines' and 'finer'.
9 and if. In this period 'and' frequently
appears as 'an'; for another instance, see 5.1.276.
10 let them...straps Similar expressions
are recorded in Tilley (G42), but all of them follow
Shakespeare's earlier use in *MND* (1595/96), in
1H4 (1597), and in this play (? 1601). *ODEP* gives
one citation from 1591, scarcely an indication of its
proverbial nature before Shakespeare.
16 tall brave. Ironic in view of Sir Andrew's own
words at 3.4.237 and 240–3. In her reply Maria
wilfully takes it as a reference to height.

MARIA What's that to th'purpose?

SIR TOBY Why, he has three thousand ducats a year.

MARIA Ay, but he'll have but a year in all these ducats. He's a very fool
and a prodigal.   20

SIR TOBY Fie, that you'll say so! He plays o'th'viol-de-gamboys, and
speaks three or four languages word for word without book, and
hath all the good gifts of nature.

MARIA He hath indeed all, most natural: for besides that he's a fool,
he's a great quarreller; and but that he hath the gift of a coward   25
to allay the gust he hath in quarrelling, 'tis thought among the
prudent he would quickly have the gift of a grave.

SIR TOBY By this hand, they are scoundrels and substractors that say
so of him. Who are they?

MARIA They that add, moreover, he's drunk nightly in your company.   30

SIR TOBY With drinking healths to my niece! I'll drink to her as long
as there is a passage in my throat and drink in Illyria; he's a coward
and a coistrill that will not drink to my niece till his brains turn
o'th'toe like a parish top. What, wench! *Castiliano vulgo*: for here

---

24 indeed all, most] *Mahood, conj. Furness;* indeed, almost F *;* indeed, – all most *Collier, conj. Upton*   **34** *Castiliano vulgo*]
F *; Castiliano volto / Hanmer*

---

18 three thousand ducats According to
Thomas Coryat, in 1611 a Venetian ducat was worth
four shillings and eightpence (i.e. twenty-three
pence).

19 he'll...ducats i.e. he will use up his estate
within a year.

19 very true.

21 viol-de-gamboys *viola da gamba* or bass
viol. The bawdy implication of playing this
instrument is discussed by Gustav Ungerer, 'The
viol da gamba as a sexual metaphor in Elizabethan
music and literature', *Renaissance and Reformation*
8:2 (May 1984), 79–90.

22 without book by memory. Again ironic in
view of Sir Andrew's words at 77–9.

24 *indeed all, ...natural (1) from nature, (2)
like a natural born idiot. Upton's conjecture allows
for Maria's play on 'natural' in these two senses.

25 gift natural ability. Affording a quibble at 27
on 'gift' as 'present'.

26 gust...in taste...for.

28 By this hand An oath derived from shaking
hands when making a promise; used also by
Malvolio at 2.3.105.

28 substractors i.e. detractors. This nonce
usage points up Sir Toby's wayward diction,
perhaps underscoring his tipsy behaviour.

33 coistrill knave. Literally, a groom. This

word, like the later 'gaskins', 'pavin' and 'galliard'
(subsequently used three times), represents Shakespeare's earliest usage, with 'gaskins' and 'pavin'
not used again. Kenneth Muir (*Shakespeare's
Sources*, 1957, revised as *The Sources of Shakespeare's
Plays*, 1978) points out that the four words appear
in Riche's *Farewell to Military Profession*, which
includes the story of 'Apolonius and Silla',
Shakespeare's main source for this play.
J. J. M. Tobin ('Gabriel Harvey in Illyria', *ES* 61
(1980), 318–28) emphasises the remarkable similarity
of diction in *TN* to that found in several works of
Nashe, particularly in the controversy with Harvey;
for evidence of similar Nashean vocabulary in
Hamlet, close in date to *TN*, see Harold Jenkins
(ed.), *Ham.*, 1982, pp. 104–6.

34 parish top A large top for public use which
was kept spinning by being lashed with a whip (a
diversion called 'top-scourging'). See *OED* sv *sb²*

34 What, wench! Sir Toby may be seeking
Maria's approval for his drinking resolution,
responding to some reproof of his deportment, or
warning her of Sir Andrew's approach.

34 *Castiliano vulgo* There have been several
attempts to explain or emend Sir Toby's tipsy
cosmopolitan phrase. Hanmer's *volto* would yield 'a
Castilian countenance', and argue for sedate and
proper behaviour in Sir Andrew's presence. Others

comes Sir Andrew Agueface. 35

Enter SIR ANDREW [AGUECHEEK]

SIR ANDREW Sir Toby Belch! How now, Sir Toby Belch?
SIR TOBY Sweet Sir Andrew!
SIR ANDREW Bless you, fair shrew.
MARIA And you too, sir.
SIR TOBY Accost, Sir Andrew, accost. 40
SIR ANDREW What's that?
SIR TOBY My niece's chambermaid.
SIR ANDREW Good Mistress Accost, I desire better acquaintance.
MARIA My name is Mary, sir.
SIR ANDREW Good Mistress Mary Accost – 45
SIR TOBY You mistake, knight. 'Accost' is front her, board her, woo her, assail her.
SIR ANDREW By my troth, I would not undertake her in this company. Is that the meaning of 'accost'?
MARIA Fare you well, gentlemen. [*Leaving*] 50
SIR TOBY And thou let part so, Sir Andrew, would thou mightst never draw sword again.
SIR ANDREW And you part so, mistress, I would I might never draw sword again. Fair lady, do you think you have fools in hand?
MARIA Sir, I have not you by th'hand. 55

35 SD AGUECHEEK] *Malone; not in* F   43 SH SIR ANDREW] F2 *(An.); Ma.* F   45 Mary Accost –] *Theobald subst.;* Mary, accost. F   50 SD *Leaving*] *This edn; not in* F

have supposed Sir Toby to be calling for a kind of wine (*Castiglione voglio*) or thinking of a Spanish ducat (*Castigliano volgo*). J. F. Killeen (*SQ* 28 (1977), 92–3) argues for its meaning 'the devil' in vulgar speech and suggests that '*Castiliano*' was perhaps a cant Italian term.

35 Agueface Like Aguecheek, the name accords with Sir Andrew's physical appearance; he is later described by Sir Toby as a 'knave, a thin-faced knave, a gull' (5.1.190–1).

38 shrew A generic usage: compare the carol at *2H4* 5.3.32–6, which has the line, 'For women are shrows [contemporary pronunciation of "shrew"], both short and tall.' Often in Shakespeare the term designates a 'scold'; for this, see the adverbial use at 1.5.133.

40 Accost A verb, though Sir Andrew persists in mistaking the word for a proper name; at 46–7 Sir Toby dilates on the word's other meanings.

42 My...chambermaid Sir Toby wilfully misunderstands in order to jest at Maria's expense;

a gentlewoman attending the countess, she is later to become Lady Belch.

43 SH *SIR ANDREW F's assignment of the SH to *Ma.* rather than to Sir Andrew (corrected to *An.* in F2) is perhaps the result of eyeskip. For later errors in speech headings, see 2.5.29, 33, 69–70 and 3.4.23, 78 nn.

46–7 front...assail 'front' = confront, come alongside (a nautical term); 'board' = to enter a ship by force (also nautical, but with a sexual innuendo as with 'woo'); 'assail' = attack (a military term).

48 undertake have to do with. Also with a sexual innuendo.

48 in this company i.e. before this audience. An interruption of dramatic illusion for comic effect. For another instance of this technique, see 3.4.108–9.

51 And...so If you let her leave thus.

54 in hand to deal with.

SIR ANDREW Marry, but you shall have, and here's my hand.

MARIA Now, sir, thought is free. I pray you bring your hand to th'buttery-bar and let it drink.

SIR ANDREW Wherefore, sweetheart? What's your metaphor?

MARIA It's dry, sir.   60

SIR ANDREW Why, I think so: I am not such an ass but I can keep my hand dry. But what's your jest?

MARIA A dry jest, sir.

SIR ANDREW Are you full of them?

MARIA Ay, sir, I have them at my fingers' ends; marry, now I let go   65
your hand, I am barren.   *Exit*

SIR TOBY O knight, thou lack'st a cup of canary. [*Hands him a cup*] When did I see thee so put down?

SIR ANDREW Never in your life, I think, unless you see canary put me down. Methinks sometimes I have no more wit than a Christian   70
or an ordinary man has, but I am a great eater of beef, and I believe that does harm to my wit.

SIR TOBY No question.

SIR ANDREW And I thought that, I'd forswear it. I'll ride home tomorrow, Sir Toby.   75

67 SD *Hands...cup*] *This edn; not in* F

56 Marry Mild expletive here and elsewhere; originally 'by the Virgin Mary'.

57 thought is free Proverbial; see Tilley T244, who cites Lyly's *Euphues and His England*, II, 60: 'Why then quoth he, doest thou thinke me a fool, thought is free my Lord quoth she.' See also *Temp.* 3.2.123, where it is the last line of a catch or part-song.

57–8 bring...drink The dialogue suggests that Maria is toying with his hand. Compare 'Didst thou not see her paddle with the palm of his hand?' (*Oth.* 2.1.253–4) and 'paddling palms and pinching fingers' (*WT* 1.2.115).

58 buttery-bar The ledge on the top of the buttery hatch on which to rest tankards.

59 your metaphor i.e. of a drinking hand.

60 dry Both 'thirsty' and 'lacking sexual vigour'. To Othello (3.4.36 ff.), Desdemona's 'moist' hand indicates her libidinous nature; to Charmian (*Ant.* 1.2.52–3), an 'oily palm' is a sign of fertility.

61–2 an ass...dry Tilley (F537) cites Shakespeare's usage here as a variation of the proverb 'Fools have wit enough to come in out of the rain.'

63 dry jest caustic joke. Otherwise called a

'privy taunt', a 'dry bob' or a 'dry mock'. Elsewhere Shakespeare plays on the alternative meaning 'insipid', as in the repartee in *LLL* 5.2.371–3 where Rosaline says, 'this I think, / When they are thirsty, fools would fain have drink', to which Berowne replies, 'This jest is dry to me.'

65 at my fingers' ends in readiness and in hand. Proverbial; Tilley F245.

66 barren i.e. bereft both of Sir Andrew's hand, which she drops, and of jests.

67 canary A sweet wine colloquially referred to by the name of the islands where it was produced. Compare Mistress Quickly's observation of Doll's rosy colour: 'i' faith, you have drunk too much canaries' (*2H4* 2.4.26).

68 put down baffled, deflated.

69–70 unless...put me down i.e. unless you should see drink (1) baffle my wits and (2) lay me flat. An ironic assertion in view of his nightly carousing.

71–2 beef...wit Beef was proverbially supposed to make a man stupid (Dent B215.1). Shakespeare's Thersites calls Ajax 'beef-witted' (*Tro.* 2.1.13).

SIR TOBY *Pourquoi*, my dear knight?

SIR ANDREW What is '*pourquoi*'? Do, or not do? I would I had
bestowed that time in the tongues that I have in fencing, dancing,
and bear-baiting. O had I but followed the arts!

SIR TOBY Then hadst thou had an excellent head of hair.   80

SIR ANDREW Why, would that have mended my hair?

SIR TOBY Past question, for thou seest it will not curl by nature.

SIR ANDREW But it becomes me well enough, does't not?

SIR TOBY Excellent; it hangs like flax on a distaff; and I hope to see
a huswife take thee between her legs and spin it off.   85

SIR ANDREW Faith, I'll home tomorrow, Sir Toby; your niece will not
be seen, or if she be, it's four to one, she'll none of me. The count
himself here hard by woos her.

SIR TOBY She'll none o'th'count; she'll not match above her degree,
neither in estate, years, nor wit. I have heard her swear't. Tut,   90
there's life in't, man.

SIR ANDREW I'll stay a month longer. I am a fellow o'th'strangest mind
i'th'world: I delight in masques and revels sometimes altogether.

SIR TOBY Art thou good at these kickshawses, knight?

SIR ANDREW As any man in Illyria, whatsoever he be, under the degree   95
of my betters, and yet I will not compare with an old man.

SIR TOBY What is thy excellence in a galliard, knight?

SIR ANDREW Faith, I can cut a caper.

82 curl by] *Theobald*; coole my F   83 me] F2; we F   83 does't] *Rowe*; dost F

76–7 Pourquoi Why. Despite his ignorance of
French at this point, Sir Andrew is able to muster
a few words at 3.1.61. Here and elsewhere
Shakespeare's French has been regularised.

78 tongues languages. There is a pun (picked up
in 82) on 'tongs' (i.e. curling tongs); in Elizabethan
English the two were homophones as indicated by
the rhymes tongues/songs in *Venus and Adonis*
775–7 and tongue/long, *Rape of Lucrece* 1465–8
(NS).

79 the arts learning. Sir Toby thinks 'the arts'
signifies something artificial as opposed to natural.

81 mended improved.

82 *curl by Theobald's reading is preferred to
F's 'coole my', a possible but meaningless
misreading of the copy.

84 distaff A staff for spinning the straight,
straw-coloured fibres of flax.

85 huswife (1) housewife (pronounced
'hussif'); (2) hussy or prostitute (with a suggestion
of venereal disease causing the hair to fall out).

88 hard near.

89 degree rank. Since Olivia is a countess, Sir
Toby's remark would seem to confirm Shakespeare's
original intention of making Orsino a duke – unless
Toby is, as usual, gulling the fatuous Sir Andrew.

91 there's…in't Tilley (L265) records the
expression as proverbial, though Shakespeare's
usage here is the earliest one cited; L269 is perhaps
its origin: 'While there's life there's hope.'

92 strangest most singular.

94 kickshawses (1) elegant trifles, (2) tidbits
served with mutton. The second meaning prompts
Sir Toby's allusion in 99. Compare *2H4* 5.1.27–8:
'a joint of mutton, and any pretty little tiny
kickshaws'. The form 'kickshaws', derived from
French *quelque chose*, is a singular.

95–6 under…old man i.e. provided he is
not above me in social rank (in accord with the
proverb 'Compare not with thy betters', Tilley
C578) and provided he is not more experienced
because of his age.

97 galliard A lively dance in triple time.

98 cut a caper leap.

SIR TOBY And I can cut the mutton to't.

SIR ANDREW And I think I have the back-trick simply as strong as any   100
man in Illyria.

SIR TOBY Wherefore are these things hid? Wherefore have these gifts
a curtain before 'em? Are they like to take dust, like Mistress Mall's
picture? Why dost thou not go to church in a galliard and come
home in a coranto? My very walk should be a jig; I would not so   105
much as make water but in a sink-a-pace. What dost thou mean?
Is it a world to hide virtues in? I did think, by the excellent
constitution of thy leg, it was formed under the star of a galliard.

SIR ANDREW Ay, 'tis strong, and it does indifferent well in a dun-coloured
stock. Shall we set about some revels?   110

SIR TOBY What shall we do else? Were we not born under Taurus?

SIR ANDREW Taurus? That's sides and heart.

SIR TOBY No, sir, it is legs and thighs. Let me see thee caper. Ha,
higher; ha, ha, excellent!

Exeunt

109 dun-coloured] *Collier²;* dam'd colour'd F; flame-colour'd *Rowe³*   110 set] *Rowe³;* sit F   112 That's] F3; That F

99 cut the mutton Mutton is a slang term for
a strumpet, a *double entendre* which Sir Andrew
recognises in his response.

100 back-trick Backward steps in a dance.
There is also the innuendo of sexual vigour.
Compare Marston, *Certaine Satyres*, 5, 47:

When strong backt Hercules in one poore night
With great, great ease, and wondrous delight
In strength of lust and Venus surquedry
Rob'd fifty wenches of virginity.

A. Davenport (ed.), *The Poems of Marston*, 1961, p.
251 n., gives instances of this usage in the drama.

103 curtain Curtains were used to protect
pictures from dust and sunlight.

103 Mistress Mall's Mall is a diminutive of
Mary, perhaps used here generically, perhaps in
reference to Maria.

105 coranto A running dance.

106 sink-a-pace A dance with five steps, as its
name (cinque pace) indicates, but with a quibble on
'sink' = a receptacle for filth and ordure.

107 virtues abilities.

108 leg...galliard i.e. determined by the
stars to dance. Compare *Ado* 2.1.335: 'there was a
star danc'd, and under that was I born'.

109 indifferent moderately.

109–10 *dun-coloured stock mouse-coloured
stocking. This emendation of F's 'dam'd colour'd'
provides a plausible explanation for Compositor B's
misreading 'dunne' or 'donne' as 'dam'd' by the
common confusion of d/e and variable minims.
Though some editors doubt that Sir Andrew would
choose dark-coloured stockings, one may note that
Augustine Phillips, a fellow sharer with Shakespeare
in the company of the Lord Chamberlain's–King's
Men, in 1605 bequeathed to his apprentice his
'mouse colloured Velvit hose'. (The will is printed
in Var. 1821, III, 472.)

111 Taurus The twelve signs of the zodiac were
believed to govern distinct areas of the body.
Taurus, the sign of the bull, was generally said to
govern the neck and throat, but Sir Toby's
correction to legs and thighs in 113 accords with his
earlier sexual innuendoes.

1.4 *Enter* VALENTINE, *and* VIOLA *in man's attire*

VALENTINE If the duke continue these favours towards you, Cesario,
you are like to be much advanced; he hath known you but three
days, and already you are no stranger.

VIOLA You either fear his humour, or my negligence, that you call in
question the continuance of his love. Is he inconstant, sir, in his   5
favours?

VALENTINE No, believe me.

VIOLA I thank you. Here comes the count.

Enter DUKE [ORSINO], CURIO, *and Attendants*

ORSINO Who saw Cesario, ho?

VIOLA On your attendance, my lord, here.   10

ORSINO [*To Curio and Attendants*] Stand you awhile aloof. Cesario,
Thou know'st no less but all: I have unclasped
To thee the book even of my secret soul.
Therefore, good youth, address thy gait unto her,
Be not denied access; stand at her doors,   15
And tell them there thy fixèd foot shall grow
Till thou have audience.

VIOLA   Sure, my noble lord,
If she be so abandoned to her sorrow
As it is spoke, she never will admit me.

ORSINO Be clamorous, and leap all civil bounds,   20
Rather than make unprofited return.

VIOLA Say I do speak with her, my lord, what then?

ORSINO O then unfold the passion of my love,
Surprise her with discourse of my dear faith;

Act 1, Scene 4   1.4] *Scena Quarta.* F   8 SD] *Follows 7 in* F   11 SD *To...Attendants*] *Mahood; not in* F

Act 1, Scene 4
Location The duke's palace (Cam.).
2–3 but three days For an account of the
double-time scheme, see p. 16 above, n. 2.
4 his humour...negligence his volatility or
my neglect of duty.
10 On your attendance Ready and waiting to
do service.
11 aloof aside. So that Curio and attendants will
not hear his directives to Viola/Cesario.
14 address thy gait go. Another instance of
Orsino's mannered style.

15 access Accented on the second syllable.
16 them i.e. servants, not doors; 'there' serves
as a fulcrum, referring to those at the doors and to
the place.
20 leap...bounds exceed the limits of proper
behaviour. An indecorum paralleling that of Sir
Toby.
21 unprofited return without advantage (to his
suit).
24 Surprise her Take her (heart) by force. A
military image (Ard.).
24 dear heartfelt.

It shall become thee well to act my woes: 25
She will attend it better in thy youth
Than in a nuncio's of more grave aspect.
VIOLA I think not so, my lord.
ORSINO   Dear lad, believe it;
For they shall yet belie thy happy years
That say thou art a man: Diana's lip   30
Is not more smooth and rubious; thy small pipe
Is as the maiden's organ, shrill and sound,
And all is semblative a woman's part.
I know thy constellation is right apt
For this affair. Some four or five attend him –   35
All if you will, for I myself am best
When least in company. Prosper well in this,
And thou shalt live as freely as thy lord
To call his fortunes thine.
VIOLA   I'll do my best
To woo your lady. [*Aside*] Yet a barful strife!   40
Whoe'er I woo, myself would be his wife.

                                              Exeunt

1.5 *Enter* MARIA *and* CLOWN [FESTE]

MARIA Nay, either tell me where thou hast been, or I will not open my
lips so wide as a bristle may enter in way of thy excuse. My lady
will hang thee for thy absence.

40 SD *Aside*] Capell; *not in* F   Act 1, Scene 5   1.5] *Scena Quinta.* F

25 become suit.
26 attend pay attention to.
27 nuncio's...aspect messenger of more dignified countenance; 'aspect' is accented on the
second syllable.
29 yet as yet.
31 rubious ruby-coloured. A Shakespearean
coinage (Onions).
31–2 small pipe...sound i.e. Cesario has a
piping voice, like that of a eunuch or a virgin (as
in *Cor.* 3.2.114), still clear and uncracked. Compare
also *Wiv.* 1.1.48, where Anne Page (not yet
seventeen) is said to speak 'small like a woman'.
33 semblative like. Properly 'semblative to'. A
Shakespearean coinage (Onions).

33 part (1) nature, (2) role. The double meaning
reflects both the dramatic and the feigned theatrical
situation: a boy playing the part of a girl who then
disguises herself as a boy and so serves as a fitting
surrogate wooer of Olivia.
34 constellation The determining configuration
of the stars at a nativity.
38 freely readily.
40 barful strife a striving full of obstacles. This
striving is specified in the next line as singular.

Act 1, Scene 5
Location Olivia's house (Rowe).

FESTE Let her hang me: he that is well hanged in this world needs to
fear no colours. 5

MARIA Make that good.

FESTE He shall see none to fear.

MARIA A good lenten answer. I can tell thee where that saying was born,
of 'I fear no colours.'

FESTE Where, good Mistress Mary? 10

MARIA In the wars, and that may you be bold to say in your foolery.

FESTE Well, God give them wisdom that have it; and those that are
fools, let them use their talents.

MARIA Yet you will be hanged for being so long absent – or to be turned
away: is not that as good as a hanging to you? 15

FESTE Many a good hanging prevents a bad marriage; and for turning
away, let summer bear it out.

MARIA You are resolute then?

FESTE Not so neither, but I am resolved on two points –

MARIA That if one break, the other will hold, or if both break, your 20
gaskins fall.

---

4 SH FESTE] F *reads / Clo. / throughout*   14 absent – or] *This edn;* absent, or F   19 points –] *NS;* points F

---

5 **fear no colours** have no fear of an enemy's
flag. Proverbial (Tilley c520). Feste quibbles on
'colours' as 'flags' and as 'false pretexts' (as in
'colorable colors', *LLL* 4.2.149–50) and 'collars',
the hangman's nooses. The same set of puns occurs
in *2H4* 5.5.85–8: '*Fal.* This that you heard was but
a color [false pretext]. *Shal.* A color that I fear you
will die in, Sir John. *Fal.* Fear no colors...'

6 **Make that good** Prove it.

8 **lenten** less than sufficient, as in the season for
fasting. Compare the reference to 'lenten entertainment' in *Ham.* 1363 (2.2.316).

8–9 **saying...colours** Colloquial transposition
'that saying of "I fear no colours" was born'.

11 **In the wars** From the literal meaning of the
proverb.

11 **that...bold to say** 'say with confidence', as
opposed to the quibbling on 'false pretexts' and
'hangman's nooses'.

12 **God give...have it** Echoing the Biblical
statement, 'For unto everie man that hathe, it shal
be given' (Matt. 25.29, and elsewhere). This
chapter of St Matthew, which includes the parable
of the talents, may have prompted Feste's pun in
the next line.

13 **talents** natural gifts of a born fool (as against
the gifts that a professional fool like Feste exploits).
There is an orthographic pun on 'talons' = claws,

which are equally natural. A similar pun occurs in
LLL 4.2.63–4: 'If a talent be a claw, look how he
claws him with a talent.'

14–15 **to be turned away** to be dismissed, with
a hint of 'turned off', hanged (*OED* Turn *v* 73d).
Abbott (416) justifies the change of construction
with 'to' on grounds of clarity.

16 **Many...marriage** Shakespeare may be
recalling his use in *MV* 2.9.82–3 of 'The ancient
saying... / Hanging and wiving goes by destiny'
(Tilley w232).

17 **bear it out** make it endurable. For the
significance of Feste's remark in relation to the
projected season of the play's action see p. 41, n. 3
above.

19 **points** (1) matters, (2) laces that tied the
breeches (upperstocks) to the doublet. Punctuation
is lacking in F, apparently because of the scant
margin.

20 **the other will hold** With a glance perhaps at the proverb (Tilley R119), 'Good riding
at two anchors...for if the one fall, the other may
hold.'

21 **gaskins** Wide breeches reaching to the knee.
They were usually loose, but some were inflated by
padding (bombasted), a pair made for the court fool
in 1575 requiring six yards of material (Linthicum,
p. 208 and n.).

FESTE Apt, in good faith, very apt. Well, go thy way; if Sir Toby would leave drinking, thou wert as witty a piece of Eve's flesh as any in Illyria.

MARIA Peace, you rogue, no more o'that; here comes my lady: make   25
your excuse wisely, you were best.   [*Exit*]

Enter LADY OLIVIA [*attended*,] *with* MALVOLIO

FESTE Wit, and't be thy will, put me into good fooling! Those wits that think they have thee do very oft prove fools, and I that am sure I lack thee may pass for a wise man. For what says Quinapalus? 'Better a witty fool than a foolish wit' – God bless thee, lady.   30

OLIVIA Take the fool away.

FESTE Do you not hear, fellows? Take away the lady.

OLIVIA Go to, y'are a dry fool: I'll no more of you; besides, you grow dishonest.

FESTE Two faults, madonna, that drink and good counsel will amend: 35
for give the dry fool drink, then is the fool not dry; bid the dishonest man mend himself; if he mend, he is no longer dishonest; if he cannot, let the botcher mend him. Anything that's mended is but patched: virtue that transgresses is but patched with sin, and sin that amends is but patched with virtue. If that this simple syllogism   40
will serve, so; if it will not, what remedy? As there is no true cuckold

26 SD.1 *Exit*] *Pope; not in* F   26 SD.2 OLIVIA *attended*,] *Capell; Olivia*, F   30 wit' –] *This edn*; wit. F

22–4 if...Illyria Feste's seeming *non sequitur* assumes the validity of the Porter's observation in *Mac.* 2.3.30–2: 'Therefore much drink may be said to be an equivocator with lechery.' Except for the conditional about Sir Toby's drinking, he implies that Maria and Sir Toby would make a good match and sexual partnership.

26 SD.2 As a countess, Olivia should be well attended on her first entrance, as Feste's reference to 'fellows' (32) and 'gentlemen' (59) indicates.

27 Wit...will In invoking 'Wit, if it be thy will' to give him 'good fooling', Feste hopes by that means (1) to chide his mistress for her folly in grieving and (2) to placate her for his 'dishonest' (34) absence. This is perhaps to be accounted for by his presence at Orsino's palace: Viola sees him there and he too has seen her (3.1.31, 34–5); by Act 5, Orsino also acknowledges that he knows him well (8).

27–8 Those...fools Compare the proverb (Tilley c582), 'He that is wise in his own conceit is a fool', which echoes Prov. 26.5.

29 Quinapalus An example of Feste's mock learning, as in 2.3.20–1.

31 Take...away Olivia's order indicates that she has overheard his barbed innuendoes. If not quite the 'bitter fool' of *Lear*, Feste is capable of many sharp passes, as Cesario remarks at 3.1.36; see also his mocking of Malvolio in 4.2 and at 5.1.349–50.

33 Go to Here and elsewhere a term of reproof or impatience.

33 dry See 1.3.63 n.

34 dishonest dishonourable (in absenting himself).

35 madonna my lady. Italian *mia donna*: Feste's characteristic manner of addressing Olivia.

35–8 amend...mend him Feste plays on the moral sense 'to make better' and on the material sense 'to make useful again'; 'mend' is simply an aphetic form of 'amend'. For other examples in *TN* of Shakespeare's use of the stem of a word in a different sense from the word itself, see 5.1.240 and 265 and nn.

38 botcher mender of old clothes.

41 so As in *TGV* 2.1.131: 'And if it please you, so; if not, why, so.'

41–2 As...calamity This perhaps means that

but calamity, so beauty's a flower. The lady bade take away the fool;
therefore I say again, take her away.

OLIVIA Sir, I bade them take away you.

FESTE Misprision in the highest degree! Lady, *cucullus non facit* 45
monachum: that's as much to say as I wear not motley in my brain.
Good madonna, give me leave to prove you a fool.

OLIVIA Can you do it?

FESTE Dexteriously, good madonna.

OLIVIA Make your proof. 50

FESTE I must catechise you for it, madonna. Good my mouse of virtue,
answer me.

OLIVIA Well, sir, for want of other idleness, I'll bide your proof.

FESTE Good madonna, why mourn'st thou?

OLIVIA Good fool, for my brother's death. 55

FESTE I think his soul is in hell, madonna.

OLIVIA I know his soul is in heaven, fool.

FESTE The more fool, madonna, to mourn for your brother's soul being
in heaven. Take away the fool, gentlemen.

OLIVIA What think you of this fool, Malvolio? Doth he not mend? 60

MALVOLIO Yes, and shall do, till the pangs of death shake him;
infirmity, that decays the wise, doth ever make the better fool.

FESTE God send you, sir, a speedy infirmity, for the better increasing
your folly! Sir Toby will be sworn that I am no fox, but he will
not pass his word for twopence that you are no fool. 65

58 soul being] *Rowe;* soul, being F

whereas the marital state of a husband may alter – for the worse – to that of a cuckold, a calamitous state of affairs necessarily alters – for the better; the first is potential; the second inevitable and hence 'true'.

42–3 beauty's...take her away Feste's comment that youthful beauty fades, taken together with his comment that misfortune can change to its opposite, draws attention to Olivia's folly of grieving for seven years apart from the 'sight / And company of men'.

45 Misprision Error (Shakespeare's most frequent usage) but also a legal term for a misdemeanour; 'in the highest degree' emphasises the gravity of the offence.

45–6 cucullus...monachum 'The hood makes not the monk.' Proverbial (Tilley H586).

46 motley The particoloured costume worn by fools; hence the frequency of their being called 'Patch', as in the string of epithets in *Err.* 3.1.32: 'Mome, malt-horse, capon, coxcomb, idiot, patch!'

49 Dexteriously An Elizabethan form, not a malapropism; the only appearance of the adverbial form in Shakespeare.

51 Good...virtue 'Good' used as a vocative, as in 'good my lord'; 'mouse', a term of endearment – but Feste's modifying phrase may glance at Olivia's small virtue of prolonged mourning. In catechising her, Feste anticipates his later impersonation of Sir Topas the curate.

53 idleness pastime.

60 mend improve (in his fooling). Olivia's laughter here will account for Malvolio's marvelling at the 'delight' (67) she takes in Feste's fooling.

62 infirmity...fool Perhaps a glance at William Wager's interlude (entered in *SR* in 1569) *The Longer Thou Livest, the More Fool Thou Art*, where the main character, Moros, is an irredeemable fool.

65 pass give.

OLIVIA How say you to that, Malvolio?

MALVOLIO I marvel your ladyship takes delight in such a barren rascal.
I saw him put down the other day with an ordinary fool that has
no more brain than a stone. Look you now, he's out of his guard
already. Unless you laugh and minister occasion to him, he is   70
gagged. I protest I take these wise men that crow so at these set
kind of fools no better than the fools' zanies.

OLIVIA O you are sick of self-love, Malvolio, and taste with a
distempered appetite. To be generous, guiltless, and of free
disposition is to take those things for bird-bolts that you deem   75
cannon bullets. There is no slander in an allowed fool though he
do nothing but rail; nor no railing in a known discreet man though
he do nothing but reprove.

FESTE Now Mercury endue thee with leasing, for thou speak'st well
of fools!   80

Enter MARIA

MARIA Madam, there is at the gate a young gentleman much desires
to speak with you.

OLIVIA From the Count Orsino, is it?

MARIA I know not, madam; 'tis a fair young man and well attended.

OLIVIA Who of my people hold him in delay?   85

MARIA Sir Toby, madam, your kinsman.

68–9 with an ordinary…stone i.e. by one who was born a fool and who entertained in an ordinary, or tavern. An apparent topical allusion: Stone was the name of a tavern-fool known for his caustic remarks and frequently referred to in popular literature; Nashe, for example, comments that *aqua fortis*, or nitric acid, has almost spoiled his nose (*Works*, III, 25). Stone is mentioned in Ben Jonson's *Volpone*; two of his barbed witticisms are recorded in Jonson, *Works*, ed. C. H. Herford and P. and E. Simpson, 11 vols., 1925–52, IX, 701.

69 out of his guard used up his tricks of defence. A term in fencing.

71 wise men…crow i.e. sane persons who laugh uproariously. A 'palpable hit' in respect to his mistress.

71–2 set kind artificial sort (as opposed to those who are 'born fools').

72 zanies Subordinates who mimicked a professional clown (from Italian *zanni*, a character in the *commedia dell'arte*).

73 of because of; 'self-love' is Malvolio's 'humour'.

74 distempered unwholesome, morbid.

74–5 free disposition generous temper or character.

75 bird-bolts Blunt arrows used for shooting small birds, perhaps with a glance at the proverb 'A fool's bolt is soon shot' (Tilley F515). Olivia's diction anticipates other allusions to the art of bird-catching, used generally in reference to Malvolio (2.5.39, 2.5.69, 4.2.45–6), and so gives point to his later triumphant vaunt about Olivia, 'I have limed her' (3.4.66).

76 allowed licensed.

77–8 railing . . . reprove A 'palpable hit' in respect to her steward, whose duty it was to 'reprove' in civil fashion. See p. 11 above.

79 Mercury…leasing let Mercury, the god of deception, endow you with the art of lying. The word 'leasing' appears only one other time in Shakespeare – *Cor.* 5.2.22.

OLIVIA Fetch him off, I pray you; he speaks nothing but madman. Fie
on him.

[Exit Maria]

Go you, Malvolio. If it be a suit from the count, I am sick, or not
at home – what you will to dismiss it.   90

Exit Malvolio

Now you see, sir, how your fooling grows old, and people dislike
it.

FESTE Thou hast spoke for us, madonna, as if thy eldest son should be
a fool: whose skull Jove cram with brains, for – here he comes –

Enter SIR TOBY *[staggering]*

one of thy kin has a most weak *pia mater*.   95

OLIVIA By mine honour, half drunk! What is he at the gate, cousin?

SIR TOBY A gentleman.

OLIVIA A gentleman? What gentleman?

SIR TOBY 'Tis a gentleman here – *[Hiccuping]* a plague o'these pickle
herring! How now, sot?   100

FESTE Good Sir Toby –

OLIVIA Cousin, cousin, how have you come so early by this lethargy?

SIR TOBY Lechery! I defy lechery. There's one at the gate.

OLIVIA Ay, marry, what is he?

SIR TOBY Let him be the devil and he will, I care not: give me faith,   105
say I. Well, it's all one.   *Exit*

OLIVIA What's a drunken man like, fool?

FESTE Like a drowned man, a fool, and a madman: one draught above

---

88 SD *Exit Maria*] Capell; not in F   94 for – …comes –] *Cam.*; for…comes. F   94 SD *staggering*] *This edn; not in* F
99 here – [*Hiccuping*.]] Rann *subst.*; heere, F   101 Toby –] *This edn;* Toby. F

---

87 **speaks…madman** Analogues to this construction are: 'She speaks poniards', *Ado* 2.1.247; 'I
will speak daggers', *Ham.* 2267 (3.2.396); and 'He
speaks plain cannon-fire, and smoke, and bounce',
John 2.1.462 (Furness).
   90 **what you will** For the significance of this
catch-phrase, see p. 1 above.
   91 **old** stale.
   93–4 **Thou hast spoke…fool** i.e. 'wisely', in
accord with the proverb 'A wise man commonly has
a fool to his heir' (Tilley M421). Commentators
have misunderstood Feste's remark, interpreting it
(in the words of one of them) as 'at best a left-handed
compliment'; see Jenkins, p. 32.
   95 *pia mater* brain. Physiologically, its covering
membrane (metonymy).

100 **sot** Both 'fool' and 'drunkard'. Armin, who
is generally believed to have played Feste, uses the
double meaning in his *Foole upon Foole or Six Sortes
of Sottes* (1600) (NS).
   102 **lethargy** stupor.
   104 **what is he** of what quality or rank is he. As
in 1.2.35.
   105 **give me faith** i.e. as opposed to good
works as a means of salvation – a source of
theological debate (NS).
   106 **it's all one** it doesn't matter. For the
repeated use of this catch-phrase, see p. 1, n. 4
above and 5.1.181 and 351 nn.
   108–9 **above heat** beyond bodily warmth. Compare *Tim.* 1.1.261: 'Ay to see meat fill knaves, and
wine heat fools'.

heat makes him a fool, the second mads him, and a third drowns
him.   110

OLIVIA Go thou and seek the crowner, and let him sit o'my coz, for
he's in the third degree of drink: he's drowned. Go look after him.

FESTE He is but mad yet, madonna, and the fool shall look to the
madman.   [*Exit*]

Enter MALVOLIO

MALVOLIO Madam, yond young fellow swears he will speak with you.   115
I told him you were sick; he takes on him to understand so much
and therefore comes to speak with you. I told him you were asleep;
he seems to have a foreknowledge of that too, and therefore comes
to speak with you. What is to be said to him, lady? He's fortified
against any denial.   120

OLIVIA Tell him he shall not speak with me.

MALVOLIO H'as been told so; and he says he'll stand at your door like
a sheriff's post, and be the supporter to a bench, but he'll speak
with you.

OLIVIA What kind o'man is he?   125

MALVOLIO Why, of mankind.

OLIVIA What manner of man?

MALVOLIO Of very ill manner: he'll speak with you, will you or no.

OLIVIA Of what personage and years is he?

MALVOLIO Not yet old enough for a man, nor young enough for a boy: 130
as a squash is before 'tis a peascod, or a codling when 'tis almost
an apple. 'Tis with him in standing water, between boy and man.
He is very well-favoured and he speaks very shrewishly. One would
think his mother's milk were scarce out of him.

OLIVIA Let him approach. Call in my gentlewoman.   135

MALVOLIO Gentlewoman, my lady calls.   *Exit*

114 SD *Exit*] *Rowe; not in* F   122 H'as] *Staunton;* Ha's F

111 **crowner** Old form of 'coroner'; not a
vulgarism.
111 **sit o'** hold an inquest on.
117 **therefore** for that reason.
118 **foreknowledge** prescience. A theological
term; used only this once by Shakespeare.
122 **H'as** Staunton's alteration of F's 'ha's' is in
accord with F at 5.1.164 and with Rowe's alteration
of F's 'has' at 5.1.181 and 269, thus retaining the
colloquial flavour of the speeches that a modernisa-
tion to 'he's' largely dissipates.
123 **sheriff's post** Posts were set before the

houses of mayors and sheriffs and were often
elaborately carved and coloured (Halliwell, cited in
Furness).
123 **supporter** prop.
131 **squash** unripe peapod (peascod).
131 **codling** unripe apple.
132 **in standing water** at the turn of the tide.
133 **well-favoured** good-looking.
133 **shrewishly** i.e. like a scold.
133–4 **One...him** Listed in Tilley (M1204) as
proverbial, but the only example antedating this
instance comes from a manuscript source.

Enter MARIA

OLIVIA Give me my veil; come throw it o'er my face.
We'll once more hear Orsino's embassy.

Enter VIOLA

VIOLA The honourable lady of the house, which is she?
OLIVIA Speak to me; I shall answer for her. Your will? 140
VIOLA Most radiant, exquisite, and unmatchable beauty – I pray you
tell me if this be the lady of the house, for I never saw her. I would
be loath to cast away my speech: for besides that it is excellently
well penned, I have taken great pains to con it. Good beauties, let
me sustain no scorn; I am very comptible, even to the least sinister 145
usage.
OLIVIA Whence came you, sir?
VIOLA I can say little more than I have studied, and that question's out
of my part. Good gentle one, give me modest assurance if you be
the lady of the house, that I may proceed in my speech. 150
OLIVIA Are you a comedian?
VIOLA No, my profound heart; and yet, by the very fangs of malice,
I swear, I am not that I play. Are you the lady of the house?
OLIVIA If I do not usurp myself, I am.
VIOLA Most certain, if you are she, you do usurp yourself: for what is 155
yours to bestow is not yours to reserve. But this is from my
commission. I will on with my speech in your praise, and then show
you the heart of my message.
OLIVIA Come to what is important in't: I forgive you the praise.
VIOLA Alas, I took great pains to study it, and 'tis poetical. 160

---

138 SD VIOLA] F2; *Uiolenta.* F   **141** beauty –] *Rowe;* beautie. F   **152–3**] yet, by…fangs of malice, I swear, I am] *This edn;* yet (by…phangs of malice, I sweare) I am F

143 cast…speech waste my efforts (on the wrong auditor, e.g. Maria).
144 con it learn it by heart.
145 sustain no scorn suffer no derision.
145 comptible sensitive. A nonce use.
145 sinister wrong.
149 modest satisfactory.
151 comedian stage player. This picks up Cesario's own theatrical diction.
152 my profound heart my wise dear one; 'heart' or 'my heart' is a familiar term of affection, as in Falstaff's address to Prince Hal, 'I speak to thee, my heart' (*2H4* 5.5.46). Cesario is still being saucy.

152–3 very fangs…play i.e. I swear, by the very teeth of spite, I am not what I impersonate (as the audience well knows). Note that 'I swear' can serve as a fulcrum, governing both the prepositional phrase and 'I am not'. See 1.4.16 for a similar construction.
154 usurp myself wrongfully possess myself.
155–6 usurp…reserve i.e. by acting wrongly in not giving yourself to a husband.
156–7 from my commission outside my mandate.
159 important significant.
159 forgive you excuse you from.

OLIVIA It is the more like to be feigned; I pray you keep it in. I heard
   you were saucy at my gates, and allowed your approach rather to
   wonder at you than to hear you. If you be not mad, be gone; if
   you have reason, be brief. 'Tis not that time of moon with me to
   make one in so skipping a dialogue.   165

MARIA Will you hoist sail, sir? Here lies your way.

VIOLA No, good swabber, I am to hull here a little longer. Some
   mollification for your giant, sweet lady! Tell me your mind, I am
   a messenger.

OLIVIA Sure you have some hideous matter to deliver, when the   170
   courtesy of it is so fearful. Speak your office.

VIOLA It alone concerns your ear. I bring no overture of war, no
   taxation of homage; I hold the olive in my hand; my words are as
   full of peace as matter.

OLIVIA Yet you began rudely. What are you? What would you?   175

VIOLA The rudeness that hath appeared in me I learned from my
   entertainment. What I am, and what I would, are as secret as
   maidenhead: to your ears, divinity; to any other's, profanation.

OLIVIA Give us the place alone; we will hear this divinity.

                                [Exeunt Maria and Attendants]

   Now, sir, what is your text?   180

VIOLA Most sweet lady —

---

179 SD *Exeunt Maria and Attendants*] Capell; *not in* F   181 lady –] *Theobald subst.*; Ladie. F

---

161 feigned fictive because 'poetical', in contrast to the deeds recorded in historical writings. See
Tilley P28: 'Painters (Travelers) and poets have
leave to lie.'

163 not mad i.e. not altogether mad (though the
negative has puzzled editors). Elsewhere Shakespeare uses intensives to qualify the degree of
madness: 'stark mad' (*Err.* 2.1.59); (*Shr.* 1.1.69;
WT 3.2.183; and 'very mad, exceeding mad' (*H8*
1.4.28).

164–5 'Tis...dialogue i.e. I am not so under
the influence of the moon – therefore lunatic – as to
take part in such a wanton or flighty conversation.
Compare the same metaphorical reference to love
in *LLL* 5.2.760–1: 'love... / All wanton as a child,
skipping and vain'.

166 Here...way Proverbial (Tilley D556).

167 swabber cleaner of decks.

167 hull lie adrift. Cesario continues the
nautical diction introduced by Maria's 'hoist sail'.

167–8 Some mollification...giant Somewhat
appease your huge protectress. A mocking allusion

to Maria's diminutive size, later twice commented
on by Sir Toby – 2.5.11 and 3.2.52.

168 mind message (Schmidt). As in *TGV*
1.1.136–40: 'Sir, I could perceive nothing at all
from her; no, not so much as a ducat for delivering
your letter: and being so hard to me that brought
your mind, I fear she'll prove as hard to you in
telling your mind.' Many editors adopt Warburton's
division of the Folio text by giving 'I am a
messenger' to Olivia, but 'mind' as 'message'
appropriately introduces Viola's identification of
herself as a 'messenger'.

170–1 when...fearful i.e. when the show of
politeness (on your part) induces apprehension. A
reference back to the report of Cesario's 'ill manner'
in 133–4.

171 Speak...office Report what you are
charged to report.

173 taxation of homage demand for tribute.

177 entertainment reception.

178 maidenhead virginity.

178 divinity sacred doctrine.

OLIVIA A comfortable doctrine, and much may be said of it. Where lies your text?

VIOLA In Orsino's bosom.

OLIVIA In his bosom? In what chapter of his bosom?   185

VIOLA To answer by the method, in the first of his heart.

OLIVIA O I have read it. It is heresy. Have you no more to say?

VIOLA Good madam, let me see your face.

OLIVIA Have you any commission from your lord to negotiate with my face? You are now out of your text, but we will draw the curtain   190
and show you the picture. [*Unveiling*] Look you, sir, such a one I was this present. Is't not well done?

VIOLA Excellently done, if God did all.

OLIVIA 'Tis in grain, sir; 'twill endure wind and weather.

VIOLA 'Tis beauty truly blent, whose red and white   195
Nature's own sweet and cunning hand laid on.
Lady, you are the cruell'st she alive,
If you will lead these graces to the grave,
And leave the world no copy.

OLIVIA O sir, I will not be so hard-hearted: I will give out divers   200
schedules of my beauty. It shall be inventoried and every particle
and utensil labelled to my will, as, *item*, two lips, indifferent red;
item, two grey eyes, with lids to them; *item*, one neck, one chin,
and so forth. Were you sent hither to 'praise me?

VIOLA I see you what you are. You are too proud;   205

191 SD *Unveiling*] *Rowe; not in* F

182–7 Much as Feste does at 51 ff., Olivia here 'catechises' Viola.

182 comfortable full of comfort, like a religious text. In this interchange, the diction conforms to that of the secular religion of love.

186 by the method (1) according to the stylistic form of her catechism, (2) according to its contents. Compare *1H6* 3.1.12–13: 'I...am not able / Verbatim to rehearse the method of my pen.'

190 out of departing from.

190–1 draw...picture Compare Pandarus's words in *Tro.* 3.2.46–7: 'Come, draw this curtain, and let's see your picture.'

192 this present i.e. just now, this present time. Not used before Shakespeare (Onions).

193 God...all Perhaps with a wry suggestion of the proverb 'God has done his part' (Tilley G188).

194 in grain fast-dyed.

195 blent blended.

197 she Compare Orlando's verses in *AYLI*

3.2.9–10: 'carve on every tree / The fair, the chaste, and unexpressive she'.

198–9 If...copy Compare *Rom.* 1.1.219–20: 'For beauty starv'd with her [Rosaline's] severity / Cuts beauty off from all posterity.' The first fourteen *Sonnets* also treat this theme.

201 schedules detailed listings. A deliberate wresting of 'copy' from 'posterity' back to its literal meaning.

201–2 particle...will every particular and every furnishing added as a codicil to my will.

202 item Latin, 'likewise'; used in enumerations.

202 indifferent somewhat.

204 'praise appraise. This usage (*OED* v¹) continued until at least 1886, perhaps the result of its being treated as an aphetic form of 'appraise', a form which Shakespeare never uses. In 159 Olivia excused Cesario from any charge to extol or praise her.

But if you were the devil, you are fair!
My lord and master loves you. O such love
Could be but recompensed, though you were crowned
The nonpareil of beauty.

OLIVIA   How does he love me?

VIOLA With adorations, fertile tears,   210
    With groans that thunder love, with sighs of fire.

OLIVIA Your lord does know my mind. I cannot love him.
    Yet I suppose him virtuous, know him noble,
    Of great estate, of fresh and stainless youth;
    In voices well divulged, free, learned, and valiant,   215
    And in dimension, and the shape of nature,
    A gracious person. But yet I cannot love him.
    He might have took his answer long ago.

VIOLA If I did love you in my master's flame,
    With such a suff'ring, such a deadly life,   220
    In your denial I would find no sense;
    I would not understand it.

OLIVIA   Why, what would you?

VIOLA Make me a willow cabin at your gate,
    And call upon my soul within the house;
    Write loyal cantons of contemnèd love,   225
    And sing them loud even in the dead of night;
    Hallow your name to the reverberate hills,
    And make the babbling gossip of the air
    Cry out 'Olivia!' O you should not rest
    Between the elements of air and earth   230

---

206 if...devil even if you were as proud as
Lucifer. See Dent L572 for a reference antedating
those in Tilley.

208–9 be but recompensed...beauty be no
more than requited even if you were crowned the
paragon of beauty.

210 fertile abundant.

215 In...free Publicly proclaimed as generous.

216 dimension...nature form and physical
appearance.

217 A gracious An attractive.

219 flame Figuratively, 'passion'.

220 deadly life death-like life. An oxymoron
characteristic of love poetry.

223 willow cabin Hut of willows as a symbol of
unrequited love. Compare *Ado* 2.1.217–19: 'I
off'red him my company to a willow-tree...to make
him a garland, as being forsaken...'

224 my soul i.e. Olivia.

225 loyal...love duteous songs of unrequited
love; 'canton', a variant form of 'canto', is used
only this once by Shakespeare.

227 Hallow Shout, halloo. The F spelling,
retained here, also suggests the meaning 'conse-
crate' as in *Sonnets* 108.8: 'Even as when first I
hallowed thy fair name'.

227 reverberate reverberating. Philip Brockbank (ed.), *Cor.*, 1976, compares it with the use of
'participate' for 'participating' in *Cor.* 1.1.102.

228 babbling...air The prating woman of the
air is the nymph Echo who wasted away for love of
Narcissus until nothing was left but her voice.

229 rest (1) remain, (2) have peace of mind.

230 Between...earth i.e. anywhere.

But you should pity me!
OLIVIA   You might do much.
What is your parentage?
VIOLA Above my fortunes, yet my state is well:
I am a gentleman.
OLIVIA   Get you to your lord.
I cannot love him. Let him send no more –   235
Unless (perchance) you come to me again,
To tell me how he takes it. Fare you well.
I thank you for your pains. Spend this for me.
VIOLA I am no fee'd post, lady; keep your purse;
My master, not myself, lacks recompense.   240
Love make his heart of flint that you shall love,
And let your fervour like my master's be
Placed in contempt. Farewell, fair cruelty.   *Exit*
OLIVIA 'What is your parentage?'
'Above my fortunes, yet my state is well: 245
I am a gentleman.' I'll be sworn thou art;
Thy tongue, thy face, thy limbs, actions, and spirit
Do give thee five-fold blazon. Not too fast! Soft, soft!
Unless the master were the man – How now?
Even so quickly may one catch the plague?   250
Methinks I feel this youth's perfections
With an invisible and subtle stealth
To creep in at mine eyes. Well, let it be.
What ho, Malvolio!

Enter MALVOLIO

MALVOLIO   Here, madam, at your service.
OLIVIA Run after that same peevish messenger,   255

249 man –] man...*NS*; man. F

233 **state** social condition.
239 **fee'd post** A messenger who expects payment.
241 **heart of flint** Proverbial (Tilley H311).
241 **that** whom.
246 **thou art** While soliloquising, Olivia thinks of Cesario in the familiar second person.
248 **five-fold blazon** A heraldic coat-of-arms, proclaimed here five times over in terms of beauty of speech, of face, of body, of demeanour, of spirit.

248 **Soft, soft** Here and elsewhere = 'Slowly, slowly'.
249 **Unless...man** Unless the servant were the master.
253 **To...eyes** The standard doctrine was that love entered through the eyes. Prospero comments on the instant enamourment of Miranda and Ferdinand: 'At the first sight / They have chang'd eyes' (*Temp.* 1.2.441–2).
255 **peevish** perverse.

The county's man. He left this ring behind him,
Would I, or not. Tell him, I'll none of it.
Desire him not to flatter with his lord,
Nor hold him up with hopes; I am not for him.
If that the youth will come this way tomorrow,   260
I'll give him reasons for't. Hie thee, Malvolio!
MALVOLIO Madam, I will.   *Exit*
OLIVIA I do I know not what, and fear to find
    Mine eye too great a flatterer for my mind.
    Fate, show thy force; ourselves we do not owe.   265
    What is decreed must be; and be this so.   [*Exit*]

2.1 *Enter* ANTONIO *and* SEBASTIAN

ANTONIO Will you stay no longer? Nor will you not that I go with you?
SEBASTIAN By your patience, no. My stars shine darkly over me; the
    malignancy of my fate might perhaps distemper yours; therefore
    I shall crave of you your leave that I may bear my evils alone. It
    were a bad recompense for your love to lay any of them on you.   5
ANTONIO Let me know of you whither you are bound.
SEBASTIAN No, sooth, sir. My determinate voyage is mere extravagancy.
    But I perceive in you so excellent a touch of modesty that you will
    not extort from me what I am willing to keep in. Therefore it
    charges me in manners the rather to express myself. You must know   10

---

256 county's] *Capell;* Countes F   266 SD *Exit*] *Rowe; Finis, Actus primus.* F   **Act 2, Scene 1** 2.1] *Actus Secundus, Scæna prima.* F

256 county's count's. Capell's emendation keeps the metrical pattern. For the alternation with 'duke', see 1.1.0 SD n.
258 flatter with encourage.
261 Hie thee Hasten.
264 My quick emotional response has subdued my judgement.
265 owe own.

Act 2, Scene 1
Location The sea coast (Capell).
1 Nor will...you? Do you not wish me to go with you? The use of a double negative is common in the period; for an example of a triple negative, see 3.1.144 and n.
3 malignancy...fate my malevolent destiny. An astrological phrase in accord with 2 but also suggesting disease in accord with the verb 'dis-

temper' = infect. Sebastian's negative view here is countered by Antonio's invoking the 'gentleness' of the gods at 32. The influence of the heavens (here, the stars) ties in with the motifs of time, fate and fortune which run throughout the play.
4 evils ills.
7 sooth indeed, truly.
7 determinate voyage intended walk (nautical diction). As a sea captain, Antonio uses it in turn at 3.3.7. His use of 'bound' at 6 above is also nautical.
7 extravagancy vagrancy. Not pre-Shakespeare (Onions).
8 touch feeling. As in *Temp.* 5.1.21–2: 'Hast thou...a touch, a feeling / Of their afflictions...?'
9–10 it...manners i.e. in courtesy, I am charged.

of me then, Antonio, my name is Sebastian (which I called
Roderigo); my father was that Sebastian of Messaline whom I know
you have heard of. He left behind him myself and a sister, both
born in an hour: if the heavens had been pleased, would we had
so ended! But you, sir, altered that, for some hour before you took   15
me from the breach of the sea was my sister drowned.

ANTONIO Alas the day!

SEBASTIAN A lady, sir, though it was said she much resembled me, was
yet of many accounted beautiful; but though I could not with such
estimable wonder overfar believe that, yet thus far I will boldly   20
publish her: she bore a mind that envy could not but call fair. She
is drowned already, sir, with salt water, though I seem to drown
her remembrance again with more.

ANTONIO Pardon me, sir, your bad entertainment.

SEBASTIAN O good Antonio, forgive me your trouble.   25

ANTONIO If you will not murder me for my love, let me be your servant.

SEBASTIAN If you will not undo what you have done, that is, kill him
whom you have recovered, desire it not. Fare ye well at once; my
bosom is full of kindness, and I am yet so near the manners of my
mother that, upon the least occasion more, mine eyes will tell tales   30
of me. I am bound to the Count Orsino's court. Farewell.   *Exit*

ANTONIO The gentleness of all the gods go with thee!
I have many enemies in Orsino's court,
Else would I very shortly see thee there.
But come what may, I do adore thee so   35
That danger shall seem sport, and I will go.   *Exit*

11–12 I...**Roderigo** No explanation is given
for Sebastian's earlier use of an alias.

12 **Messaline** The reference is uncertain,
though the 'Massilians' (i.e. people of ancient
Massila, now Marseilles) are mentioned with the
Illyrians in Plautus's *Menaechmi* I, 235, in the
context of one twin searching for his fellow
(L. G. Salingar, *TLS*, 3 June 1955, p. 235).

14 **in an hour** within the same hour.

15 **some hour** about an hour.

16 **breach** surf.

19–20 **with...wonder** with such an admiring
judgement (Schmidt, Onions). Such disordered
sequence (the rhetorical figure hysteron proteron)
Puttenham describes as putting the cart before the
horse. Sebastian's locution serves both to call
attention to Viola's beauty and to depreciate it with

becoming modesty, the audience having seen that
brother and sister are identical in appearance.

21 **publish** proclaim. A link with Olivia's giving
out 'divers schedules' of her beauty at 1.5.200–1.

22–3 **with salt water...more** The drowning-
in-tears image is frequent in Shakespeare, as in *The
Rape of Lucrece* 1680: 'To drown one woe, one pair
of weeping eyes'.

24 **your...entertainment** my bad hospitality.

26 **murder me...love** i.e. cause me to die of
grief as the result of separation.

28 **recovered** rescued.

29 **kindness** emotion.

29–31 **the manners...me** Sebastian acknowledges the proclivity of women to weep; compare
H5 4.6.30–2: 'I had not so much of man in me, /
And all my mother came into mine eyes / And gave
me up to tears.'

2.2 *Enter* VIOLA *and* MALVOLIO *at several doors*

MALVOLIO Were you not even now with the Countess Olivia?
VIOLA Even now, sir; on a moderate pace, I have since arrived but
   hither.
MALVOLIO She returns this ring to you. You might have saved me my
   pains to have taken it away yourself. She adds, moreover, that you   5
   should put your lord into a desperate assurance: she will none of
   him. And one thing more, that you be never so hardy to come again
   in his affairs, unless it be to report your lord's taking of this. Receive
   it so.
VIOLA She took the ring of me. I'll none of it.   10
MALVOLIO Come, sir, you peevishly threw it to her; and her will is,
   it should be so returned. If it be worth stooping for, there it lies,
   in your eye; if not, be it his that finds it.   *Exit*
VIOLA I left no ring with her: what means this lady?
   Fortune forbid my outside have not charmed her!   15
   She made good view of me, indeed so much
   That, methought, her eyes had lost her tongue,
   For she did speak in starts distractedly.
   She loves me sure; the cunning of her passion
   Invites me in this churlish messenger.   20
   None of my lord's ring? Why, he sent her none;
   I am the man; if it be so, as 'tis,

Act 2, Scene 2 2.2] *Scæna Secunda.* F 17 That, methought,] F ; That sure methought F2

Act 2, Scene 2
  Location A street (Capell).
  0 SD *several* separate.
  6 desperate assurance certainty that there is
no hope.
  7 so hardy so bold as. See Abbott 281 for the
frequent omission of 'as' in this construction.
  8 taking of this response (1) to this ultimatum
and (2) to the ring.
  8–9 Receive it so Take the ring back on this basis.
  10 Having left no ring behind, Cesario, sensitive
to Olivia's predicament, dissembles in the presence
of her messenger.
  11 peevishly ill-manneredly. Although Malvolio
appropriates Olivia's diction (1.5.255) here, he then
develops it in accordance with his own sense of
Cesario's earlier unseemly deportment (1.5.128).
  11 threw it Malvolio's elaboration; Olivia
simply said that he had 'left' it (1.5.256).

  13 in your eye in plain sight.
  15 charmed enchanted. A fact Olivia later
acknowledges (3.1.97).
  16 made...of me looked at me closely.
  17–18 her eyes...distractedly i.e. as a result
of her fixed staring, Olivia spoke only disjointedly,
by fits and starts.
  19 sure certainly (adverb).
  19–20 the cunning...messenger i.e. she
shows the crafty aspect of her emotional state in
soliciting me by means of this rude messenger.
Compare *A Lover's Complaint* 295. 'For lo his
passion, [is] but an art of craft.'
  21 None of...ring *Not* what Malvolio says but
what Olivia has said at 1.5.257: 'I'll none of it.'
  22 I...man i.e. of her choice. As in *AYLI*
3.3.2–4: 'And how, Audrey? am I the man yet?
Doth my simple feature content you?'

Poor lady, she were better love a dream.
Disguise, I see thou art a wickedness,
Wherein the pregnant enemy does much.   25
How easy is it for the proper-false
In women's waxen hearts to set their forms!
Alas, our frailty is the cause, not we,
For such as we are made of, such we be.
How will this fadge? My master loves her dearly,   30
And I (poor monster) fond as much on him
As she (mistaken) seems to dote on me.
What will become of this? As I am man,
My state is desperate for my master's love;
As I am woman – now alas the day! –   35
What thriftless sighs shall poor Olivia breathe?
O time, thou must untangle this, not I;
It is too hard a knot for me t'untie.   [*Exit*]

2.3 *Enter* SIR TOBY *and* SIR ANDREW

SIR TOBY Approach, Sir Andrew. Not to be abed after midnight is to
  be up betimes, and *diluculo surgere*, thou know'st –
SIR ANDREW Nay, by my troth, I know not; but I know to be up late
  is to be up late.

---

28 our] F2; O F   29 made of,] *Rann, conj. Tyrwhitt;* made, if F   32 As] *Dyce²;* And F   36 breathe] F2; breath F
38 SD *Exit*] *Rowe; not in* F   Act 2, Scene 3   2.3] *Scæna Tertia.* F   2 *diluculo*] *Rowe; Deliculo* F   2 know'st –] *Theobald
subst.;* know'st. F

25 **pregnant enemy** ready foe. Perhaps Cupid, perhaps the devil – the two perhaps not differentiated at this point. The adjective is used again at 3.1.74.
26 **proper-false** goodlooking but deceitful (men).
27 To impress their images on women's soft hearts.
28–9 **Alas...be** Viola accounts for women's susceptibility to love on the basis of their nature, thus excusing both Olivia's enamourment and her own (expressed at 31–2).
30 **fadge** turn out well.
31 **monster** i.e. responding both as a man (33) and as a woman (35).
31 **fond** dote. Among illustrative examples (sv *v* 2), *OED* cites a line from John Palsgrave's translation of the comedy *Acolastus* (1540): 'I fonde, or dote upon a thyng for inordynate love.'

32 *As F's reading 'And' seems a clear instance of dittography from the preceding line, blurring the sharp parallelism of the rest of the passage.
33 **As I am man** i.e. since I am disguised as a man.
34 **My state...for** My condition is hopeless in respect to.
36 **thriftless** unprofitable.
36 **breathe** 'breath', F's spelling, is frequently not distinguished in this period from 'breathe' as in *LLL* 5.2.722 (F): 'I breath free breath.'

Act 2, Scene 3
Location Olivia's house (Rowe).
2 **betimes** early.
2 *diluculo surgere* From William Lily's Latin *Grammar: diluculo surgere saluberrimum est* (to rise at daybreak is extremely healthful). Lily's *Grammar* was a standard school textbook from the sixteenth century to the nineteenth.

SIR TOBY A false conclusion: I hate it as an unfilled can. To be up after   5
 midnight and to go bed then is early; so that to go to bed after
 midnight is to go to bed betimes. Does not our lives consist of the
 four elements?
SIR ANDREW Faith, so they say, but I think it rather consists of eating
 and drinking.   10
SIR TOBY Th'art a scholar; let us therefore eat and drink. Marian, I
 say, a stoup of wine!

Enter CLOWN [FESTE]

SIR ANDREW Here comes the fool, i'faith.
FESTE How now, my hearts? Did you never see the picture of 'We
 Three'?   15
SIR TOBY Welcome, ass. Now let's have a catch.
SIR ANDREW By my troth, the fool has an excellent breast. I had rather
 than forty shillings I had such a leg, and so sweet a breath to sing,
 as the fool has. In sooth, thou wast in very gracious fooling last
 night, when thou spok'st of Pigrogromitus, of the Vapians passing   20
 the equinoctial of Queubus. 'Twas very good, i'faith: I sent thee
 sixpence for thy leman; hadst it?

12 SD FESTE] *This edn; not in* F   22 leman] *Theobald;* Lemon F

5 **unfilled can** empty drinking-vessel.

8 **four elements** i.e. fire, air, water and earth, which were believed to compose all matter; the four humours (choler, blood, phlegm and melancholy or black bile) which composed the fluids of the human body corresponded to them, providing an analogy between the little world of man (the microcosm) and the universe (the macrocosm).

11 **Th'art a scholar** i.e. in confirming Sir Toby's own predilection.

11 **Marian** i.e. 'Maid Marian', a reference to the disreputable character who led morris dances and May games, popular diversions opposed by the puritans. Another sobriquet for Maria, whom Sir Toby earlier called his 'niece's chambermaid' (1.3.42).

14 **my hearts** See 1.5.152 n.

14–15 **picture... Three** A sign-board representing two fools or two asses and inscribed 'We Three', the spectator making the third (NS).

16 **Welcome, ass** Sir Toby's salutation to the 'fool' plays on the two forms (fool or ass) which the sign-board might carry. See above.

16 **catch** A song with three successive vocal parts.

17 **breast** voice. Synonymous with 'breath' (18).

18 **forty shillings** The precise amount that Slender (*Wiv.* 1.1.198–9) would give to have his copy of the 'Book of Songs and Sonnets' at hand in his attempt to woo Mistress Page. To the NS editors, the similarity of details of character in the two plays suggests that the same actor played both Sir Andrew and Slender. This was perhaps John Sincler, Sincklo or Sinklo, a member of Shakespeare's company at this time who was conspicuous for his thinness.

18 **such a leg** Probably said in admiration of Feste's ability to dance, the complementary feature of his ability to sing. In commending the 'excellent constitution' of Sir Andrew's leg at 1.3.107–8, Sir Toby had attributed it to the astral influence of a 'galliard' at his birth. Still, there are other admiring references in Shakespeare simply to a well-turned leg; Romeo's, for example, according to the Nurse, 'excels all men's' (*Rom.* 2.5.41).

20–1 **Pigrogromitus...Queubus** Further instances of Feste's mock learning (see 1.5.29).

21 **equinoctial** The equinoctial line; terrestrial equator. Used figuratively and humorously.

22 **leman** sweetheart.

FESTE   I did impeticos thy gratillity: for Malvolio's nose is no whipstock;
my lady has a white hand, and the Myrmidons are no bottle-ale
houses.   25
SIR ANDREW   Excellent! Why this is the best fooling, when all is done.
Now a song.
SIR TOBY   Come on, there is sixpence for you. Let's have a song.
SIR ANDREW   There's a testril of me, too; if one knight give a –
FESTE   Would you have a love song or a song of good life?   30
SIR TOBY   A love song, a love song.
SIR ANDREW   Ay, ay. I care not for good life.

(*Clown* [*Feste*] *sings*)

O mistress mine, where are you roaming?
O stay and hear, your true love's coming,
That can sing both high and low.   35
Trip no further, pretty sweeting;
Journeys end in lovers meeting,
Every wise man's son doth know.
SIR ANDREW   Excellent good, i'faith.
SIR TOBY   Good, good.   40

29 a –] F2; a F   32 SD *Feste*] *This edn; not in* F

23 **impeticos** Burlesque word meaning 'im-
pocket', perhaps intending to suggest 'impetticoat',
a form that many editors adopt.
23 **gratillity** little tip. A perversion of 'gratuity'
to emphasise its smallness.
23 **for...whipstock** This perhaps means
that Malvolio's nose (for smelling out faults in
others) does not give him the right to punish; hence
Feste need have no fear of him. Literally, his nose
is no handle to a whip.
24 **my lady...hand** This perhaps means that
my lady (the Countess Olivia) is a gentlewoman, the
term to be taken in two senses: (1) of noble birth
and (2) kindly (in contrast to the just-mentioned
Malvolio). See 66 below and n.
24–5 **Myrmidons...houses** Meaning uncertain, often explained simply as the fool's 'nonsense'. The Myrmidons were the followers of
Achilles; 'bottle-ale' is used as a term of abuse in
2H4 (2.4.131), which suggests that it refers to
the inferior kind of beer served in low taverns.
26 **when...done** Proverbial (Dent A211.1)
for 'when all is said and done'.
29 **testril** A perversion of 'tester', a sixpence;
'unconscious imitation' of Feste's 'gratillity' (NS).

29 **give a –** The line in F ends at the margin
without punctuation; either the mark or, as
some think, words have been dropped from the
text.
30 **song of good life** A generic reference to the
extolling of the shepherd's life in contrast to that of
kings and worldlings. See Hallett Smith's chapter on
the pastoral in *Elizabethan Poetry*, 1952, pp. 13, 30
and n., where he alludes to more than forty-five
Elizabethan examples based on this topos.
32 **Ay...life** Not having 'followed the arts', Sir
Andrew understands Feste to mean a song having
a moral import, perhaps even a metrical psalm.
33–8, 41–6 Though there are three contemporary
musical settings for 'O mistress mine', the words
are thought to be Shakespeare's own. The difficulty
in reconciling the settings with the text suggests that
a popular tune antedated the earliest of these and
that each of three composers reworked it in turn.
See Seng (pp. 94–100) for a full discussion of the
issues frequently debated. The words would seem
to have a particular relevance to Olivia's folly in
shunning the 'sight / And company of men', to
which Feste alluded in 1.5.27–30.

FESTE [*Sings*]   What is love? 'Tis not hereafter;
                            Present mirth hath present laughter;
                            What's to come is still unsure.
                            In delay there lies no plenty,
                            Then come kiss me, sweet and twenty;   45
                            Youth's a stuff will not endure.

SIR ANDREW A mellifluous voice, as I am true knight.

SIR TOBY A contagious breath.

SIR ANDREW Very sweet, and contagious, i'faith.

SIR TOBY To hear by the nose, it is dulcet in contagion. But shall we   50
make the welkin dance indeed? Shall we rouse the night owl in a
catch that will draw three souls out of one weaver? Shall we do
that?

SIR ANDREW And you love me, let's do't: I am dog at a catch.

FESTE By'r lady, sir, and some dogs will catch well.   55

SIR ANDREW Most certain. Let our catch be, 'Thou knave'.

FESTE 'Hold thy peace, thou knave', knight? I shall be constrain'd in't
to call thee knave, knight.

SIR ANDREW 'Tis not the first time I have constrained one to call me
knave. Begin, fool. It begins, 'Hold thy peace.'   60

FESTE I shall never begin if I hold my peace.

SIR ANDREW Good, i'faith. Come, begin.

                                                            (*Catch sung*)

---

41 SD *Sings*] Cam.; *not in* F   57 knight?] *Capell;* knight. F

43 still 'always', here and frequently elsewhere.

45 sweet and twenty sweet and twenty times
sweet. An intensive, as in *Wiv.* 2.1.195–6: 'Good
even and twenty, good Master Page!' Substantiation
for this reading is provided by its use in *The Wit
of a Woman* (1604, sig. D2ᵛ): 'Sweet and twenty, all
sweet and sweet, why thou sweet Schoolemaster, all
my lesson is of Love, a sweet Love lesson...' (cited
by R. Proudfoot, *S.Sur.* 29 (1976), 179, but with
a different reference).

48 contagious breath A 'catchy voice' (Furness)
but with a play on 'contagious' or 'pestilent'
(in reference to the plague) and breath or
'exhalation', as in *JC* 1.2.244–7: 'the
rabblement...utter'd such a deal of stinking
breath'.

50 To hear...contagion If one *hears* through
the nose in the same way that one catches the
pestilence through it, the voice is (indeed) sweetly
infectious.

51 make...dance make (the stars) in the sky
dance. Compare *Cor.* 5.4.49–51: 'The trumpets,
sackbuts, psalteries, and fifes, / Tabors and

cymbals, and the shouting Romans, / Make the sun
dance' (Kittredge).

52 catch...weaver Compare *Ado* 2.3.59–60:
'Is it not strange that sheep's guts should hale souls
out of men's bodies?' As refugees from the Low
Countries and frequently Calvinists, weavers were
accustomed to singing psalms, not catches; compare
1H4 2.4.133–4: 'I would I were a weaver, I could
sing psalms, or any thing.'

54 dog an adept. As in *TGV* 4.4.11–13: 'I
would have (as one should say) one that takes upon
him to be a dog indeed, to be, as it were, a dog at all
things.' Feste then literalises the metaphor in the
next line.

55 By'r lady By Our Lady.

57 Hold...knave The words of the round are
'Hold thy piece, thou knave, and I prithee hold thy
piece', with the result that each of the singers is
called 'knave' in turn. The text derives from
Thomas Ravenscroft's *Deuteromelia* (1609, sig. C4),
as printed in Seng, p. 101, who also notes (p. 103)
that an earlier musical version (*c.* 1580) exists in
King's College, Cambridge, MS. KC 1, no. 32.

Enter MARIA

MARIA What a caterwauling do you keep here! If my lady have not
called up her steward Malvolio and bid him turn you out of doors,
never trust me.   65
SIR TOBY My lady's a Cataian, we are politicians, Malvolio's a
Peg-a-Ramsey, and [*Sings*] 'Three merry men be we.' Am not I
consanguineous? Am I not of her blood? Tilly vally! 'Lady!'
[*Sings*] 'There dwelt a man in Babylon, lady, lady.'
FESTE Beshrew me, the knight's in admirable fooling.   70
SIR ANDREW Ay, he does well enough if he be disposed, and so do I,
too; he does it with a better grace, but I do it more natural.
SIR TOBY [*Sings*] O'the twelfth day of December –

67 SD *Sings*] NS; not in F   68 'Lady!'] NS, conj. Furness; Ladie F   69 SD *Sings*] Rowe subst.; not in F
73 SD *Sings*] Rowe subst.; not in F   73 O'] NS, conj. Walker; O F   73 December –] Theobald subst.; December. F

66 **Cataian** A form of 'Cathayan', i.e. native of
Cathay (China), used as a term of reproach in *Wiv.*
2.1.144–6: 'I will not believe such a Cataian, though
the priest o'th'town commended him for a true
man.' Although in his cups, Sir Toby seems
unlikely to mean anything more than that the
countess can be relied on not to execute the order
to which Maria has just referred, even as Feste, who
also risked being turned out, has just implied that
she was both of noble birth and kind (24 above).
Ard. usefully quotes a contemporary description
that accounts for the opprobrium of the name: 'the
Cathaiens...knowe not what we meane, when we
speake of faithfulnesse, or trustinesse' (John
Boemus, trans. William Watreman, *Fardle of
Facions* (1555), sig. M4ᵛ).
66 **politicians** schemers.
67 **Peg-a-Ramsey** A generic reference that has
occasioned much editorial debate; it was the name
both of a popular tune (the music is given in
William Chappell's *Old English Popular Music*, rev.
H. Ellis Woolridge, 2 vols., 1893, I, 248) and of a
dance to which Nashe alludes (*Works*, III, 122).
67 **Three...we** Four lines of what may be the
source of this fragment of song appeared in Peele's
The Old Wives' Tale (1595), where it is called an 'old
proverb' (Tilley M590):

Three merrie men, and three merrie men,
And three merrie men be wee.
I in the wood, and thou on the ground,
And Jacke sleeps in the tree.

A musical version, deriving from a manuscript commonplace book in the hand of John
Playford (*c.* 1650), is given in Chappell, *Popular
Music of the Olden Time*, 2 vols., 1855–9, I, 216
(reprinted in E. W. Naylor, *Shakespeare and Music*,
1931, p. 182, and John H. Long, *Shakespeare's Use
of Music*, 1955, p. 174); another version (given in

Louis C. Elson, *Shakespeare in Music*, 1901, p. 214)
seems to have been used for a number of Robin
Hood ballads (Seng, pp. 102–3, where he also
indicates the popularity of the song from frequent
allusions to it in the seventeenth century).
67–8 **Am I...'Lady'** Since Sir Toby is of
Olivia's blood – i.e. 'consanguineous' – he reacts
with some fervour ('Tilly vally!' = 'Fiddle-
faddle!') when Maria refers to her in formal terms
as 'my lady' rather than as earlier 'Your cousin, my
lady' (1.3.3–4).
69 **There...lady** Based on the Biblical story
of Susanna and the Elders, the ballad exists in
numerous versions, one of which was entered in
SR for Thomas Colwell in 1562/3. A version of it
is included in *Roxburghe Ballads*, ed. William
Chappell and J. W. Ebsworth, 9 vols., 1871–99, I,
190–3 (Seng, pp. 103–4). Claude M. Simpson (*The
British Broadside Ballad and Its Music*, 1966) gives
the tune as that of a popular ballad on King
Solomon by William Elderton, typified by the use
of a short refrain 'Lady, Lady' (pp. 410–12).
70 **Beshrew me** Curse me. Used here as a
simple asseveration.
71 **disposed** inclined to merriment.
72 **natural** naturally. The adjectival form is
used instead of the adverbial in order to play on
'born idiot' as at 1.3.24.
73 **O'...December** Not certainly identified.
Kittredge suggests it is a line from the ballad of
'Musselburgh Field' (*The English and Scottish
Popular Ballads*, ed. F. J. Child, 10 parts, 1882–98,
VI, 378) which reads 'the tenth day of December'.
Shakespeare could conceivably have altered this to
suit the title of the play, though a later version of
it (*Choyce Drollery: Songs & Sonnets* (1656), p. 78)
reads 'twelfth' (Seng, p. 103).

MARIA For the love o'God, peace!

Enter MALVOLIO

MALVOLIO My masters, are you mad? Or what are you? Have you no   75
wit, manners, nor honesty but to gabble like tinkers at this time
of night? Do ye make an alehouse of my lady's house, that ye squeak
out your coziers' catches without any mitigation or remorse of
voice? Is there no respect of place, persons, nor time in you?

SIR TOBY We did keep time, sir, in our catches. Sneck up!   80

MALVOLIO Sir Toby, I must be round with you. My lady bade me tell
you that, though she harbours you as her kinsman, she's nothing
allied to your disorders. If you can separate yourself and your
misdemeanours, you are welcome to the house; if not, and it would
please you to take leave of her, she is very willing to bid you farewell.   85

SIR TOBY [*Sings*] Farewell, dear heart, since I must needs be gone.

MARIA Nay, good Sir Toby.

FESTE [*Sings*] His eyes do show his days are almost done.

MALVOLIO Is't even so?

SIR TOBY [*Sings*] But I will never die.   90

FESTE [*Sings*] Sir Toby, there you lie.

86, 88, 90, 91 SD *Sings*] *Hanmer subst.; not in* F

76 **wit...honesty** judgement, breeding, decency.

77–8 **squeak out** shrill out.

78 **coziers'** cobblers'.

78 **mitigation or remorse** abating or softening.

79 **respect of** regard for.

80 **Sneck up** Shut up. Literally, 'shut the doors', in reference to Malvolio's duty to secure the house. From the time of Robert Nares's *Glossary* (1822) the word, which *OED* gives as chiefly Scottish and Northern, has usually been identified with 'snick' or 'sneck up', meaning 'be hanged'.

82–3 **nothing...disorders** no kin to your bad conduct. As Jessica says of Shylock (*MV* 2.3.18–19): 'But though I am a daughter to his blood, / I am not to his manners.'

83 **and** from.

86–96 **Farewell...dare not** From 'Corydon's Farewell to Phyllis' in Robert Jones's *The First Booke of Songes and Ayres* (1600, sigs. D4ᵛ–E1). Sir Toby and Feste sing a composite of the first two stanzas:

(1)

Farewel dear love since thou wilt needs be gon,
mine eies do shew my life is almost done,

nay I will never die,
so long as I can spie,
there be many mo
though that she do go
there be many mo I feare not,
why then let her goe I care not.

(2)

Farewell, farewell, since this I finde is true,
I will not spend more time in wooing you:
But I will seeke elswhere,
If I may find her there,
Shall I bid her goe,
What and if I doe?
Shall I bid her go and spare not,
Oh no no no no I dare not.

For a listing of texts and settings, see Seng, pp. 106–7.

87 **Nay...Toby** Maria is still remonstrating with Sir Toby and his vocalising, but the 'nay' perhaps refers to some amorous stage business here on the part of Sir Toby.

91 **Sir...lie** The stichomythic exchange would seem to preclude any stage business here, such as Sir Toby's falling down.

MALVOLIO This is much credit to you.

SIR TOBY [*Sings*] Shall I bid him go?

FESTE [*Sings*] What and if you do?

SIR TOBY [*Sings*] Shall I bid him go, and spare not? 95

FESTE [*Sings*] O no, no, no, no, you dare not.

SIR TOBY Out o'time, sir? Ye lie! Art any more than a steward? Dost thou think because thou art virtuous there shall be no more cakes and ale?

FESTE Yes, by St Anne, and ginger shall be hot i'th'mouth too. 100
[*Exit*]

SIR TOBY Th'art i'th'right. Go, sir, rub your chain with crumbs. A stoup of wine, Maria!

MALVOLIO Mistress Mary, if you prized my lady's favour at anything more than contempt, you would not give means for this uncivil rule; she shall know of it, by this hand. *Exit* 105

MARIA Go shake your ears.

SIR ANDREW 'Twere as good a deed as to drink when a man's a-hungry, to challenge him the field, and then to break promise with him, and make a fool of him.

SIR TOBY Do't, knight. I'll write thee a challenge, or I'll deliver thy 110 indignation to him by word of mouth.

93–6 SD *Sings*] *Rowe subst.; not in* F   97 time, sir?] *Theobald; tune, sir,* F   100 SD *Exit*] *Ard.; not in* F

---

97 *Out o'time Sir Toby is reverting to his original riposte to Malvolio in 80. F's 'tune' can be accounted for on the grounds of frequent misreading in Secretary hand of i:u followed by a nasal. Q2 *Ham.* 1814 (3.1.158) has 'Like sweet bells jangled out of time' where F reads 'tune'; the reverse error occurs in *Mac.* 4.3.235: 'This tune [F 'time'] goes manly.' Compare also *R2* 5.5.42–3: 'How sour sweet music is / When time is broke, and no proportion kept!' On the other hand, Dent (T598.1) gives 'out of tune' as proverbial, referring to *OED* Tune *sb* 3b and meaning 'out of order'; while this reading accords in general with Malvolio's remonstrations in 75–85, it does not pick up any specific charge with which Sir Toby can quibble.

98–9 cakes and ale Metaphoric for parish celebrations at Christmas and Easter time; in the view of a strict puritan like Phillip Stubbes (*Anatomy of Abuses*, ed. F. J. Furnivall, 1877–9, I, 151) these included 'swilling and gulling, night and day'.

100 St Anne Mother of the Virgin, according to the apocryphal Book of James. St Anne was venerated in the Middle Ages but her cult was derided by Luther and later reformers; thus Feste's asseveration is a further dig at Malvolio's would-be puritan tendencies. It is used only here and in *Shr.* 1.1.250.

100 ginger Used to spice ale; 'canded, greene, or condited', it was considered an aphrodisiac according to Gerard's *Herball* (1633 edn), p. 62 (Furness).

100 SD F gives no exit for Feste, who clearly is not present at 146 when Maria outlines her plot.

101 rub...crumbs i.e. polish up the insignia of your steward's office with crumbs from the buttery.

104 give...rule provide drink to encourage this unmannerly regimen.

106 Go...ears A contemptuous dismissal (Tilley E16). Compare 'turn him off / (Like to the empty [unburdened] ass) to shake his ears / And graze in commons' (*JC* 4.1.25–7).

107 a-hungry This conjunction Abbott (24) explains as the result of a corruption of Anglo-Saxon intensive 'of' and compares Matt. 25.35: 'For I was an hungred and ye gave me meat.' It is another verbal mannerism that Sir Andrew shares with Slender (*Wiv.* 1.1.270). See 2.3.18 n.

108 the field to single combat.

MARIA Sweet Sir Toby, be patient for tonight. Since the youth of the count's was today with my lady, she is much out of quiet. For Monsieur Malvolio, let me alone with him. If I do not gull him into an ayword, and make him a common recreation, do not   115 think I have wit enough to lie straight in my bed. I know I can do it.

SIR TOBY Possess us, possess us, tell us something of him.

MARIA Marry, sir, sometimes he is a kind of puritan.

SIR ANDREW O if I thought that, I'd beat him like a dog!   120

SIR TOBY What, for being a puritan? Thy exquisite reason, dear knight?

SIR ANDREW I have no exquisite reason for't, but I have reason good enough.

MARIA The devil a puritan that he is, or anything constantly but a time-pleaser, an affectioned ass, that cons state without book and   125 utters it by great swarths. The best persuaded of himself: so crammed (as he thinks) with excellencies, that it is his grounds of faith that all that look on him love him; and on that vice in him will my revenge find notable cause to work.

SIR TOBY What wilt thou do?   130

MARIA I will drop in his way some obscure epistles of love, wherein by the colour of his beard, the shape of his leg, the manner of his gait, the expressure of his eye, forehead, and complexion, he shall find himself most feelingly personated. I can write very like my lady

114 **let me alone** leave him to me. An idiom used again at 3.4.84, 95 and 153.

114 **gull** deceive. The compatibility of Maria and Sir Toby is highlighted: she has in mind a trick to gull Malvolio, while Sir Toby is gulling Sir Andrew throughout the action. Both victims are labelled 'gulls'.

115 **an ayword** a proverb. Maria threatens to make Malvolio's name synonymous with 'gull'. Kökeritz explains this nonce usage (p. 313) as equivalent to 'a nayword', with detached 'n' on the analogy of the modern 'adder' (formed by erroneous word-division in the Middle Ages so that 'a nadder' became 'an adder'). Though editors frequently emend to 'nayword', they do so by reference to *Wiv.* 2.2.126 and 5.2.5, where it means 'password' and hence represents a homonym.

115 **recreation** sport, diversion.

118 **Possess** Inform.

119 **kind of puritan** i.e. morally straitlaced, but not an adherent of a specific religious group, as Maria makes clear at 124. Sir Andrew, however, understands him to be a party member.

121 **exquisite** excellent.

124 **constantly** consistently.

125 **time-pleaser** time-server. As in *Cor.* 3.1.43–5: 'you repin'd...call'd them / Time-pleasers, flatterers, foes to nobleness'.

125 **affectioned** affected.

125–6 **cons state...swarths** memorises the rules for appearing dignified in speech and deportment and discloses them in great sweeps. A 'swarth' = swath, the quantity of corn etc. that can be cut down with one sweep of the scythe.

126 **The best persuaded** Having the best opinion.

127–8 **it is...of faith** i.e. all the elements of his creed are united in this opinion (Kittredge). The lack of concord between subject and verb is not unusual in Elizabethan English.

131 **obscure** ambiguously worded.

131 **epistles** Plural for singular. Similarly with 'letters' (139), though at 147 and elsewhere in the play a single missive is specified. Shakespeare's general practice as to singular and plural form is divided.

133 **expressure** expression.

134 **feelingly personated** precisely represented.

your niece; on a forgotten matter we can hardly make distinction   135
of our hands.

SIR TOBY Excellent, I smell a device.

SIR ANDREW I have't in my nose, too.

SIR TOBY He shall think by the letters that thou wilt drop that they
come from my niece, and that she's in love with him.   140

MARIA My purpose is indeed a horse of that colour.

SIR ANDREW And your horse now would make him an ass.

MARIA Ass, I doubt not.

SIR ANDREW O 'twill be admirable!

MARIA Sport royal, I warrant you: I know my physic will work with   145
him. I will plant you two, and let the fool make a third, where he
shall find the letter. Observe his construction of it. For this night,
to bed, and dream on the event. Farewell.   *Exit*

SIR TOBY Good night, Penthesilea.

SIR ANDREW Before me, she's a good wench.   150

SIR TOBY She's a beagle, true bred, and one that adores me. What
o'that?

SIR ANDREW I was adored once, too.

SIR TOBY Let's to bed, knight. Thou hadst need send for more money.

SIR ANDREW If I cannot recover your niece, I am a foul way out.   155

SIR TOBY Send for money, knight; if thou hast her not i'th'end, call
me 'cut'.

---

135 on a forgotten matter i.e. when we have forgotten the circumstances in which it was written or the topic it concerned.

136 hands handwriting.

137 smell perceive. A frequent metaphor in Shakespeare; see *WT* 4.4.642–3: 'I smell the trick on't', and *1H4* 1.3.277, where Hotspur says of Worcester's plot 'I smell it.'

137 device clever stratagem or invention. It is also the term Malvolio uses (5.1.339) to refer to the plot against Malvolio.

143 Ass Used either (1) as a vocative or (2) as an object; some editors suggest a play on 'ass' and 'as'.

145 physic medicine (for purging Malvolio's self-love).

146 let...third Maria's language makes clear that the fool is not now present, and it is Fabian, in fact, who makes up the trio of observers in 2.5.

147 construction interpretation.

148 event outcome.

149 Penthesilea Queen of the Amazons. Another of Sir Toby's playful sobriquets for Maria, commenting again on her diminutive size, as at 1.5.167–8, 2.3.151, 2.5.11 and 3.2.52.

150 Before me On my soul. Modelled on 'before my God' (Onions).

151 beagle A small hunting-dog noted for its keenness of smell. Again a comment on Maria's diminutive size. The choice of diction says something again about Sir Toby's idiosyncratic speech since the term 'beagle' was generally one of opprobrium, as in *Tim.* 4.3.174–5 and many times elsewhere in drama.

153 I was...too Compare Sir Andrew's plaintive statement with that of Menelaus (*Tro.* 4.5.26): 'I had good argument for kissing, once' (Kenneth Palmer (ed.), *Tro.*, 1982).

155 recover obtain (and so regain expenses).

155 a foul way out grievously out of pocket.

156 Send for money Sir Toby has successfully importuned him 'some two thousand strong, or so' (3.2.43–4); at 1.3.18 he is said to have three thousand ducats a year.

157 cut Proverbial term of abuse (Tilley C940). It refers either to a horse with a cut tail or to one that has been gelded. It was considered a stupid beast; hence Falstaff's remark in *1H4* 2.4.193–4: 'if I tell thee a lie, spit in my face, call me horse'. For the obscene usage, see 2.5.72–3 and n.

SIR ANDREW If I do not, never trust me; take it how you will.

SIR TOBY Come, come, I'll go burn some sack; 'tis too late to go to
bed now. Come, knight, come, knight.   160

Exeunt

2.4 *Enter* DUKE [ORSINO], VIOLA, CURIO, *and others* [*both Lords and Musicians*]

ORSINO Give me some music –
            [*Musicians step forward*]
                              Now good morrow, friends;
Now, good Cesario – but that piece of song,
That old and antique song we heard last night;
Methought it did relieve my passion much,
More than light airs and recollected terms   5
Of these most brisk and giddy-pacèd times.
Come, but one verse.

CURIO He is not here, so please your lordship, that should sing it.

ORSINO Who was it?

CURIO Feste, the jester, my lord, a fool that the Lady Olivia's father   10
took much delight in. He is about the house.

ORSINO Seek him out, and play the tune the while.

[*Exit Curio*]

Act 2, Scene 4   2.4] *Scena Quarta.* F   0 SD *both Lords and Musicians*] *This edn; not in* F   1–2 music – [*Musicians step forward.*] Now…friends; / …Cesario –] *This edn;* Musick; Now…friends. / …*Cesario,* F; music. Now – [*musicians enter* good morrow, friends…. / …*Cesario, NS;* music – [*to others*] Now…friends; / [*to Viola*] Now…*Cesario –conj. Ard.*   12 SD.1 *Exit Curio*] Pope; *not in* F

159 burn…sack heat some canary wine with sugar.

Act 2, Scene 4
  Location The palace (Rowe).
  0 SD *and…Musicians* Possibly lords or musicians but better both lords *and* musicians; 'lords' corresponds to the directive at 1.1.0 SD and again at 5.1.5; 'and musicians' solves the problem presented in the first two lines. See next note.
  1–2 The punctuation of these lines in F offers difficulties as to whom the duke is addressing and, consequently, as to the staging. If F's 'and others' (0 SD) is taken to refer both to 'lords' and 'musicians' (as here) there is an easy solution: the musicians come forward after the duke's opening call for music, whereupon he interrupts his demand for a specific piece in order to greet them and

Cesario. Such an arrangement removes any notion that Cesario is being asked to sing and thus obviates the revisionist theory that makes Feste a substitute singer. See p. 34 above. This solution concurs in part with that in NS (though it is offered there in support of revision) and in part with the suggestions of Ard. (which, however, except for the correction in 1 follows F's punctuation of a full stop in place of a semi-colon).
  2 but only.
  3 antique old and quaint. Frequently not distinguished from 'antic' in pronunciation (as here), meaning or orthography; compare 'these antic fables' (*MND* (Q2; F 1793) 5.1.3).
  4 passion pangs of unrequited love.
  5 recollected artificial. In contrast with the 'old and plain' song, which is the way Orsino characterises it in 41.

(*Music plays*)

Come hither, boy; if ever thou shalt love,
In the sweet pangs of it, remember me:
For such as I am, all true lovers are,   15
Unstaid and skittish in all motions else,
Save in the constant image of the creature
That is beloved. How dost thou like this tune?
VIOLA It gives a very echo to the seat
Where love is throned.
ORSINO   Thou dost speak masterly.   20
My life upon't, young though thou art, thine eye
Hath stayed upon some favour that it loves;
Hath it not, boy?
VIOLA   A little, by your favour.
ORSINO What kind of woman is't?
VIOLA   Of your complexion.
ORSINO She is not worth thee then. What years, i'faith?   25
VIOLA About your years, my lord.
ORSINO Too old, by heaven! Let still the woman take
An elder than herself; so wears she to him;
So sways she level in her husband's heart;
For, boy, however we do praise ourselves,   30
Our fancies are more giddy and unfirm,
More longing, wavering, sooner lost and worn,
Than women's are.
VIOLA   I think it well, my lord.
ORSINO Then let thy love be younger than thyself,
Or thy affection cannot hold the bent: 35

15–18 For...beloved Compare 1.1.9–15 where, by his analogy of love and the 'never-surfeited sea', Orsino suggests the inconstancy of (male) lovers, a point that he (inconstantly) denies here and (inconstantly) reaffirms at 31–3.

16 motions else other thoughts and feelings.

19 seat i.e. the heart.

22 stayed...favour fixed upon some countenance.

23 by your favour it you please. A courteous formula, but also a quibble on 'near to your countenance' (Abbott 145).

24 complexion temperament. Dictated by a mixture of the four humours; see 2.3.8 n.

27 still Carries here the two senses: (1) nonetheless and (2) ever.

28 wears...him becomes fit to (and for) him

like a garment. Perhaps echoing the proverb 'Win it and wear it' (Tilley w408).

29 sways she level (1) rules, (2) swings in perfect balance (NS).

31 fancies loves.

32 worn worn out. Following Hanmer, many editors emend to 'won', but the duke is continuing his earlier metaphorical use of 'wear'; see 28 and n.

33 I...well I believe it. The expression appears again in *MM* 2.4.130, where Angelo is agreeing with Isabella's comment that women are frail, soft and 'credulous to false imprints'. Her attitude agrees with that expressed in Viola's soliloquy at 2.2.26–9.

35 hold the bent keep its intensity. A metaphor from the extent to which a bow can be made taut.

For women are as roses, whose fair flower,
Being once displayed, doth fall that very hour.
VIOLA And so they are. Alas, that they are so:
To die, even when they to perfection grow!

Enter CURIO *and* CLOWN [FESTE]

ORSINO O fellow, come, the song we had last night.   40
Mark it, Cesario, it is old and plain;
The spinsters and the knitters in the sun,
And the free maids that weave their thread with bones,
Do use to chant it; it is silly sooth,
And dallies with the innocence of love   45
Like the old age.
FESTE Are you ready, sir?
ORSINO Ay, prithee sing.

(Music)
The Song
Come away, come away, death,
And in sad cypress let me be laid.   50
Fie away, fie away, breath,
I am slain by a fair cruel maid;
My shroud of white, stuck all with yew,
O prepare it.
My part of death no one so true   55
Did share it.

39 SD FESTE] *This edn; not in* F   51 Fie...fie] F; Fly...fly *Rowe*   53–6] *As Pope; two lines in* F, *ending*...prepare
it / ...share it

39 **even when** just when.
41 **plain** artless.
42 **spinsters** spinners.
43 **free...bones** i.e. carefree maidens who
make lace by weaving the thread on bone bobbins.
44 **silly sooth** simple truth.
45 **dallies** sports with.
46 **Like...age** As in former (and better) times.
48 SD **The Song** Although the original music is
not known, it was clearly a folk song. Katherine
Garvin (*N&Q* 170 (9 May 1936), 326–8, cited by
Seng, p. 110) speculates that it may refer to the Old
French *chansons de toile* popular in the twelfth
century. Sung by women, the words suggest patient
devotion towards men who treat them badly. To
support her suggestion, she argues that Shakespeare
knew Huguenots in London, many of whom were
lacemakers and clothworkers; he lodged for a time

with a maker of ornamental headdresses (by 1604
but perhaps earlier). Seng records the earliest of
modern settings as one by Thomas Arne (1710–78),
included in *The Shakespeare Vocal Album*, 1864,
p. 90.
49 **Come away** Come hither.
50 **sad cypress** A coffin of cypress wood or a
bier covered with cypress boughs; the tree was
emblematic of mourning.
51 **Fie...fie away** Seng (p. 112) points out that
there is a song in Thomas Ravenscroft's *Melismata*
(1611, sig. C2) which begins 'Fie away, fie away, fie,
fie, fie', thus supporting the wording in F. Following
Rowe, editors usually emend to 'Fly...fly away'.
53 **yew** Like the cypress, a tree associated with
mourning.
55–6 **My part...share it** No one ever died for
love who was so constant as I.

Not a flower, not a flower sweet,
On my black coffin let there be strown;
Not a friend, not a friend greet
My poor corpse, where my bones shall be thrown: 60
A thousand thousand sighs to save,
Lay me, O where
Sad true lover never find my grave,
To weep there.

ORSINO There's for thy pains. [*Gives money*]   65

FESTE No pains, sir, I take pleasure in singing, sir.

ORSINO I'll pay thy pleasure then.

FESTE Truly, sir, and pleasure will be paid, one time or another.

ORSINO Give me now leave to leave thee.

FESTE Now the melancholy god protect thee, and the tailor make thy   70
doublet of changeable taffeta, for thy mind is a very opal. I would
have men of such constancy put to sea, that their business might
be everything and their intent everywhere, for that's it that always
makes a good voyage of nothing. Farewell.   *Exit*

ORSINO Let all the rest give place.
[*Curio and attendants retire*]
Once more, Cesario,   75
Get thee to yond same sovereign cruelty.
Tell her my love, more noble than the world,
Prizes not quantity of dirty lands;
The parts that fortune hath bestowed upon her
Tell her I hold as giddily as fortune;   80

61–4] As Pope; *two lines in* F, *ending*…where / …there   65 SD *Gives money*] Collier²; *not in* F   75 SD *Curio*…*retire*]
Cam.; *not in* F

68 pleasure…another Feste plays on the
proverbial idea that pleasure must be paid for with
pain (Tilley P420, with variant forms).

69 Give…thee Orsino dismisses Feste cour-
teously and wittily, employing the rhetorical trick of
using the same word in different senses (antaclasis).
This is one of Shakespeare's favourite devices: see
for example 3.1.1–9, 3.2.39, 42–3.

70 melancholy god Saturn, who determined
the melancholy temperament which would vary
according to social types. Of these, the melancholy
of a lover is a composite, as Jaques explains in *AYLI*
4.1.10–15, and hence the worst. At 109 below, it is
described as a 'green and yellow melancholy'.

71 doublet…taffeta jacket of iridescent silk.

71 opal Shakespeare's apt characterisation of
this iridescent stone (and his only other reference
to it) is in the catalogue in *A Lover's Complaint*:
'The heaven-hu'd sapphire and the opal blend /
With objects manifold' (215–16).

73 intent port of call.

73–4 for that's…nothing i.e. that's what
makes a so-called 'good' voyage but, in fact, one
without profit. Tilley (E194) cites the proverb 'He
that is everywhere is nowhere.'

79–80 The parts…as fortune i.e. the social
status and wealth that chance to be Olivia's, he
evaluates as lightly as fickle fortune herself.

But 'tis that miracle and queen of gems
That nature pranks her in attracts my soul.
VIOLA But if she cannot love you, sir?
ORSINO I cannot be so answered.
VIOLA   Sooth, but you must.
    Say that some lady, as perhaps there is,   85
    Hath for your love as great a pang of heart
    As you have for Olivia. You cannot love her.
    You tell her so. Must she not then be answered?
ORSINO There is no woman's sides
    Can bide the beating of so strong a passion   90
    As love doth give my heart; no woman's heart
    So big, to hold so much. They lack retention.
    Alas, their love may be called appetite,
    No motion of the liver, but the palate,
    That suffers surfeit, cloyment, and revolt,   95
    But mine is all as hungry as the sea,
    And can digest as much. Make no compare
    Between that love a woman can bear me,
    And that I owe Olivia.
VIOLA   Ay, but I know –
ORSINO What dost thou know?   100
VIOLA Too well what love women to men may owe.
    In faith, they are as true of heart as we.
    My father had a daughter loved a man
    As it might be perhaps, were I a woman,
    I should your lordship.
ORSINO   And what's her history?   105
VIOLA A blank, my lord. She never told her love,
    But let concealment like a worm i'th'bud

---

84 I] *Hanmer;* It F   95 suffers] *Rowe;* suffer F   99 know –] *Rowe;* know. F

81–2 **that miracle...in** i.e. the inestimable beauty with which nature has decked her, as opposed to the 'dirty lands' which fortune has bestowed on her.

84 *I Hanmer's emendation of F's 'It' is sanctioned by Cesario's use of the second person in reply.

90 **bide** endure.

92 **retention** the power to retain. A medical term following on 'woman's sides' and 'heart' and looking toward 'digest' at 97.

93 **appetite** no more than desire. Like the appetite for music in 1.1.1–3.

94 **No...liver** No impulse (i.e. emotion) in the liver. The liver was considered the throne of the passions, as in 1.1.37–8.

95 **suffers...revolt** experiences satiety and revulsion; 'cloyment' is a nonce usage. Orsino's words here about the quality of women's love provide an ironic comment on his opening speech in Act 1.

97 **compare** comparison.

99 **owe** bear. As also at 101.

107 **concealment...bud** secrecy like a canker worm destroying the budding rose. In *Temp.* 1.2.416, it is 'grief' that is 'beauty's canker'.

> Feed on her damask cheek. She pined in thought,
> And with a green and yellow melancholy
> She sat like Patience on a monument,   110
> Smiling at grief. Was not this love indeed?
> We men may say more, swear more, but indeed
> Our shows are more than will: for still we prove
> Much in our vows, but little in our love.
> ORSINO But died thy sister of her love, my boy?   115
> VIOLA I am all the daughters of my father's house,
> And all the brothers, too – and yet I know not.
> Sir, shall I to this lady?
> ORSINO   Ay, that's the theme.
> To her in haste; give her this jewel; say   120
> My love can give no place, bide no denay.

> *Exeunt*

117 too –] *Rowe;* too: F

108 damask mingled red and white. Like the 'damask'd' roses of *Sonnets* 130.5.

109 green...melancholy The pallor typical of a melancholic lover, according to Jaques Ferrand's *'Erotomania*, is either a mixture of white and yellow or of white, yellow and green (French edn 1612, trans. 1640, p. 121, quoted in Lawrence Babb, *The Elizabethan Malady*, 1951, p. 136).

111 Smiling...grief Most editors assume that 'grief' is a generalised, rather than a personified, abstraction, but the monument is perhaps graced with two figures. 'Patience' and 'Monument' are capitalised in F, but not 'grief'. Capitalisation is of little expressive significance in the *STM* manuscript (Hand D) or in texts believed to have been set from foul papers. That Shakespeare conceived of Patience as smiling is supported by *Per.* 5.1.137–9: 'Yet thou dost look / Like Patience gazing on king's graves, and smiling / Extremity out of act.' For an

account of contemporary representations of the figure of Patience, frequently coupled with other virtues such as Fortitude and Hope, see W. S. Heckscher, 'Shakespeare in his relationship to the visual arts', *Research Opportunities in Renaissance Drama* 13–14 (1970–1), 35–56. Alternatively, 'grief' can simply refer to the cause of suffering or sorrow (Onions).

113 Our...will Our display is greater than our determination.

113 still we prove always we demonstrate.

117 and yet...not Though Viola's 'own escape' has allowed her to take hope in a like escape for Sebastian; she is uncertain.

119 give...jewel This Viola does not do; instead the emphasis at 3.1 is on the ring Olivia sent 'in chase' of her (2.2).

120 give...denay yield no ground, endure no denial.

2.5 *Enter* SIR TOBY, SIR ANDREW, *and* FABIAN

SIR TOBY Come thy ways, Signior Fabian.

FABIAN Nay, I'll come. If I lose a scruple of this sport, let me be boiled to death with melancholy.

SIR TOBY Wouldst thou not be glad to have the niggardly rascally sheep-biter come by some notable shame?   5

FABIAN I would exult, man. You know he brought me out o'favour with my lady about a bear-baiting here.

SIR TOBY To anger him, we'll have the bear again; and we will fool him black and blue, shall we not, Sir Andrew?

SIR ANDREW And we do not, it is pity of our lives.   10

SIR TOBY Here comes the little villain.

Enter MARIA

How now, my metal of India?

MARIA Get ye all three into the box-tree. Malvolio's coming down this walk. He has been yonder i'the sun practising behaviour to his own shadow this half hour. Observe him, for the love of mockery, for   15
I know this letter will make a contemplative idiot of him. Close, in the name of jesting!

[The men hide]

Act 2, Scene 5 2.5] *Scena Quinta.* F   11 SD] *Dyce; after 10* F   17 SD *The men hide] Capell subst.; not in* F

Act 2, Scene 5
Location Olivia's garden (Pope).
0 SD Fabian, rather than Feste as Maria originally specified, makes up the trio of observers. See 2.3.146 n.
1 Come thy ways Come along.
2 Nay i.e. protesting that he needs no urging.
2 scruple Figuratively, 'the least bit'; literally, a third of a dram.
2–3 boiled…melancholy A jest, in that 'boil' and (black) 'bile', the cause of the cold and dry humour of melancholy, were homonyms up through the eighteenth century and continued so in dialectal pronunciation.
5 sheep-biter An opprobrious term for a dissembler. Nashe applies it to merchants turned usurers (*Works*, II, 98); to a pander (II, 260–1), leering 'like a sheep-biter', of whom he also says, 'If he be halfe a puritan, and have scripture continually in his mouth, hee speeds the better'; and directly to a puritan in an anti-Martinist tract (III, 372), 'What say you [Martin] to that zealous sheepbyter of your owne edition in Cambridge?'

7 bear-baiting One of the many Sabbath pastimes to which the puritans objected (along with plays and interludes).
8–9 fool…blue Figuratively, 'bruise him with fooling'.
10 it is…lives Proverbial (in the singular) for 'we do not deserve to live' (Dent P368.1).
11 little villain Used as a term of endearment, as in *Tro.* 3.2.33 – Cressida 'the prettiest villain' – and to comment again on Maria's diminutive size.
12 metal of India i.e. like pure gold from the 'bountiful' mines of India (*1H4* 3.1.166–7). 'India' was also used to refer to the East Indies, which had recently been more fully delineated than ever before on a new map ('with the augmentation of the Indies'), to which Maria refers in 3.2.62–3. F's 'mettle' was simply a variant spelling of 'metal' which, used figuratively (*OED* Metal *sb* 1f), referred to the character of an individual. Thus for Shakespeare's period there was no pun involved.
13 box-tree An evergreen shrub.
16 contemplative idiot meditative fool.
16 Close Keep still and out of sight.

Lie thou there [*Drops a letter*]; for here comes the trout that must
be caught with tickling.   *Exit*

Enter MALVOLIO

MALVOLIO 'Tis but fortune; all is fortune. Maria once told me she did   20
affect me, and I have heard herself come thus near, that should she
fancy, it should be one of my complexion. Besides, she uses me with
a more exalted respect than any one else that follows her. What
should I think on't?

SIR TOBY Here's an overweening rogue!   25

FABIAN O peace! Contemplation makes a rare turkey-cock of him; how
he jets under his advanced plumes!

SIR ANDREW 'Slight, I could so beat the rogue!

FABIAN Peace, I say!

MALVOLIO To be Count Malvolio!   30

SIR TOBY Ah, rogue!

SIR ANDREW Pistol him, pistol him!

FABIAN Peace, peace!

MALVOLIO There is example for't: the Lady of the Strachy married
the yeoman of the wardrobe –   35

---

18 SD *Drops a letter*] *Theobald subst.; not in* F   29 SH FABIAN] *NS, conj. Cam.; To.* F   33 SH FABIAN] *NS, conj. Cam.;*
To. F   35 wardrobe –] *This edn; wardrobe.* F

18–19 trout...tickling Proverbial (Tilley T537 and, for later entries, Dent) for the use of flattery to beguile a person just as the fish was caught by being 'rubbed and clawed' (Thomas Cogan, *The Haven of Health* (1584), sig. S4).

20 she i.e. Olivia.

20–1 did affect me was fond of me.

21–2 should...complexion should she love, it would be one of my appearance and temperament. Temperament was dictated by the mixture of the four humours; see 2.3.8 n.

23 follows her i.e. in her service and as a suitor (*OED* Follow *v* 3b). This second meaning provides the evidence, in Maria's words (3.4.34), of Malvolio's 'ridiculous boldness'.

26 Contemplation Thought. Picking up Maria's diction in 16.

26 rare extraordinary (intensive).

26 turkey-cock Symbol of foolish vanity.

27 jets...advanced plumes struts under his raised feathers. In view of Malvolio's social pretensions, 'advanced' applies both literally and metaphorically.

28 'Slight By God's light. A mild oath characteristic of Sir Andrew; he uses it again at 3.2.9. By 1633, it was considered an asseveration and not an oath (Furness).

29 SH *FABIAN Following on a conjecture in

Cam., NS assigns this speech and also 33 to Fabian, rather than to Sir Toby as F does, since it is Fabian who tries to quiet the other two in 26, and again at 37, 43, 48 and 53. Such restraint accords with his character and position as gentleman servitor to the countess and contrasts with that of her irrepressible kinsman. F abbreviates the speech headings here as *Fa.* or *Fab.* and *To.* (though elsewhere as *Tob.*), and majuscule T was easily confused in Secretary hand with other letters. Samuel A. Tannenbaum points out (*The Handwriting of the Renaissance*, 1930, p. 115) that Thomas Heywood was in the habit of crossing his T's, thus making them look exactly like F's.

32 Pistol him Shoot him.

34–5 The Lady...wardrobe The allusion has yet to be explained and has occasioned many attempted emendations. Sisson (I, 188–91) connects William Strachey, a shareholder in the rival Blackfriars Theatre, with David Yeomans, a 'tyreman' of that company in 1606, but such a topical reference would have had to be a late addition, an unlikely possibility if F's text derived from a scribal copy of foul papers. See Textual Analysis, p. 165 below. Others assume that Strachy is a place-name, and still others (like Dr Johnson) that it is a reference to 'some old story'.

SIR ANDREW Fie on him, Jezebel!

FABIAN O peace! Now he's deeply in. Look how imagination blows him.

MALVOLIO Having been three months married to her, sitting in my state –

SIR TOBY O for a stone-bow to hit him in the eye!

MALVOLIO Calling my officers about me, in my branched velvet gown,   40
having come from a day-bed, where I have left Olivia sleeping –

SIR TOBY Fire and brimstone!

FABIAN O peace, peace!

MALVOLIO And then to have the humour of state; and after a demure
travel of regard – telling them I know my place, as I would they   45
should do theirs – to ask for my kinsman Toby –

SIR TOBY Bolts and shackles!

FABIAN O peace, peace, peace! Now, now.

MALVOLIO Seven of my people, with an obedient start, make out for
him. I frown the while, and perchance wind up my watch, or play   50
with my – some rich jewel. Toby approaches; curtsies there to me –

SIR TOBY Shall this fellow live?

FABIAN Though our silence be drawn from us by th'ears, yet peace!

MALVOLIO I extend my hand to him thus, quenching my familiar smile
with an austere regard of control –   55

SIR TOBY And does not 'Toby' take you a blow o'the lips then?

---

38 state –] *Pope;* state. F   41 sleeping –] *Cam.;* sleeping. F   45–6 regard – ...theirs –] *Capell;* regard: ...theirs: F
46 Toby –] *Rowe;* Toby. F   51 my – some] *Collier;* my some F   51 me –] *Cam. subst.;* me. F   53 by th'ears] *Hanmer;*
with cars F   55 control –] *Cam. subst.;* controll. F

36 **Jezebel** The proud widow of Ahab, King of Israel, who was cast down to the street to become the food for dogs (2 Kings 19).

37 **blows** inflates.

38 **state** Canopied chair of state.

39 **stone-bow** A cross-bow that shot stones in place of arrows.

40 **branched** wrought, embroidered with flowers (Linthicum, p. 126).

44 **humour of state** caprice of rank.

44–5 **demure...regard** sober survey (of the officers of the household).

46 **kinsman Toby** Malvolio's dropping the formality of Sir Toby's title here and at 51 elicits a response both vehement and mocking (56).

47 **Bolts** Irons (to fasten the shackles on Malvolio).

49 **with...start** jumping out in obsequious obedience.

49 **make out** go.

50–1 **play with my –** For a moment Malvolio forgets that in his new status he will not be wearing his steward's chain.

51 **curtsies** bows (in deference). A variant of the two-syllable verb 'courtesy'.

53 ***by th'ears** i.e. by what we hear and by force. As in *2H4* 2.4.289–90, where Hal says punningly to Falstaff, 'I come to draw you out by the ears.' Hanmer's emendation of F's 'with cars' is reasonable in terms of a misreading of Secretary hand since 'c' and 'e' are frequently confused, and a malformed 'by' (or 'bi') + 'th' could be read as 'wy' (or 'wi') + 'th'. Editors who retain the F reading, because Shakespeare elsewhere uses 'car' to mean 'chariot', similarly assume the meaning to be 'by force or torment'.

55 **austere...control** severe glance of command.

56 **take...a blow** Sixteenth-century idiom for 'give...a blow'.

MALVOLIO Saying, 'Cousin Toby, my fortunes having cast me on your
   niece, give me this prerogative of speech – '
SIR TOBY What, what?
MALVOLIO 'You must amend your drunkenness.'   60
SIR TOBY Out, scab!
FABIAN Nay, patience, or we break the sinews of our plot.
MALVOLIO 'Besides, you waste the treasure of your time with a foolish
   knight – '
SIR ANDREW That's me, I warrant you.   65
MALVOLIO 'One Sir Andrew – '
SIR ANDREW I knew 'twas I, for many do call me fool.
MALVOLIO [*Taking up the letter*] What employment have we here?
SIR TOBY Now is the woodcock near the gin.
FABIAN O peace, and the spirit of humours intimate reading aloud to   70
   him!
MALVOLIO By my life, this is my lady's hand: these be her very c's,
   her u's, and her t's, and thus makes she her great P's. It is, in
   contempt of question, her hand.
SIR ANDREW Her c's, her u's, and her t's: why that?   75
MALVOLIO [*Reads*] 'To the unknown beloved, this, and my good
   wishes' – her very phrases! By your leave, wax. Soft! And the
   impressure her Lucrece, with which she uses to seal: 'tis my lady.
   To whom should this be? [*Opens the letter*]
FABIAN This wins him, liver and all.   80

58 speech –] *Cam.;* speech. F   64 knight –'] *Cam.;* knight. F   66 Andrew –'] *Theobald; Andrew.* F   68 SD
Taking...letter] *Rowe;* not in F   69 SH SIR TOBY] *Conj. NS; Fa.* F   70 SH FABIAN] *Conj. NS; To.* F   76 SD
Reads] *Capell;* not in F   77 wishes' –] *Cam. subst.;* Wishes: F   79 SD *Opens the letter*] *NS subst.;* not in F

62 **sinews** Used metaphorically to mean
'strength' (Schmidt).
68 **employment** business.
69 **woodcock** Proverbial symbol of stupidity
(Tilley W746). In exorcising Malvolio's devil (4.2),
Feste remarks that even the soul of his grandam
had passed into a woodcock (45–6).
69 **gin** snare or trap. Aphetic form of 'engine'.
*69–71 The speeches of Fabian and Sir Toby
have been redistributed, in accord with 29 n. above.
70–1 **the spirit...him** may a capricious impulse
suggest his reading it aloud.
72–3 **her very c's...t's** A *double entendre*,
incorporating a slang reference to the female
pudenda (Kökeritz, p. 133, n. 1). Other examples
from the drama are cited in NS.

73 **her great P's** Another *double entendre*. It also
indicates that, despite the use of upper case in F,
the other letters should be minuscules.
73–4 **in contempt of** beyond.
77 **By...wax** For a comparable conventional
apology addressed to the seal on a letter, see *Cym.*
3.2.35: 'Good wax, thy leave.'
78 **impressure...Lucrece** The wax is
impressed with the device Olivia has chosen for her
seal; it represents Lucretia, the Roman matron who
committed suicide after she was violated by Sextus
Tarquinius. Shakespeare had told the story at
length in *The Rape of Lucrece* (1594).
80 **liver and all** through and through. Literally,
the liver (the seat of the passions, as at 1.1.37–8) is
affected and everything else too.

MALVOLIO [*Reads*]   Jove knows I love,
But who?
Lips, do not move:
No man must know.
'No man must know.' What follows? The numbers altered! 'No   85
man must know'! If this should be thee, Malvolio!
SIR TOBY Marry, hang thee, brock!
MALVOLIO [*Reads*]   I may command where I adore,
But silence, like a Lucrece knife,
With bloodless stroke my heart doth gore;   90
M.O.A.I. doth sway my life.
FABIAN A fustian riddle!
SIR TOBY Excellent wench, say I.
MALVOLIO 'M.O.A.I. doth sway my life.' Nay, but first let me see, let
me see, let me see.   95
FABIAN What dish o'poison has she dressed him!
SIR TOBY And with what wing the staniel checks at it!
MALVOLIO 'I may command where I adore.' Why, she may command
me: I serve her; she is my lady. Why, this is evident to any formal
capacity. There is no obstruction in this, and the end – what should   100
that alphabetical position portend? If I could make that resemble
something in me – Softly! 'M.O.A.I.' –
SIR TOBY O ay, make up that! He is now at a cold scent.
FABIAN Sowter will cry upon't for all this, though it be as rank as a
fox.   105

81 SD *Reads*] *Capell; not in* F   81–4] *As verse, Capell; as prose,* F   88 SD *Reads*] *Capell; not in* F   88–91] *As Hanmer; as two lines* F   96 dish o'] *Dyce;* dish a F   97 staniel] *Hanmer;* stallion F   100 end –] *Cam.;* end. F   101–2 portend? ...me –] *Capell;* portend, ...me? F   102 me – Softly! 'M.O.A.I.' –] *Cam. subst.;* me? Softly, *M.O.A.I.* F

85 **numbers** versification (of 88–91).
87 **brock** badger. An animal noted for its evil odour; hence a term of opprobrium.
91 **M.O.A.I....life** Compare Orlando's verses (*AYLI* 3.2.1–10) which contain the line 'Thy huntress' name that my full life doth sway'.
92 **fustian** affected, pretentious. A figurative usage, from the fact that the cloth served as a substitute for silk (Linthicum, pp. 108–9); thus Pistol (*2H4* 2.4.189) is called a 'fustian rascal' and Cassio (*Oth.* 2.3.280) describes himself as discoursing 'fustian' in his drunken state.
96 **What dish** What a dish. The omission of the article after 'what' in the sense of 'what kind of' (Abbott 86) is common, as in *JC* 1.3.42: 'Cassius, what night is this!'
96 **dressed** prepared (for).
97 **wing** speed.

97 ***staniel** kestrel. An inferior kind of hawk.
97 **checks** is led astray. A figurative usage, from the ease with which the staniel may be diverted from its course by a chance bird. The image is used again at 3.1.54–5.
99–100 **any...capacity** any normal person. As in *Err.* 5.1.104–5: 'With wholesome syrups, drugs, and holy prayers, / To make of him a formal man again'.
100 **obstruction** difficult meaning.
101 **position** arrangement.
103 **O ay** Echoing letters of the riddle.
103 **make up** construe, make sense of.
104–5 **Sowter...fox** Even though the scent (the clue to the riddle) be as strong as the smell of a fox, Sowter (literally, 'cobbler') will cry out in triumph or 'give tongue' to his success.

MALVOLIO 'M' – Malvolio. 'M' – why, that begins my name!

FABIAN Did not I say he would work it out? The cur is excellent at
faults.

MALVOLIO 'M' – but then there is no consonancy in the sequel that
suffers under probation. 'A' should follow, but 'O' does.   110

FABIAN And O shall end, I hope.

SIR TOBY Ay, or I'll cudgel him and make him cry 'O'!

MALVOLIO And then 'I' comes behind.

FABIAN Ay, and you had any eye behind you, you might see more
detraction at your heels than fortunes before you.   115

MALVOLIO 'M.O.A.I.' This simulation is not as the former, and yet,
to crush this a little, it would bow to me, for every one of these
letters are in my name. Soft, here follows prose. [*Reads*] 'If this
fall into thy hand, revolve. In my stars I am above thee, but be not
afraid of greatness. Some are born great, some achieve greatness,   120
and some have greatness thrust upon 'em. Thy fates open their
hands; let thy blood and spirit embrace them, and, to inure thyself
to what thou art like to be, cast thy humble slough and appear fresh.
Be opposite with a kinsman, surly with servants; let thy tongue tang
arguments of state; put thyself into the trick of singularity. She thus   125

---

106 'M' – Malvolio. 'M' –] *Cam. subst.; M. Malvolio, M.* F   118 SD *Reads*] *Capell; not in* F   120 born] *Douai
MS., Rowe;* become F   120 achieve] F2*;* atcheeues F

107–8 **excellent at faults** clever at finding the
scent again after the trail is lost. A 'fault' is a break
in the scent. The hunting diction continues here,
but ironically, implying that Malvolio will follow up
a false scent and so be easily duped.

109–10 **no consonancy . . . probation** no consistency in what follows that will hold up under
examination.

111 **And O . . . end** And misery shall conclude.
(The verb is intransitive.) 'O' here is a substantive,
as in *Rom.* 3.3.90: 'Why should you fall into so deep
an O?' In the next line, it is an exclamation,
expressing pain or shock. Dr Johnson suggests that
it refers to the hangman's noose.

113–14 **I . . . Ay . . . eye** Playing on the sound of
the letter 'I' in the riddle (as on the letter 'O' in
the preceding lines).

114 **eye behind you** Kittredge notes that the
virtue Prudence was characterised as having a third
eye in the back of her head.

115 **fortunes** possessions, wealth. To accord
with his wish to be 'Count Malvolio'.

116 **simulation** surface resemblance (*OED sv sb*
2).

117 **crush** force.

117 **bow** yield.

119 **revolve** turn (it) over in your mind.

119 **my stars** i.e. the determinants of my wealth
and rank.

120 ***born** Rowe's emendation of F's 'become' is
substantiated by the quotations in 3.4.37 and
5.1.349.

120 **achieve** F2's correction of F's 'atcheeves' is
also substantiated by the quotations at 3.4.39 and
5.1.349.

121–2 **open their hands** offer bounty. As in *H8*
3.2.184: 'my hand has open'd bounty to you'.

122 **blood and spirit** i.e. mettle.

122 **inure** accustom.

123 **like** likely.

123 **cast . . . slough** abandon your lowly demeanour as a snake sloughs off its old skin.

123 **fresh** new; 'fresh and new' are used as
synonyms in *Wiv.* 4.5.8.

124 **Be opposite** In 3.4.60 Malvolio interprets
this as to 'appear stubborn' to Sir Toby.

124–5 **tang . . . state** sound forth on the subject
of statecraft.

125 **put . . . singularity** adopt the habit of
eccentricity.

advises thee that sighs for thee. Remember who commended thy
yellow stockings and wished to see thee ever cross-gartered: I say,
remember. Go to, thou art made if thou desir'st to be so; if not,
let me see thee a steward still, the fellow of servants, and not worthy
to touch Fortune's fingers. Farewell. She that would alter services   130
with thee,
The Fortunate-Unhappy.'

Daylight and champain discovers not more! This is open. I will be
proud, I will read politic authors, I will baffle Sir Toby, I will wash
off gross acquaintance, I will be point-device, the very man. I do   135
not now fool myself to let imagination jade me; for every reason
excites to this, that my lady loves me. She did commend my yellow
stockings of late, she did praise my leg being cross-gartered; and
in this she manifests herself to my love, and with a kind of
injunction drives me to these habits of her liking. I thank my stars,   140
I am happy. I will be strange, stout, in yellow stockings, and
cross-gartered, even with the swiftness of putting on. Jove and my

---

131–3 thee, The Fortunate-Unhappy.' Daylight] *Capell subst.*; thee; tht fortunate vnhappy daylight F

127 yellow stockings A symbol here of love;
used frequently elsewhere in the drama to indicate
marriage and jealousy after marriage (Linthicum, p.
48, with many citations from the drama).

127 cross-gartered i.e. the garters are placed
below the knee, crossed at the back, brought round
above the knee and tied at the side. They were
fashionable, according to Linthicum (p. 264 and
nn.) from the 1560s until *c.* 1600. For the fashion
in 1562, see illustration 5, p. 14 above. Earlier
('Malvolio's cross-gartered yellow stockings', *MP*
25 (1927–8), 92 n.), Linthicum offered the likely
suggestion that cross-gartering may have been
taken to indicate a hopeful as opposed to a despair-
ing lover. This would be in accord with Malvolio's
declaration that 'every reason' impels him to conclude that Olivia loves him (136–7). Shakespeare
certainly makes clear that the opposite mode of
dress was the sign of an unhappy lover. Valentine is
said to have chided Sir Proteus for going ungartered, the reason being that, in contrast to the smiling Malvolio, he could not as a result of tears see to
garter his hose (*TGV* 2.1.73, 76–7); Rosalind
specifies that the hose of one suffering the 'quotid-
ian of love' should be ungartered (*AYLI* 3.2.378),
and so Ophelia describes Hamlet (*Ham.* F 976
(2.1.77)).

128 thou art made i.e. you are favoured by
fortune, literally – by the economic status of the
Countess Olivia – and metaphorically – by the
goddess Fortuna.

130–1 alter services...thee exchange places,
becoming subservient to his mastery.

133 champain open country.

133 discovers reveals.

134 politic authors i.e. writers from whom he
can learn to 'tang arguments of state' (see
124–5 n.).

134 baffle use (him) contemptuously. The literal
meaning is 'deprive Sir Toby of his knighthood',
'degrade him'. The tables are turned in 5.1.348
when Olivia says to him, 'Alas, poor fool, how have
they baffled thee!'

135 gross base.

135 point-device i.e. precisely as described in
the letter.

136 jade me make me ridiculous. Literally, a
'jade' is a vicious or worthless horse.

137 excites to this impels this (thought).

140 habits Both (1) dress (as in his comment at
3.4.65 on 'the habit of some sir of note') and (2)
deportment.

141 happy blessed by fortune.

141 strange distant.

141 stout proud.

142 Jove Editors have taken the use of 'Jove'
here and elsewhere in the play (some nine times) as
suggesting late revision to comply with the 1606
statute of non-profanity on the stage, but as Turner

stars be praised! Here is yet a postscript. [*Reads*] 'Thou canst not choose but know who I am. If thou entertain'st my love, let it appear in thy smiling; thy smiles become thee well. Therefore in my presence still smile, dear my sweet, I prithee.' Jove, I thank thee. I will smile; I will do every thing that thou wilt have me.　　*Exit*

FABIAN I will not give my part of this sport for a pension of thousands to be paid from the sophy.

SIR TOBY I could marry this wench for this device —

SIR ANDREW So could I, too.

SIR TOBY And ask no other dowry with her but such another jest.

SIR ANDREW Nor I neither.

FABIAN Here comes my noble gull-catcher.

Enter MARIA

SIR TOBY Wilt thou set thy foot o'my neck?

SIR ANDREW Or o'mine either?

SIR TOBY Shall I play my freedom at tray-trip and become thy bondslave?

SIR ANDREW I'faith, or I either?

SIR TOBY Why, thou hast put him in such a dream that when the image of it leaves him, he must run mad.

MARIA Nay, but say true, does it work upon him?

SIR TOBY Like acqua-vitae with a midwife.

MARIA If you will then see the fruits of the sport, mark his first approach before my lady. He will come to her in yellow stockings, and 'tis a colour she abhors, and cross-gartered, a fashion she detests; and he will smile upon her, which will now be so unsuitable to her

---

143 SD *Reads*] *Collier; not in* F　146 dear] F2 (deere); deero F　154 SD *Enter Maria*] *Capell; after 152* F

has pointed out ('The text of *Twelfth Night*'), the use of 'God' sixteen times (as well as four instances of the contracted forms – 'slight, 'slid and 'odds) scarcely supports that notion. It would indeed be unthinkable, as he notes, for God to be invoked at 3.1.38.

149 sophy Title of the Shah of Persia, deriving from the surname of the dynastic rulers from *c.* 1500 to 1736. Together with the second reference to the sophy (3.4.236), this has been taken to reflect current interest in the accounts (published 1600 and 1601) of Sir Anthony Sherley's adventures when serving as an ambassador for the shah.

153 Nor I neither For examples of double (and triple) negatives, see 3.1.144 n.

154 gull-catcher One who preys on the credulity of others; as Maria with Malvolio, so Sir Toby with Sir Andrew.

157 play wager.

157 tray-trip A dice game in which the winner threw a three (a 'tray' or, as in *LLL* F 2137 (5.2.232), a 'trey').

163 acqua-vitae A 'hot infusion', in Autolycus's words (*WT* 4.4.786–7); it is elsewhere specified as favoured by an Irishman (*Wiv.* 2.2.303–4) and by Juliet's nurse (*Rom.* 3.2.88) but not by a midwife.

165–6 yellow...detests Olivia's antipathy to yellow stockings and cross-garters is, of course, pointedly at odds with Malvolio's notion (137–8) that she had commended them.

disposition, being addicted to a melancholy as she is, that it cannot
but turn him into a notable contempt. If you will see it, follow me.
SIR TOBY To the gates of Tartar, thou most excellent devil of wit!   170
SIR ANDREW I'll make one, too.

                                                                        Exeunt

3.1 *Enter* VIOLA *and* CLOWN [FESTE, *playing on a pipe and tabor*]

VIOLA Save thee, friend, and thy music! Dost thou live by thy tabor?
FESTE No, sir, I live by the church.
VIOLA Art thou a churchman?
FESTE No such matter, sir. I do live by the church; for I do live at my
     house, and my house doth stand by the church.   5
VIOLA So thou mayst say the king lies by a beggar, if a beggar dwell
     near him; or the church stands by thy tabor if thy tabor stand by
     the church.
FESTE You have said, sir. To see this age! A sentence is but a cheveril
     glove to a good wit – how quickly the wrong side may be turned   10
     outward!
VIOLA Nay, that's certain: they that dally nicely with words may
     quickly make them wanton.

---

171 SD *Exeunt*] *Exeunt.* / *Finis Actus secundus* F   Act 3, Scene 1 3.1] *Actus Tertius, Scæna prima.* F
0 SD FESTE, *playing…tabor*] Collier² ; *not in* F   6 king] F2 ; kings F

---

170 **Tartar** Tartarus, equivalent to the Christian
hell.

Act 3, Scene 1
Location Olivia's garden (Capell).
0 SD A pipe and tabor (small drum) were
traditional stage properties of the clown, and
Viola's first words indicate that he enters playing.
1 **Save thee** May God preserve thee.
1 **live by** make your living by. A question that
induces Feste's quibbling in the next line where he
uses 'by' to mean 'beside'.
3 **churchman** ecclesiastic. A mocking retort in
view of the dress the fool was probably wearing; see
1.5.21 and 46 nn.
4 **No such matter** Nothing of the kind.
Dent lists this idiomatic phrase as proverbial
(M754.1).
6 **the king…beggar** Viola perhaps here
assumes Feste's musical knowledge to include the
ballad of the 'illustrate King Cophetua' and the

'pernicious and indubitate beggar Zenelophon'
(*LLL* 4.1.65–6).
6 **lies by** Quibbling on (1) lies near and (2) lies
with.
7 **stands by…stand by** Quibbling on the
literal meaning ('is placed near') and the figurative
('is maintained by').
9 **You have said** 'You are right.' Dent (S118.1)
records this as proverbial.
9 **sentence** (1) opinion, (2) judgement, or even
(3) axiom.
9 **cheveril** kidskin. A soft and pliable kind of
leather, aptly used in reference both to 'wit' (as here
and in *Rom.* 2.4.83) and to 'conscience' (as in *H8*
2.3.32 and Tilley C608). Pronounced *chevril*.
10–11 **wrong side…outward** Dent (S431.1)
records this as proverbial.
12 **dally nicely** play curiously.
13 **wanton** wayward. Viola's diction, beginning
in 6, carries sexual overtones which Feste then
exploits. Compare *Venus and Adonis* 105–6, 'And
for my sake [Mars] hath learn'd… / To toy, to
wanton, dally, smile and jest.'

FESTE I would therefore my sister had had no name, sir.

VIOLA Why, man?   15

FESTE Why, sir, her name's a word, and to dally with that word might
make my sister wanton; but, indeed, words are very rascals, since
bonds disgraced them.

VIOLA Thy reason, man?

FESTE Truth, sir, I can yield you none without words, and words are   20
grown so false, I am loath to prove reason with them.

VIOLA I warrant thou art a merry fellow and car'st for nothing.

FESTE Not so, sir, I do care for something; but in my conscience, sir,
I do not care for you: if that be to care for nothing, I would it would
make you invisible.   25

VIOLA Art not thou the Lady Olivia's fool?

FESTE No, indeed, sir. The Lady Olivia has no folly. She will keep no
fool, sir, till she be married, and fools are as like husbands as
pilchards are to herrings – the husband's the bigger. I am indeed
not her fool but her corrupter of words.   30

VIOLA I saw thee late at the Count Orsino's.

FESTE Foolery, sir, does walk about the orb like the sun; it shines
everywhere. I would be sorry, sir, but the fool should be as oft
with your master as with my mistress: I think I saw your wisdom
there.   35

VIOLA Nay, and thou pass upon me, I'll no more with thee. Hold,
there's expenses for thee. [*Gives a coin*]

FESTE Now Jove, in his next commodity of hair, send thee a beard!

---

29 pilchards] *Capell*, Pilchers F   37 SD *Gives…coin*] *Hanmer subst.; not in* F

17–18 words…disgraced them words are
untrustworthy in that promises (bonds) are no
longer to be relied on. Julia (*TGV* 2.7.75) says of
Proteus: 'His words are bonds.'

20 none no explanation.

21 reason with them anything rational by them.

23–5 I do care…invisible Asserting that he
does care for something, Feste excludes Viola; if
that is to care 'for nothing', as she has just said, then
he wishes that as a 'no-thing' she should also not
be visible.

23 in my conscience in truth.

28–9 fools are…the bigger Feste establishes
his disparaging comment by a familiar comparison:
Nashe terms pilchards 'counterfets to the red
Herring, as Copper to Golde, or Ockamie [a
silver-coloured alloy] to silver' (*Works*, III, 192).

31 late lately.

32 orb The earth, the centre of the universe in
the Ptolemaic system.

32–3 sun…everywhere Compare the proverb
(Tilley s985), 'The sun shines upon all alike.'

33–4 I would be…mistress I should be sorry
unless a fool (i.e. Viola) would be as often with your
master as (one is) with my mistress. 'Would' is used
for 'should' just as 'should' is for 'would'; see
Abbott (120, 331), though he interprets the generic
'fool' as Feste's reference to himself, thus missing
the mockery of the next line.

34 your wisdom A mocking title to point up
Viola's role as her master's fool.

36 pass (1) give sentence, (2) thrust (a fencing
term, here used of Feste's barbs). Compare Jonson's
Every Man in His Humour (1601), 1.3.207 ff.
(modernised):

Matheo How mean you 'pass upon me'?

Bobadill Why, thus, sir, make a thrust at me – come in
upon my time; control your point, and make a full
career [lunge] at the body.

38 commodity consignment.

VIOLA By my troth, I'll tell thee, I am almost sick for one – [*Aside*]
  though I would not have it grow on my chin. Is thy lady within?   40
FESTE Would not a pair of these have bred, sir?
VIOLA Yes, being kept together and put to use.
FESTE I would play Lord Pandarus of Phrygia, sir, to bring a Cressida
  to this Troilus.
VIOLA I understand you sir; 'tis well begged. [*Gives another coin*]   45
FESTE The matter, I hope, is not great, sir – begging but a beggar:
  Cressida was a beggar. My lady is within, sir. I will conster to them
  whence you come. Who you are, and what you would are out of
  my welkin – I might say 'element', but the word is overworn.

                                                          Exit

VIOLA This fellow is wise enough to play the fool,   50
  And to do that well craves a kind of wit;
  He must observe their mood on whom he jests,
  The quality of persons, and the time;

---

39 SD *Aside*] Cam.; *not in* F   45 SD *Gives...coin*] Collier² *subst.; not in* F

---

39 sick for one (1) lovesick for one who has a beard, (2) longing to be able to grow a beard.

41 bred produced more. The double meaning is that the coin would multiply (1) if there was another coin to mate with, (2) if the coin was put out to interest. Viola acknowledges both meanings in the next line; 'use' is interest paid on borrowed money, but it also refers to sexual activity. Compare the Lord Chief Justice's charge against Falstaff (*2H4* 2.1.114–16): 'You have...practic'd upon the easy-yielding spirit of this woman, and made her serve your uses both in purse and in person.'

43 Pandarus Cressida's uncle, who acted as a pander in order to bring his niece and Troilus together, as set forth in Chaucer's great love poem *Troilus and Criseyde*. Close to the time when he was writing *TN*, Shakespeare turned this Chaucerian material into dramatic form but giving it a dark and cynical tone. Here Feste is applying the names of the lovers to the coin he has received and the one he hopes to receive, but the implicit suggestion is that he will bring Olivia and Cesario together.

46 The matter...beggar Having been rewarded a second time for his willingness to bring this Troilus (literally, the coin and, figuratively, Troilus's surrogate, Cesario) to a Cressida, Feste says it is no great thing for him to beg for a beggar like Cressida, thus denying Viola's 'well-begged' of the previous line. According to the *Testament of Cresseid*, Robert Henryson's fifteenth-century continuation of the story, she became a leper and was forced to beg for her living.

47 conster Though simply a variant of 'construe', F's spelling is retained for the sake of euphony; from early on up to the nineteenth century, the stress was on the first syllable.

49 welkin sky. Most often in poetical use.

49 element Referring to one of the four elements, each of which was regarded as the natural habitat for particular sorts of creatures – the air for birds, and so on; but since 'element' could also refer to the sky (as in 1.1.26), Feste is punning as well as remarking on his incapacity to say 'who' Cesario is or 'what' it is he wants.

49 overworn It seems that Feste is referring to 'element' as one of Malvolio's special words: note his supercilious remark to Sir Toby, Maria and Fabian at 3.4.106. For another example of a special word, see 4.2.73 and n. Editors have often accepted that Shakespeare is glancing here at the frequent use of the word by the character representing Jonson in *Satiromastix* (1601), Dekker's contribution to the current 'war of the theatres'. But throughout *TN* Shakespeare comments on affectations of diction by means of Orsino's stilted language, Viola's variability, Sir Toby's waywardness, Sir Andrew's inadequacy and Feste's nice dallying.

50 Playing on the proverbial statement 'No man can play the fool so well as the wise man' (Tilley M321) and perhaps also 'He is not wise who cannot play the fool' (Tilley M428).

53 quality (1) nature, (2) rank.

Not, like the haggard, check at every feather
That comes before his eye. This is a practice,   55
As full of labour as a wise man's art:
For folly that he wisely shows is fit;
But wise men, folly-fall'n, quite taint their wit.

Enter SIR TOBY *and* [SIR] ANDREW

SIR TOBY Save you, gentleman.
VIOLA And you, sir.   60
SIR ANDREW *Dieu vous garde, monsieur.*
VIOLA *Et vous aussi; votre serviteur.*
SIR ANDREW I hope, sir, you are, and I am yours.
SIR TOBY Will you encounter the house? My niece is desirous you
    should enter, if your trade be to her.   65
VIOLA I am bound to your niece, sir; I mean, she is the list of my voyage.
SIR TOBY Taste your legs, sir; put them to motion.
VIOLA My legs do better understand me, sir, than I understand what
    you mean by bidding me taste my legs.
SIR TOBY I mean, to go, sir, to enter.   70
VIOLA I will answer you with gait and entrance – but we are prevented.

Enter OLIVIA *and* GENTLEWOMAN [MARIA]

Most excellent accomplished lady, the heavens rain odours on you!

---

54 Not] *Rann, conj. Johnson;* And F   58 wise men, …fall'n] *Capell;* wisemens folly falne F   58 SD SIR ANDREW]
Rowe; Andrew. F   71 SD MARIA] *Rowe;* Gentlewoman. F

---

54 *Not Rann's emendation of F's 'And', conjectured by Dr Johnson, is required in order to make Cesario's point about Feste's judicious wit (57).
54 **like the haggard…feather** like the wild hawk, seize on every prey.
55 **practice** professional exercise.
57 **wisely shows** judiciously reveals.
57 **is fit** suits the purpose.
58 *folly-fall'n having stooped to folly.
58 **quite taint** completely infect.
61–2 *Dieu…serviteur* 'God keep you, sir.' 'And you too. At your service.' Sir Andrew here both understands and responds (in his way) to the conventional French salutations; as Sir Toby says (1.3.22), he can speak 'three or four languages word for word' (though at 1.3.77 he could not grasp the meaning of *pourquoi*).
64 **encounter** i.e. go to meet. Another of Sir Toby's verbal affectations.
65 **trade** business (of any kind). It also suggests

a commercial venture, which is the meaning Viola picks up in the next line.
66 **bound to** (1) intending to go to, (2) confined to.
66 **list** boundary. As in *1H4* 4.1.51–2: 'The very list, the very utmost bound / Of all our fortunes'. But also, affectedly, 'goal' or 'destination' (Schmidt).
67 **Taste** Try. Used in the same sense at 3.4.207: 'to taste their valour'.
68–9 **My legs…mean** A Launce-like quibble, as in *TGV* 2.5.32: 'Why, stand-under and under-stand is all one.'
71 **I…entrance** I will respond by going and entering. With a quibble on 'gate' (the spelling in F) and 'entrance'.
71 **prevented** anticipated.
72 **the heavens…you** For Shakespeare's use of the optative subjunctive with the omission of 'may', see Abbott 365, where he observes that this usage gives 'great vigour' to a line.

SIR ANDREW That youth's a rare courtier – 'rain odours' – well.

VIOLA My matter hath no voice, lady, but to your own most pregnant
and vouchsafed ear.   75

SIR ANDREW 'Odours', 'pregnant', and 'vouchsafed': I'll get 'em all
three all ready.

OLIVIA Let the garden door be shut, and leave me to my hearing.
                         [*Exeunt Sir Toby, Sir Andrew, and Maria*]
Give me your hand, sir.

VIOLA My duty, madam, and most humble service.   80

OLIVIA What is your name?

VIOLA Cesario is your servant's name, fair princess.

OLIVIA My servant, sir? 'Twas never merry world
          Since lowly feigning was called compliment.
          Y'are servant to the Count Orsino, youth.   85

VIOLA And he is yours, and his must needs be yours:
          Your servant's servant is your servant, madam.

OLIVIA For him, I think not on him; for his thoughts,
          Would they were blanks, rather than filled with me!

VIOLA Madam, I come to whet your gentle thoughts   90
          On his behalf.

OLIVIA   O by your leave, I pray you!
          I bade you never speak again of him;
          But would you undertake another suit
          I had rather hear you to solicit that,
          Than music from the spheres.

VIOLA   Dear lady –   95

---

73 courtier – 'rain odours' –] *NS*; Courtier, raine odours, F   77 all ready] *Malone*; already F   78 SD *Exeunt...Maria*]
Rowe; not in F   95 lady –] *Theobald subst.*; Lady. F

---

73 **'rain odours' – well** Sir Andrew's 'well'
may suggest that he is commenting (1) admiringly
(as 76–7 would indicate) or (2) adversely on
Cesario's wrenched metaphor (catachresis). For
another example of wrenching, compare Falstaff's
'Let the sky rain potatoes' (*Wiv.* 5.5.18–19).

74 **pregnant** ready. As at 2.2.25.

75 **vouchsafed** proffered.

76–7 **get...ready** keep them in mind for ready
use. Perhaps he writes in his 'tables' or commonplace book.

78 **hearing** audience. Compare the mocking
response to similar inflated diction in *Wiv.* 2.2.40–3:
Quickly. Shall I vouchsafe your worship a word or two?
Falstaff. Two thousand,...and I'll vouchsafe thee the
hearing.

83–4 **'Twas never...Since** A proverbial
expression used to introduce a variety of

conclusions – since there were so many puritans,
since there was so much preaching, etc. (Dent
w878.1).

84 **lowly feigning** pretended humility.

86 **he is yours** he is your servant. Used here to
mean 'suitor'; Viola then immediately reverts to its
complimentary use.

88 **For** As regards.

89 **blanks** empty (like sheets of paper). Compare
Sonnets 77.9–10: 'Look what thy memory cannot
Commit to these waste blanks'; though
'blanks' in this instance is Theobald's conjecture
for 'blacks', it is a satisfactory one since n:c were
easily confused in Secretary hand.

95 **music...spheres** In their rotations, the
crystalline spheres containing the planets and the
fixed stars were held to create a ravishing harmony
inaudible to mortal ears.

OLIVIA Give me leave, beseech you. I did send,
        After the last enchantment you did here,
        A ring in chase of you. So did I abuse
        Myself, my servant, and, I fear me, you.
        Under your hard construction must I sit,   100
        To force that on you in a shameful cunning
        Which you knew none of yours. What might you think?
        Have you not set mine honour at the stake,
        And baited it with all th'unmuzzled thoughts
        That tyrannous heart can think? To one of your receiving   105
        Enough is shown; a cypress, not a bosom,
        Hides my heart: so, let me hear you speak.
VIOLA I pity you.
OLIVIA   That's a degree to love.
VIOLA No, not a grise; for 'tis a vulgar proof
       That very oft we pity enemies.   110
OLIVIA Why then, methinks 'tis time to smile again.
        O world, how apt the poor are to be proud!
        If one should be a prey, how much the better

97 here] *Warburton, conj. Thirlby;* heare F   105–9 think…receiving / …bosom, / …speak. / …proof] F; …think /
…shown / …heart / …grise / …proof / NS   107 my] F; my poore F2

96 Give me…beseech you In moving from
courteous formula (91) to entreaty, Olivia betrays
her intensity both by the abrupt grammatical shift
from second to first person and by omission of the
subject for the second verb (beseech).
98 abuse (1) deceive, (2) disgrace. Both senses
are probably intended.
99 I fear me i.e. I am afraid. This old form of
reflexive is common in Elizabethan English.
100 hard construction harsh interpretation;
'construction' is used in the same sense at 2.3.147.
Elsewhere Shakespeare has 'illegitimate construction' (*Ado* 3.4.50); 'merciful construction' (*H8*
Epilogue 10); and 'good construction' (*Cor.* 5.6.20).
101 that the ring.
101 in…cunning by means of a disgraceful
trick.
102 knew none knew was none. The verb is
understood.
103–5 Have you…think The image is of
bear-baiting, with Olivia tied to the stake and set
on by all the unrestrained thoughts, like unmuzzled
dogs, that a cruel heart (like Cesario's) can conceive.
105–9 *The lineation of F, retained here, has
occasioned much editorial rearranging; that of NS,
with lines ending '…think / …shown / …heart

/ …grise / …proof' has a good deal to commend
it, in that making 105 short ('That…can think')
suggests a break in Olivia's delivery.
105 receiving understanding.
106 cypress A light transparent material
resembling cobweb lawn or crape. Olivia's revealing
her feelings here parallels the situation at their first
meeting when she metaphorically drew 'the
curtain' and unveiled herself to Viola.
108 degree step. In the next line, 'grise' has the
same meaning.
109 vulgar proof common experience.
111 Ironic in that she has at least the 'pity' of
an enemy.
112 how…proud how ready the deprived are to
be full of self-esteem. Again, ironic.
113–14 If…wolf This seems to mean that if one
must be a victim, how much better it would be to
succumb to the lion (i.e. the duke) rather than the
wolf (i.e. Cesario, a professed enemy). The name
Orsino means 'little bear' but this point need not
have occurred to Shakespeare here. Compare the
proverb 'The lion spares the suppliant' (Tilley
L316). Mahood takes 'lion' to refer to Cesario as a
king of men, 'wolf' (since she does not equate it with
anyone) apparently to the species of animal.

To fall before the lion than the wolf!
                    (*Clock strikes*)
The clock upbraids me with the waste of time.   115
Be not afraid, good youth; I will not have you –
And yet when wit and youth is come to harvest,
Your wife is like to reap a proper man.
There lies your way, due west.

VIOLA   Then westward ho!
Grace and good disposition attend your ladyship!   120
You'll nothing, madam, to my lord by me?

OLIVIA Stay!
I prithee tell me what thou think'st of me.

VIOLA That you do think you are not what you are.

OLIVIA If I think so, I think the same of you.   125

VIOLA Then think you right: I am not what I am.

OLIVIA I would you were as I would have you be.

VIOLA Would it be better, madam, than I am?
I wish it might, for now I am your fool.

OLIVIA [*Aside*] O what a deal of scorn looks beautiful   130
In the contempt and anger of his lip!
A murd'rous guilt shows not itself more soon,
Than love that would seem hid. Love's night is noon.
Cesario, by the roses of the spring,
By maidhood, honour, truth, and everything,   135
I love thee so that, maugre all thy pride,
Nor wit nor reason can my passion hide.

122–3 Stay! / …me] *Capell subst.; one line in* F   130 SD *Aside*] *Staunton; not in* F

118 **proper** handsome, fine.
119 **westward ho** The cry of the Thames watermen for passengers going to Westminster.
120 **Grace…disposition** The favour of heaven and a happy frame of mind (Kittredge).
121 **You'll nothing** i.e. send no message.
124 Three layers of meaning: (1) you do not consider that you are a noblewoman; (2) you do not imagine you are in love with a woman, and therefore (3) you do not believe you are out of your mind. In each, the negative is transferred to the main verb.
125 Understanding Viola-Cesario to intend only the third meaning, Olivia retorts in kind.
126 Viola takes the retort literally, fully concurring that she is not what she seems to be.

131 **contempt…his lip** i.e. characterised by a drooping lip, as in *WT* 1.2.371–3: 'when he, / Wafting his eyes to th'contrary and falling / A lip of much contempt'.
132 Compare the proverbial 'Murder will out' (Tilley M1315).
133 **Love's…noon** i.e. as clear or evident as midday: as the proverb has it, 'Love cannot be hid' (Tilley L500 and L490). Dent adds Olivia's aphoristic statement to Tilley's N167, 'Dark night is Cupid's day', but the implication here is utterly at odds with the salacious use of that proverb.
136 **maugre…pride** in spite of all your unkindness. In this line Olivia shifts to the familiar second-person singular.

Do not extort thy reasons from this clause,
For that I woo, thou therefore hast no cause;
But rather reason thus with reason fetter: 140
Love sought is good, but giv'n unsought is better.
VIOLA By innocence I swear, and by my youth,
I have one heart, one bosom, and one truth,
And that no woman has; nor never none
Shall mistress be of it, save I alone.   145
And so, adieu, good madam; never more
Will I my master's tears to you deplore.
OLIVIA Yet come again: for thou perhaps mayst move
That heart which now abhors to like his love.

Exeunt

3.2 *Enter* SIR TOBY, SIR ANDREW, *and* FABIAN

SIR ANDREW No, faith, I'll not stay a jot longer!
SIR TOBY Thy reason, dear venom, give thy reason.
FABIAN You must needs yield your reason, Sir Andrew.
SIR ANDREW Marry, I saw your niece do more favours to the count's
servingman than ever she bestowed upon me. I saw't i'th'orchard.   5
SIR TOBY Did she see thee the while, old boy? Tell me that.
SIR ANDREW As plain as I see you now.
FABIAN This was a great argument of love in her toward you.
SIR ANDREW 'Slight! Will you make an ass o'me?
FABIAN I will prove it legitimate, sir, upon the oaths of judgement and   10
reason.

Act 3, Scene 2   3.2] *Scæna Secunda.* F   6 thee the] F3; the F

138–41 Do not...better Do not forcibly extract your argument from the proposition that because I woo you, you have no motive or reason (to love); rather, thus shackle one reason to another, which is, that love sought is good but given unsought is better; 'clause' as 'proposition' is a nonce usage.

144 nor...none See 2.5.153 for an example of a double negative and *AYLI* 1.2.27–8 for another instance of a triple one.

Act 3, Scene 2
Location Olivia's house (Rowe).
2 dear venom Sir Toby responds with this vocative to the virulence of Sir Andrew's statement (metonymy – here, a substitution of the cause for the effect).

5 orchard A walled or enclosed garden, as in 3.1.78.
8 argument proof.
9 'Slight See 2.5.28 n.
9 Will you...me Dent (A379.1) lists this as proverbial.
10 legitimate logically admissible (Schmidt, Onions). Curiously the earliest example given in the *OED* is from the eighteenth century.
10–11 oaths...reason sworn testimony of judgement and reason. Fabian here and Sir Toby in the next line are trying to muddle Sir Andrew by mixing (1) logical and legal and (2) abstract and concrete terms.

SIR TOBY And they have been grand-jurymen since before Noah was
a sailor.

FABIAN She did show favour to the youth in your sight only to
exasperate you, to awake your dormouse valour, to put fire in your   15
heart, and brimstone in your liver. You should then have accosted
her, and with some excellent jests, fire-new from the mint, you
should have banged the youth into dumbness. This was looked for
at your hand, and this was balked. The double gilt of this
opportunity you let time wash off, and you are now sailed into the   20
north of my lady's opinion, where you will hang like an icicle on
a Dutchman's beard unless you do redeem it by some laudable
attempt, either of valour or policy.

SIR ANDREW And't be any way, it must be with valour, for policy I
hate. I had as lief be a Brownist as a politician.   25

SIR TOBY Why then, build me thy fortunes upon the basis of valour.
Challenge me the count's youth to fight with him, hurt him in eleven
places – my niece shall take note of it – and assure thyself, there
is no love-broker in the world can more prevail in man's commen-
dation with woman than report of valour.   30

FABIAN There is no way but this, Sir Andrew.

SIR ANDREW Will either of you bear me a challenge to him?

SIR TOBY Go, write it in a martial hand, be curst and brief; it is no
matter how witty, so it be eloquent, and full of invention. Taunt
him with the licence of ink. If thou 'thou'st' him some thrice, it   35

---

15 to awake...valour The dormouse sleeps
throughout the winter.

16 accosted A well-selected word on Fabian's
part since its meaning had been spelled out to Sir
Andrew at 1.3.46–7.

18 banged Figuratively, 'struck'.

19 balked neglected.

19 double gilt Gilt plate twice washed with gold
(NS).

20–2 sailed...beard Editors agree that this is
a topical reference to the arctic voyage made by the
Dutchman William Barents in 1596–7; an English
translation of the account by Gerrit de Veer,
detailing the harsh suffering of the crew, had been
entered in the *SR* in June 1598, making the allusion
timely. See also 62–3 n.

23 policy strategy. In the next lines Sir Andrew
takes this in its derogatory sense of 'scheming', as
with 'politicians' (2.3.66).

25 Brownist A member of the extreme separatist
sect established by Robert Browne, notorious in this
period for his writing of controversial tracts.

26, 27 me Sir Toby's use of the ethical dative
here and again at 3.4.148 is intended to convey his
sympathetic concern.

27 to fight i.e. by offering to fight.

29 love-broker go-between. The only instance
in Shakespeare.

29–30 in man's...woman in commending a
man to a woman.

33 curst harsh. As in *2H6* 3.2.311–15: 'terms /
As curst, as harsh, and horrible to hear... / As
lean-fac'd Envy in her loathsome cave'.

34 invention untruth. Compare *AWW*
3.6.97–8: 'but return with an invention, and clap
upon you two or three probable [plausible] lies'.

35 licence of ink the freedom that the distance
of a written taunt confers.

35 If thou 'thou'st' i.e. if you use the familiar
form employed in addressing intimates and
servants. To use it with a stranger would be
offensive.

shall not be amiss, and as many lies as will lie in thy sheet of paper, although the sheet were big enough for the bed of Ware in England, set 'em down. Go, about it! Let there be gall enough in thy ink; though thou write with a goose-pen, no matter. About it!

SIR ANDREW Where shall I find you? 40

SIR TOBY We'll call thee at the cubiculo. Go!

Exit Sir Andrew

FABIAN This is a dear manikin to you, Sir Toby.

SIR TOBY I have been dear to him, lad, some two thousand strong, or so.

FABIAN We shall have a rare letter from him, but you'll not deliver't? 45

SIR TOBY Never trust me then, and by all means stir on the youth to an answer. I think oxen and wainropes cannot hale them together. For Andrew, if he were opened and you find so much blood in his liver as will clog the foot of a flea, I'll eat the rest of th'anatomy.

FABIAN And his opposite, the youth, bears in his visage no great presage 50 of cruelty.

Enter MARIA

SIR TOBY Look where the youngest wren of mine comes –

MARIA If you desire the spleen, and will laugh yourselves into stitches, follow me. Yond gull Malvolio is turned heathen, a very renegado;

---

45 deliver't?] *Dyce;* deliver't. F   52 mine] F; nine *Theobald*

---

37 **bed of Ware** This carved bed, famous among the Elizabethans, was ten-feet square and could accommodate a dozen people.

38 **gall** Punning on (1) the figurative meaning, 'venom', and (2) the literal, the growth on oak trees used in making ink.

39 **goose-pen** A pen made from the quill of a goose and, here, used by a goose.

41 **call...cubiculo** call for you at the bedchamber. Sir Toby is affecting either the ablative form of Latin *cubiculum* or the Italian *cubiculo.*

42 **dear...you** little plaything dear to you. In the next line Sir Toby plays on the second meaning by stressing how 'costly' he has been to Sir Andrew.

45 **rare** extraordinary.

46 **Never...then** Have no fear. But on learning how 'excellently ignorant' the written challenge is, Sir Toby determines (at 3.4.158–9) to deliver it in his own words.

47 **wainropes** wagon ropes.

47 **hale** drag.

48 **opened** dissected.

48–9 **blood...liver** A liver lacking in blood –

that is, white and pale – was, according to Falstaff (*2H4* 4.3.104–6), 'the badge of pusillanimity and cowardice'.

49 **anatomy** skeleton. Here it means the rest of the body as well but suggests that it is only skin and bones (*OED* sv *sb* 6); compare the description of Pinch in *Err.* 5.1.238–9: 'a hungry lean-fac'd villain / A mere anatomy'.

50 **opposite** adversary.

52 **of mine** Used to indicate affection, as with 'my Ariel' (*Temp.* 1.2.188), 'my Oberon' (*MND* 4.1.76) and 'my eyas-musket [young hawk]' *Wiv.* 3.3.22). Since the wren is a diminutive bird, Sir Toby again remarks on Maria's small stature. Most editors follow Theobald and emend to 'of nine' and explain that the last of nine eggs to be hatched would be the smallest specimen, though not explaining the significance of 'nine' as against ten or any other number of eggs, as Furness notes.

53 **spleen** a fit of laughter. The spleen was believed to be the seat of laughter.

54 **renegado** apostate.

for there is no Christian that means to be saved by believing rightly   55
can ever believe such impossible passages of grossness. He's in
yellow stockings.

SIR TOBY And cross-gartered?

MARIA Most villainously. Like a pedant that keeps a school i'th'church.
I have dogged him like his murderer. He does obey every point of   60
the letter that I dropped to betray him. He does smile his face into
more lines than is in the new map with the augmentation of the
Indies; you have not seen such a thing as 'tis. I can hardly forbear
hurling things at him; I know my lady will strike him. If she do,
he'll smile and take't for a great favour.   65

SIR TOBY Come bring us, bring us where he is.

Exeunt

3.3 *Enter* SEBASTIAN *and* ANTONIO

SEBASTIAN I would not by my will have troubled you,
          But since you make your pleasure of your pains,
          I will no further chide you.

ANTONIO I could not stay behind you. My desire,
          More sharp than filèd steel, did spur me forth;   5
          And not all love to see you (though so much
          As might have drawn one to a longer voyage),
          But jealousy what might befall your travel,
          Being skilless in these parts which to a stranger,

---

66 SD] *Exeunt omnes* F   Act 3, Scene 3   3.3] *Scæna Tertia* F

56 **such…grossness** such grossly unbeliev-
able statements (as those in Maria's letter). The
implication is that Malvolio has adopted them as his
creed.

59 **pedant…church** i.e. ostentatious (like a
pedantic schoolmaster). For cross-gartering, see
2.5.127 n. NS suggests that teaching in a church
rather than in a schoolhouse proper was becoming
obsolete at this date and such a 'pedant' might
seem something of an oddity.

62–3 **more lines…Indies** This is accepted as
a reference to a new map based on the Mercator
principles of projection, prepared by Edward
Wright and others and printed in 1600. It shows the
East Indies more fully than in earlier maps, gives
a slight suggestion of the unknown continent of

Australia, and also, for the first time in English
maps, Novaya Zemlya, this last as a result of
Barents's arctic voyage in 1596–7 (see 20–2 n). A
facsimile of it is included in the second volume of
Voyages and Works of John Davis, ed.
A. H. Markham, 1880, Hakluyt Society, vol. 59,
and there is a note on the 'new map' by C. H. Coote
in the first volume. The rhumb lines form a
veritable network, prompting Maria's image.

Act 3, Scene 3
  Location The street (Rowe).
  6 **all** only.
  6 **so much** enough (love).
  8 **jealousy** apprehension.
  9 **skilless in** ignorant of.

Unguided, and unfriended, often prove   10
Rough and unhospitable. My willing love,
The rather by these arguments of fear,
Set forth in your pursuit.

SEBASTIAN   My kind Antonio,
I can no other answer make but thanks,
And thanks, and ever thanks; and oft good turns   15
Are shuffled off with such uncurrent pay;
But were my worth, as is my conscience, firm,
You should find better dealing. What's to do?
Shall we go see the relics of this town?

ANTONIO Tomorrow, sir; best first go see your lodging.   20

SEBASTIAN I am not weary, and 'tis long to night.
I pray you, let us satisfy our eyes
With the memorials and the things of fame
That do renown this city.

ANTONIO   Would you'd pardon me.
I do not without danger walk these streets.   25
Once in a sea-fight 'gainst the count his galleys
I did some service, of such note indeed
That were I tane here, it would scarce be answered.

SEBASTIAN Belike you slew great number of his people?

ANTONIO Th'offence is not of such a bloody nature,   30
Albeit the quality of the time and quarrel
Might well have given us bloody argument.
It might have since been answered in repaying

15 And thanks, and ever thanks; and oft] *Theobald*; And thankes: and ever oft F   29 people?] *Dyce*; people. F

9–11 to a stranger...unhospitable Illyria was noted for its pirates, as in *2H6* 4.1.108, 'Bargulus, the strong Illyrian pirate'; in *MM* 4.3.71, the Ragusan 'Ragozine, a most notorious pirate'; and here in 5.1.58 (Hotson, pp. 151–2). This view of what Illyria is like contrasts markedly with the sentimental–romantic milieu of the two noble households.

12 The rather The more quickly. Comparative form of the obsolete adverb 'rathe'.

15 *thanks...oft This line, defective in F (and hence omitted in the later Folios), has occasioned many emendations, all of them closely related. Theobald's, adopted here, acknowledges either scribal or compositorial error in the omission of two words ('thanks', 'and') which have already appeared in the line.

16 uncurrent pay coins no longer in circulation. By extension, 'valueless rewards'.

17 worth wealth.

17 conscience sense of being indebted.

18 dealing treatment.

19 relics i.e. 'memorials' and 'things of fame', as in 23.

26 count his i.e. count's (an old genitive form).

28 scarce hardly.

28 answered (1) accounted for, (2) atoned for (by 'repaying', as in 33).

29 Belike I suppose.

31–2 Albeit...argument Although the nature of the occasion and the dispute might well have given us cause for shedding blood. Antonio's statement here does not concur with what Orsino says of that 'scathful grapple' at 5.1.45–8.

What we took from them, which for traffic's sake
Most of our city did. Only myself stood out,   35
For which if I be lapsèd in this place
I shall pay dear.
SEBASTIAN   Do not then walk too open.
ANTONIO It doth not fit me. Hold, sir, here's my purse.
In the south suburbs at the Elephant
Is best to lodge; I will bespeak our diet,   40
Whiles you beguile the time, and feed your knowledge
With viewing of the town; there shall you have me.
SEBASTIAN Why I your purse?
ANTONIO Haply your eye shall light upon some toy
You have desire to purchase; and your store,   45
I think, is not for idle markets, sir.
SEBASTIAN I'll be your purse-bearer and leave you for
An hour.
ANTONIO   To th'Elephant.
SEBASTIAN   I do remember.

                                                       Exeunt

3.4 *Enter* OLIVIA *and* MARIA *[following]*

OLIVIA *[Aside]* I have sent after him; he says he'll come –
How shall I feast him? What bestow of him?

Act 3, Scene 4 3.4 *Scæna Quarta.* F   0 SD *following*] *This edn; not in* F   1 SD *Aside*] *Staunton; not in* F

34 traffic's sake the sake of trading.

35 stood out i.e. refused to pay.

36 lapsèd apprehended. Perhaps associated with 'fall into the laps of' (Onions).

38 fit conform to my situation.

39 Elephant Shakespeare is recalling the Oliphant (a common Elizabethan spelling), an inn located on the Bankside in Elephant Alley. Next to it was the Horseshoe Inn, with a way leading from Horseshoe Yard to the Globe. Formerly the Red Hart, the inn (called the Oliphant in 1598) dates from the early part of the fourteenth century and in 1507 was acquired by the Tallow Chandlers' Company, which continued to retain the property (M. F. Monier-Williams, *Records of the Worshipful Company of Tallow Chandlers*, 1897, pp. 113–14, and [W. W. Braines], *The Site of the Globe Playhouse, Southwark*, 1921, rev. edn 1924, p. 80). Robin Hood has called my attention to an eighteenth-century engraving of an original painting of the time of Edward VI's coronation, 1547, which

shows the inn seventh from the left from the top of Goat Stairs.

40 bespeak our diet order our meals. Meanwhile Sebastian (in the next line) 'feeds' his knowledge by sightseeing.

41 beguile pass. Literally, 'deceive', as in *MND* 5.1.40–1: 'How shall we beguile / The lazy time, if not with some delight?'

44 Haply Perhaps.

45–6 your store…markets your supply of money does not extend to unnecessary purchases.

Act 3, Scene 4
Location Olivia's garden (Capell).

1 he says It is necessary to understand an introductory 'if', the broken sequence indicating that Olivia is musing to herself; not until 51–2 does she ascertain that Cesario has returned, even if reluctantly.

2 of him The use of 'of' for 'on' is frequent (Abbott 175); for another example, see 5.1.297.

For youth is bought more oft than begged or borrowed.
I speak too loud –
Where's Malvolio? He is sad and civil,   5
And suits well for a servant with my fortunes.
Where is Malvolio?

MARIA He's coming, madam, but in very strange manner. He is sure
possessed, madam.

OLIVIA Why, what's the matter? Does he rave?   10

MARIA No, madam, he does nothing but smile. Your ladyship were best
to have some guard about you, if he come, for sure the man is
tainted in's wits.

OLIVIA Go call him hither.

[Exit Maria]

I am as mad as he
If sad and merry madness equal be.   15

Enter [MARIA *with*] MALVOLIO

How now, Malvolio?

MALVOLIO Sweet lady, ho, ho!

OLIVIA Smil'st thou? I sent for thee upon a sad occasion.

MALVOLIO Sad, lady? I could be sad. This does make some obstruction
in the blood, this cross-gartering, but what of that? If it please the   20
eye of one, it is with me as the very true sonnet is: 'Please one,
and please all.'

OLIVIA Why, how dost thou, man? What is the matter with thee?

4–5] *As two lines, Pope; as one* F   8–9 He's...madam.] *As prose, Pope; as verse,* F (He's...Madame:/ But...Madam.)
14 Go...he] *As Capell; two lines,* F (Go...hither. / *Enter Maluolio.* / I...hee,)   14 SD *Exit Maria*] *Dyce; not in* F
15 SD *Maria with*] *Dyce subst.; not in* F   19–22 Sad...all] *As prose, Pope; as verse,* F (Sad...sad: / ...blood: / .. that?
/ ...true / ...all.)   23 SH OLIVIA] F2 (*Ol.*); *Mal.* F   23] *As prose, Pope; as verse,* F (man? / What...thee?)

3 Olivia's rather cynical observation combines
the proverbial 'better to buy than to borrow' (Tilley
B783) with 'beg' meaning (1) to ask alms and (2)
to petition the Court of Wards for the custody of
a (wealthy) minor.

5 **sad and civil** grave (as again in 18) and
circumspect.

9 **possessed** (1) taken over by the devil or (2)
mad. Feste (as Sir Topas) acknowledges both
meanings in 4.2.

13 **tainted** diseased. As in 3.1.58, where Viola
aptly observes that wise men who have fallen into
folly 'quite taint their wit'.

15 i.e. if a melancholic disorder is equated with
a smiling one.

19 I...sad I could be melancholic. The result of
'this cross-gartering', as he explains in the next line.

21 **sonnet** song.

21–2 **Please one...all** From 'A prettie newe
Ballad intytuled: The Crowe sits upon the Wall /
Please one and please all' entered in the *SR* in
January 1592, and attributed to the player Richard
Tarlton in the new *STC*. Stanza 10, of its seventeen
(not nineteen as Furness has it), gives an indication
that Malvolio, if he remembers more than the
refrain, could find justification for 'such impossible
passages of grossness' (3.2.56) as Maria ordered
in her letter:

Let her have her own will,
Thus the crow pypeth still,
Whatever she command
See that you do it out of hand.

23 SH *OLIVIA F's *Mal.* is another instance of
misassigning; corrected in F2.

MALVOLIO Not black in my mind, though yellow in my legs. It did
  come to his hands, and commands shall be executed. I think we   25
  do know the sweet Roman hand.
OLIVIA Wilt thou go to bed, Malvolio?
MALVOLIO To bed? Ay, sweetheart, and I'll come to thee.
OLIVIA God comfort thee! Why dost thou smile so and kiss thy hand
  so oft?   30
MARIA How do you, Malvolio?
MALVOLIO At your request!
  Yes, nightingales answer daws!
MARIA Why appear you with this ridiculous boldness before my lady?
MALVOLIO 'Be not afraid of greatness': 'twas well writ.   35
OLIVIA What mean'st thou by that, Malvolio?
MALVOLIO 'Some are born great – '
OLIVIA Ha?
MALVOLIO 'Some achieve greatness – '
OLIVIA What say'st thou?   40
MALVOLIO 'And some have greatness thrust upon them.'
OLIVIA Heaven restore thee!
MALVOLIO 'Remember who commended thy yellow stockings – '
OLIVIA Thy yellow stockings?
MALVOLIO 'And wished to see thee cross-gartered.'   45
OLIVIA Cross-gartered?
MALVOLIO 'Go to, thou art made, if thou desir'st to be so – '
OLIVIA Am I made?

---

24 Not black...in my legs i.e. not a
melancholic (from an excess of black bile). Nashe
refers to wearing the two colours in a song (in
Summers Last Will and Testament, Works, III, 239),
and a popular ballad tune was called 'Black and
Yellow'; the music is reproduced in Edward
Rimbault, *Musical Illustrations of Bishop Percy's
Reliques of Antient English Poetry*, 1850, p. 11
(Linthicum, p. 50).

24–6 It...Roman hand 'It' is Maria's letter; in
the first clause Malvolio answers to what he takes
as Olivia's opening words in the letter, 'If this fall
into thy hand' (2.5.118–19). His pronouns in this
speech modulate crazily from 'my' to 'it' to an
impersonal 'his' to an (?) intimate or (?) regal 'we'.

26 sweet Roman hand A fashionable Italian
style of handwriting rather than the native English
(Secretary) hand.

28 Ay...to thee Apparently a line from a
popular ballad; on 1 August 1586, a ballad called

'An answere to "goo to bed swete harte"' was
entered to Edward White (*SR*, II, 209). By singing
his response, Malvolio could tone down his
forwardness.

32 At your request At the request of one like
you (now subordinate to me). A response in accord
with the directive in Maria's letter (2.5.124) to be
'surly with servants'.

33 The lineation follows F and perhaps suggests
the pacing for delivery (R. Flatter, *Shakespeare's
Producing Hand*, 1948, pp. 150–1). There was no
reason for the compositor to set the lines so except
that he was following copy.

33 daws jackdaws. Thought to be stupid birds.

43 thy Olivia is startled by the familiar forms
used by her servant here and at 45 and 47 ('thee'
and 'thou'). This accounts for her amazed echoing
of Malvolio's words. Some editors emend 'thy' (44)
to 'my' on the grounds that Olivia is taking his
words as if directed to her, as she surely does in 48.

MALVOLIO 'If not, let me see thee a servant still.'
OLIVIA Why, this is very midsummer madness.   50

Enter SERVANT

SERVANT Madam, the young gentleman of the Count Orsino's is
   returned; I could hardly entreat him back. He attends your
   ladyship's pleasure.
OLIVIA I'll come to him.

                                                        [*Exit Servant*]
   Good Maria, let this fellow be looked to. Where's my cousin Toby?   55
   Let some of my people have a special care of him; I would not have
   him miscarry for the half of my dowry.

                                           [*Exeunt Olivia and Maria*]
MALVOLIO O ho, do you come near me now? No worse man than Sir
   Toby to look to me! This concurs directly with the letter: she sends
   him on purpose that I may appear stubborn to him; for she incites   60
   me to that in the letter. 'Cast thy humble slough', says she; 'be
   opposite with a kinsman, surly with servants, let thy tongue tang
   with arguments of state, put thyself into the trick of singularity',
   and consequently sets down the manner how: as a sad face, a
   reverend carriage, a slow tongue, in the habit of some sir of note,   65
   and so forth. I have limed her, but it is Jove's doing, and Jove make
   me thankful! And when she went away now, 'Let this fellow be
   looked to' – 'Fellow'! Not 'Malvolio', nor after my degree, but

54 SD *Exit Servant*] Capell; *not in* F   57 SD *Exeunt...Maria*] Capell; *exit* F   62 tang] F2; *langer* F

50 midsummer Proverbial season for madness. Compare 'dog days' and Tilley M1117, 'It is midsummer moon [i.e. lunacy] with you', but here perhaps an allusion to the projected season of the play's action. See p. 41, n. 3 above.

57 miscarry come to harm.

58 come near touch closely, affect (Onions, sv near). As in *Oth.* 4.1.198–9: 'for if it touch not you, it comes near nobody', and *1H4* 1.2.13: 'Indeed you come near me now, Hal.' Dent (N56.1) dates this idiomatic expression from *c.* 1585. Malvolio takes Olivia's last words to mean that up to this point she has been dissembling her real feelings in front of Maria.

62 *tang F2's correction of 'langer' is accounted for by the earlier use (2.5.124) of the word which Malvolio is recalling. The compositor may have read a final tick or finishing stroke as a superscript 'er' – a very common breviograph. Some editors

delete the following preposition though there is no real reason to do so.

64 consequently accordingly.

66 limed i.e. caught her like a bird entangled by lime, a glutinous substance. Thus Ursula says of Beatrice, 'She's limed, I warrant you' (*Ado* 3.1.104).

66–7 Jove's doing...thankful Luce refers this to Ps. 118.23: 'This was the Lord's doing, and it is marvelous in our eyes.' Should the audience detect the Biblical allusion, it would be one more comic foible on Malvolio's part.

68 Fellow Malvolio conveniently forgets the phrasing of Maria's letter – 'the fellow [companion] of servants' – taking it now only in reference to Olivia.

68 after my degree according to my rank in the hierarchy of servants.

'fellow'. Why, everything adheres together, that no dram of a
scruple, no scruple of a scruple, no obstacle, no incredulous or   70
unsafe circumstance – what can be said? Nothing that can be can
come between me and the full prospect of my hopes. Well, Jove,
not I, is the doer of this, and he is to be thanked!

Enter [SIR] TOBY, FABIAN, *and* MARIA

SIR TOBY Which way is he, in the name of sanctity? If all the devils
of hell be drawn in little, and Legion himself possessed him, yet   75
I'll speak to him.

FABIAN Here he is, here he is. How is't with you, sir?

SIR TOBY How is't with you, man?

MALVOLIO Go off, I discard you. Let me enjoy my private. Go off!

MARIA Lo, how hollow the fiend speaks within him! Did not I tell you?   80
Sir Toby, my lady prays you to have a care of him.

MALVOLIO Ah ha! Does she so?

SIR TOBY Go to, go to; peace, peace! We must deal gently with him.
Let me alone. How do you, Malvolio? How is't with you? What,
man, defy the devil! Consider, he's an enemy to mankind.   85

MALVOLIO Do you know what you say?

MARIA La you, and you speak ill of the devil, how he takes it at heart!
Pray God he be not bewitched!

---

73 SD SIR] *Capell subst.; not in* F   78 SH SIR TOBY] *NS, anon. conj. Cam.; not in* F, *which treats the line as part of Fabian's speech at* 77

---

69 adheres accords.

69–70 dram of a scruple a third of a scruple.
Scruple refers to an apothecary's measure and used
figuratively means 'a small amount' (as in 2.5.2) as
well as 'doubt' or 'hesitation'. Falstaff (*2H4*
1.2.130–1) also plays on these meanings: 'the wise
may make some dram of a scruple, or indeed a
scruple itself'.

70 incredulous incredible. Not pre-
Shakespearean (Onions).

71 unsafe circumstance unreliable evidence (of
the facts).

74 sanctity Sir Toby invokes 'sanctity' before
encountering the possessed Malvolio, as Hamlet
(*Ham.* F 623 (1.4.39)) does before encountering
the ghost: 'Angels and ministers of grace defend
us' (NS).

75 drawn in little (1) portrayed in miniature (as
'his picture in little', *Ham.* F 1412 (2.2.366)); (2)
contracted into one body.

75 Legion A reference to the unclean spirit in

Mark 5.8–9, who when asked his name answered,
'My name is Legion: for we are manie'; the gloss
reads 'above 6000 in nombre'.

78 *How...man Assigned to Fabian in F, but
the use of 'man' here, as opposed to Fabian's earlier
'sir', accords with Sir Toby's habit of familiar
address at 85, 98, 100. Compositorial confusion
between *Tob.* and *Fab.* (or *To.* and *Fa.*) seems to
have occurred earlier at 2.5.29, 33, 70–1; here, as
NS notes, the two questions are printed on separate
lines.

79 private privacy. Not pre-Shakespearean
(Onions).

80 hollow falsely. A figurative use (see *OED* sv
adv 1) but perhaps with an overtone of 'sepulchral'.

84 Let me alone Leave him to me.

85 defy renounce. As in *Lear* 3.4.97–8: 'defy the
foul fiend'.

87 La you Look you (Onions).

88 bewitched Different from demoniac possession and needing different treatment.

FABIAN Carry his water to th'wise woman.

MARIA Marry, and it shall be done tomorrow morning if I live. My lady 90
would not lose him for more than I'll say.

MALVOLIO How now, mistress?

MARIA O Lord!

SIR TOBY Prithee, hold thy peace; this is not the way. Do you not see
you move him? Let me alone with him. 95

FABIAN No way but gentleness; gently, gently: the fiend is rough, and
will not be roughly used.

SIR TOBY Why, how now, my bawcock? How dost thou, chuck?

MALVOLIO Sir!

SIR TOBY Ay, biddy, come with me. What, man, 'tis not for gravity 100
to play at cherry-pit with Satan. Hang him, foul collier!

MARIA Get him to say his prayers, good Sir Toby, get him to pray.

MALVOLIO My prayers, minx!

MARIA No, I warrant you, he will not hear of godliness.

MALVOLIO Go hang yourselves all! You are idle, shallow things; I am 105
not of your element. You shall know more hereafter.   *Exit*

SIR TOBY Is't possible?

FABIAN If this were played upon a stage now, I could condemn it as
an improbable fiction.

SIR TOBY His very genius hath taken the infection of the device, man. 110

MARIA Nay, pursue him now, lest the device take air and taint.

89 i.e. for inspecting his urine for a medical diagnosis; 'wise women' were those skilled in occult arts such as fortune-telling and palmistry and, according to Thomas Heywood in the *Wise Woman of Hogsden* (1638), 'casting of Waters' (cited in Furness); the term is equivalent to a harmless or 'good' witch.

95 move excite.

95 Let me alone As in 84 above.

96 rough violent.

98 bawcock...chuck Terms of endearment; 'bawcock' (*beau coq*) is masculine (as in *WT* 1.2.121) and 'chuck' (= chick, like 'biddy' in Sir Toby's next speech) usually feminine (as in *Mac.* 3.2.45). Such language, as Kittredge notes, enrages Malvolio even more.

100 gravity i.e. a grave person.

101 play at cherry-pit be on familiar terms with. From the child's game of tossing cherry pits into a hole.

101 foul collier i.e. 'the fiend' of 96, from the proverb (Tilley L287) 'Like will to like, quoth the devil to the collier.' As a dealer in pit-coal, a collier was assumed to be like the devil, black in heart as

well as in appearance. An interlude dating from 1568 by Ulpian Fulwell uses this proverb as its title; *ODEP* dates it from *c.* 1559.

105 idle foolish.

105–6 I am...element I am out of your sphere. Shakespeare is again having sport with the word 'element' and its 'overworn' use, either as Malvolio's special word or, perhaps, Jonson's. (See 3.1.49 and n.)

108–9 If...fiction Like 1.3.48, the line is guaranteed to evoke audience-response, but it is also a typically Shakespearean comment on the unreality of theatrical illusion.

110 genius nature. In this period 'genius' was more frequently used to refer to the tutelary spirit (or angel) guarding an individual.

110 device stratagem.

111 take air (1) become infectious, (2) become known. The first meaning accords with Sir Toby's medical image; compare *Lear* 2.4.163–4: 'Strike her young bones, / You taking airs, with lameness!'

111 taint be spoiled. Continues the disease image.

FABIAN Why, we shall make him mad indeed.

MARIA The house will be the quieter.

SIR TOBY Come, we'll have him in a dark room and bound. My niece
is already in the belief that he's mad. We may carry it thus for our   115
pleasure, and his penance, till our very pastime, tired out of breath,
prompt us to have mercy on him; at which time we will bring the
device to the bar and crown thee for a finder of madmen. But see,
but see!

Enter SIR ANDREW

FABIAN More matter for a May morning!   120

SIR ANDREW Here's the challenge; read it. I warrant there's vinegar
and pepper in't.

FABIAN Is't so saucy?

SIR ANDREW Ay, is't. I warrant him; do but read.

SIR TOBY Give me. [*Reads*] 'Youth, whatsoever thou art, thou art but   125
a scurvy fellow.'

FABIAN Good, and valiant.

SIR TOBY [*Reads*] 'Wonder not, nor admire not in thy mind, why I do
call thee so, for I will show thee no reason for't.'

FABIAN A good note! That keeps you from the blow of the law.   130

SIR TOBY [*Reads*] 'Thou com'st to the Lady Olivia, and in my sight
she uses thee kindly. But thou liest in thy throat. That is not the
matter I challenge thee for.'

FABIAN Very brief, and to exceeding good sense [*Aside*] – less.

SIR TOBY [*Reads*] 'I will waylay thee going home, where if it be thy   135
chance to kill me –'

FABIAN Good.

125, 128, 131, 135, 138, 140 SD *Reads*] *Capell; not in* F   134 sense [*Aside*] – less] NS *subst.;* sence-less F

114 **we'll...bound** The usual treatment for
madness. Compare *Err.* 4.4.92–4: 'Mistress, both
man and master is possess'd: / ...They must be
bound and laid in some dark room.'

115 **carry** manage.

118 **bar** i.e. to be judged.

118 **a finder of madmen** Like those acting
under the writ *De lunatico inquirendo* which 'found'
(i.e. declared) an individual mad.

120 **matter . . . morning** i.e. fit for May-day
plays or games. Also perhaps an allusion to the
season which the play seems intended to represent.
See p. 41, n. 3 above.

123 **saucy** (1) salty, (2) impertinent. The first
meaning carries the sense 'bitter'; compare 'salt
scorn' (*Tro.* 1.3.370).

124 **I warrant him** I can assure him (i.e.
Cesario). Used as an asseveration.

125 **thou** This is in accord with Sir Toby's
advice at 3.2.35–6.

128 **admire** marvel.

130 **blow of the law** legal punishment (for
breach of the peace). All Sir Andrew's taunts, as NS
notes, are carefully hedged.

132 **liest...throat** Proverbial charge of menda-
city (Tilley T268).

SIR TOBY [*Reads*] 'Thou kill'st me like a rogue and a villain.'

FABIAN Still you keep o'th'windy side of the law. Good.

SIR TOBY [*Reads*] 'Fare thee well, and God have mercy upon one of   140
our souls! He may have mercy upon mine, but my hope is better,
and so look to thyself. Thy friend, as thou usest him, and thy sworn
enemy,
                                        Andrew Aguecheek.'

If this letter move him not, his legs cannot. I'll give't him.   145

MARIA You may have very fit occasion for't; he is now in some
commerce with my lady and will by and by depart.

SIR TOBY Go, Sir Andrew, scout me for him at the corner of the orchard
like a bumbaily. So soon as ever thou seest him, draw, and as thou
draw'st, swear horrible; for it comes to pass oft that a terrible oath,   150
with a swaggering accent sharply twanged off, gives manhood more
approbation than ever proof itself would have earned him. Away!

SIR ANDREW Nay, let me alone for swearing.   *Exit*

SIR TOBY Now will not I deliver his letter; for the behaviour of the
young gentleman gives him out to be of good capacity and breeding;   155
his employment between his lord and my niece confirms no less.
Therefore this letter, being so excellently ignorant, will breed no
terror in the youth; he will find it comes from a clodpole. But, sir,
I will deliver his challenge by word of mouth, set upon Aguecheek
a notable report of valour, and drive the gentleman (as I know his   160
youth will aptly receive it) into a most hideous opinion of his rage,
skill, fury, and impetuosity. This will so fright them both that they
will kill one another by the look, like cockatrices.

---

138 **rogue and a villain** In Sir Andrew's ambiguous style, the terms could refer equally well to 'thou' or to 'me'.

139 **windy...law** The seaman sails towards the wind to avoid being driven on to rocks on the leeside; hence the 'windy side' is the 'safe side'; compare *Ado* 2.1.314–15 where the merry heart of Beatrice keeps on 'the windy side of care'.

141 **but my...better** but I hope for something better (than God's mercy on my soul), i.e. to be allowed to win.

142 **as thou usest him** in so far as you treat him (like a friend).

145 **If this letter...cannot** Sir Toby plays on 'move' as (1) incite and (2) propel.

146–7 **in...commerce** in some transaction.

147 **by and by** very soon.

148 **me** Another example of Sir Toby's use of the ethical dative, as in 3.2.26, 27.

149 **bumbaily** A bailiff who attempts to apprehend a debtor from behind. The only instance in Shakespeare, and the earliest cited in *OED*.

151–2 **gives...approbation** gives more credit to manliness.

153 **Indeed, as for swearing, leave it to me.** As in *Shr.* 4.2.71: 'Take [in] your love, and then let me alone.' Up to this point, Sir Andrew's skill has been limited to the imprecation ''Slight'' (2.5.28, 3.2.9).

158 **clodpole** blockhead.

160–1 **his youth...it** because of his inexperience he will readily believe it.

163 **cockatrices** Also called 'basilisks'. The belief that these fabulous serpents possessed a 'death-[darting] eye' (*Rom.* 3.2.47) had become proverbial (Tilley C495, Dent C496.2 and B99.1).

FABIAN Here he comes with your niece; give them way till he take leave
and presently after him.   165

Enter OLIVIA *and* VIOLA

SIR TOBY I will meditate the while upon some horrid message for a
challenge.
                              [Exeunt Sir Toby, Fabian, and Maria]
OLIVIA I have said too much unto a heart of stone,
    And laid mine honour too unchary on't;
    There's something in me that reproves my fault,   170
    But such a headstrong potent fault it is,
    That it but mocks reproof.
VIOLA With the same 'haviour that your passion bears
    Goes on my master's griefs.
OLIVIA Here, wear this jewel for me; 'tis my picture.   175
    Refuse it not; it hath no tongue to vex you.
    And, I beseech you, come again tomorrow.
    What shall you ask of me that I'll deny,
    That honour, saved, may upon asking give?
VIOLA Nothing but this – your true love for my master.   180
OLIVIA How with mine honour may I give him that
    Which I have given to you?
VIOLA   I will acquit you.
OLIVIA Well, come again tomorrow. Fare thee well.
    A fiend like thee might bear my soul to hell.   *[Exit]*

Enter SIR TOBY *and* FABIAN

SIR TOBY Gentleman, God save thee.   185
VIOLA And you, sir.
SIR TOBY That defence thou hast, betake thee to't. Of what nature the

---

165 SD *Enter...*VIOLA] *This edn; after 163* F   167 SD *Exeunt...Maria]* Capell; Exeunt. F2; *not in* F   169 on't] F; out
Theobald   184 SD *Exit]* F2; *not in* F

164 **give them way** keep out of their way.
165 **presently** immediately. As at 5.1.161.
166 **horrid** Literally, 'bristling'.
168 **a heart of stone** Then proverbial (Tilley H311), if now a cliché.
169 **And placed** (or staked) my reputation too heedlessly on (that heart of stone). Following Theobald, many editors emend 'on't' to 'out', justifying the change on the grounds of an easy compositorial error.
174 **Goes...griefs** The use of a singular verb ending in *s* preceding a plural noun is common, as in *TGV* 2.4.71–2: '(for far behind his worth / Comes all the praises that I now bestow)...'
175 Olivia's gift of a jewelled miniature recalls the earlier situation of her unveiling the 'picture' of herself to Cesario.
182 **acquit you** release you (from that gift).
184 **like thee** in your likeness.
187 **That defence thou hast** Whatever skill in fencing you have.

wrongs are thou hast done him, I know not; but thy intercepter, full
of despite, bloody as the hunter, attends thee at the orchard-end.
Dismount thy tuck, be yare in thy preparation, for thy assailant is   190
quick, skilful, and deadly.

VIOLA You mistake, sir. I am sure no man hath any quarrel to me. My
remembrance is very free and clear from any image of offence done
to any man.

SIR TOBY You'll find it otherwise, I assure you. Therefore, if you hold   195
your life at any price, betake you to your guard; for your opposite
hath in him what youth, strength, skill, and wrath can furnish man
withal.

VIOLA I pray you, sir, what is he?

SIR TOBY He is knight, dubbed with unhatched rapier, and on carpet   200
consideration, but he is a devil in private brawl. Souls and bodies
hath he divorced three, and his incensement at this moment is so
implacable that satisfaction can be none but by pangs of death and
sepulchre. Hob nob is his word: give't or take't.

VIOLA I will return again into the house and desire some conduct of   205
the lady. I am no fighter. I have heard of some kind of men that
put quarrels purposely on others to taste their valour; belike this
is a man of that quirk.

SIR TOBY Sir, no. His indignation derives itself out of a very competent
injury; therefore get you on and give him his desire. Back you shall   210
not to the house, unless you undertake that with me which with
as much safety you might answer him; therefore on, or strip your

192 sir. I am sure no] *NS*; sir, I am sure, no F   209 competent] F4; computent F

189 **despite** ill will.
189 **bloody…hunter** bloodthirsty like a hunting
dog after its prey.
190 **Dismount thy tuck** i.e. unsheathe your
(small) rapier. 'Dismount' is properly used of a
cannon; Sir Toby's inflated diction is a further
means of intimidation.
190 **yare** prompt.
192 **to** with. The same idiomatic use of the
preposition appears in *Ado* 2.1.236–7: 'The Lady
Beatrice hath a quarrel to you.'
196 **opposite** opponent.
199 **what is he** i.e. of what quality and rank. As
at 1.2.35 and 1.5.104. This contrasts with 'what
manner of man is he' at 223.
200 **unhatched** Either 'unhacked' or 'never
drawn from its scabbard'.
200–1 **on carpet consideration** dubbed for

domestic (rather than military) service and perhaps
in return for payment. Nashe (*Works*, I, 353)
describes 'carpet knights' as being 'the basest
cowards under heaven, covering an apes hart with
a lion's case, and making false alarums when they
mean nothing but a May-game' (compare 120
above). See also Benedict's reference to 'quondam
carpetmongers' in *Ado* 5.2.32–3, specifying the
inadequacy of such famous lovers as Leander and
Troilus.
204 **Hob…word** 'Have it or have it not' is his
motto. Tilley (H479) dates its earliest use to 1530.
205 **conduct** escort.
207 **put** foist.
207 **taste** try.
209 ***competent** sufficient.
211 **undertake that** i.e. fight a duel.
212–13 **strip…naked** fully unsheathe your sword.

sword stark naked; for meddle you must, that's certain, or forswear
to wear iron about you.

VIOLA This is as uncivil as strange. I beseech you, do me this courteous   215
office as to know of the knight what my offence to him is. It is
something of my negligence, nothing of my purpose.

SIR TOBY I will do so. Signior Fabian, stay you by this gentleman till
my return.   *Exit [Sir] Toby*

VIOLA Pray you, sir, do you know of this matter?   220

FABIAN I know the knight is incensed against you, even to a mortal
arbitrement, but nothing of the circumstance more.

VIOLA I beseech you, what manner of man is he?

FABIAN Nothing of that wonderful promise, to read him by his form,
as you are like to find him in the proof of his valour. He is indeed,   225
sir, the most skilful, bloody, and fatal opposite that you could
possibly have found in any part of Illyria. Will you walk towards
him? I will make your peace with him if I can.

VIOLA I shall be much bound to you for't. I am one that had rather
go with sir priest than sir knight. I care not who knows so much   230
of my mettle.

Exeunt

Enter [SIR] TOBY *and* [SIR] ANDREW

SIR TOBY Why, man, he's a very devil. I have not seen such a firago.
I had a pass with him, rapier, scabbard, and all, and he gives me

---

219 SD *Sir*] *Capell; not in* F   231 SD.2 SIR…SIR] *Capell; not in* F

---

213 **meddle** become involved.
215 **uncivil** discourteous.
216 **know of** enquire from.
217 **something…purpose** the result of some oversight, nothing intentional.
221–2 **mortal arbitrement** settlement to the death.
224 **to read** to judge.
230 **sir priest** The designation of one who has taken a Bachelor of Arts degree and by courtesy extended to a clergyman lacking the degree. Thus 'Sir Topas the curate' in 4.2.
231 SD F's unnecessary *Exeunt*, occasioning the re-entry of Viola and Fabian at 246, poses something of a problem, since their departure clears the stage as if it were the end of the scene, which it is not. Moreover, Sir Toby has directed Fabian (218–19) to stay with Viola until his return; he then alarms Sir Andrew by declaring that Fabian is scarcely able to hold Cesario 'yonder' (238–9), a

suggestion of some stage business within view of the audience. Capell solved the problem by deleting the directives for exiting and re-entry, a procedure that is frequently adopted in modern texts and productions. On an Elizabethan stage, presumably Viola and Fabian could still be seen ('yonder') through the doorway through which they exit. Sir Toby and Sir Andrew then enter through the second door and proceed down stage so that when Fabian and Viola re-enter, they are positioned diagonally, permitting Sir Toby, as well as Fabian, to accost each in turn and to incite each of them with the same words, 'There's no remedy' (251, 258). The duellists would thus be at centre stage when Antonio enters. See illustration 1*b*, p. 3.
232 **firago** virago. For comic effect Sir Toby applies a term applicable to a woman to one whom he supposes to be a man (Kittredge).
233 **pass** bout. Its more usual meaning is 'lunge' or 'thrust'.

the stuck-in with such a mortal motion that it is inevitable; and on
the answer, he pays you as surely as your feet hits the ground they   235
step on. They say he has been fencer to the sophy.

SIR ANDREW Pox on't. I'll not meddle with him.

SIR TOBY Ay, but he will not now be pacified. Fabian can scarce hold
him yonder.

SIR ANDREW Plague on't, and I thought he had been valiant, and so   240
cunning in fence, I'd have seen him damned ere I'd have challenged
him. Let him let the matter slip, and I'll give him my horse, Grey
Capilet.

SIR TOBY I'll make the motion. Stand here, make a good show on't.
This shall end without the perdition of souls. [*Aside*] Marry, I'll   245
ride your horse as well as I ride you.

Enter FABIAN *and* VIOLA

[*To Fabian*] I have his horse to take up the quarrel. I have
persuaded him the youth's a devil.

FABIAN He is as horribly conceited of him and pants and looks pale,
as if a bear were at his heels.   250

SIR TOBY [*To Viola*] There's no remedy, sir. He will fight with you
for's oath sake. Marry, he hath better bethought him of his quarrel,
and he finds that now scarce to be worth talking of. Therefore, draw
for the supportance of his vow. He protests he will not hurt you.

235 hits] F; hit *Rowe*   238–9 Ay...yonder] *As prose, Capell; as verse,* F   245 SD *Aside*] *Theobald; not in* F
247 SD *To Fabian*] *Rowe; not in* F   251 SD *To Viola*] *Capell; not in* F

234 **stuck-in** thrust. Sir Toby's form of Italian *stoccata*. Compare *Ham.* 3152 (4.7.161): 'If he by chance escape your venom'd stuck' and *Wiv.* 2.1.225–6: 'your passes, stoccadoes, and I know not what'.

234 **inevitable** unavoidable. As in *Ant.* 4.14.64–7: 'when I should see... / Th'inevitable prosecution of / Disgrace and horror... / Thou then wouldst kill me'.

234–5 **on the answer...surely** on the return he pays you home (with a mortal hit). Compare Falstaff (*1H4* 2.4.192–3): 'Two I am sure I have paid, two rogues in buckrom suits.'

235 **hits** Sir Toby's use of the singular here is either a colloquial touch (since it is retained in the three later Folios) or a misprint (with a final flourish read as s); many editors, following Rowe, correct to the plural form.

236 **fencer to the sophy** Accepted as a topical reference to a second Sherley, this time Sir Robert, who was serving in the shah's military organisation; see 2.5.149 n. for the reference to Sir Anthony.

242–3 **Grey Capilet** The Elizabethans typically used a characterising word when naming horses; the queen, for example, owned 'Grey Markham', called after a standard bearer of the royal guard of Gentlemen Pensioners; 'Roan Barbary' was Richard II's favourite mount, and 'Bay Curtal' was a prized possession of Lafew's (*AWW* 2.3.59).

244 **motion** offer.

245 **perdition** loss. But in accord with Sir Toby's inflated diction, it probably carries an overtone of 'damnation'.

246 **ride you** Figuratively, 'make a fool of', with an obvious quibble.

247 **I have...quarrel** I have the promise of his horse to settle the quarrel. See 274–5.

249 **He...conceited of him** He is possessed of as fearsome an idea of him.

252 **oath sake** oath's sake.

252 **quarrel** grounds for challenging.

254 **supportance** upholding.

VIOLA [*Aside*] Pray God defend me! A little thing would make me tell   255
    them how much I lack of a man.
FABIAN Give ground if you see him furious.
SIR TOBY Come, Sir Andrew, there's no remedy: the gentleman will
    for his honour's sake have one bout with you; he cannot by the
    duello avoid it, but he has promised me, as he is a gentleman and   260
    a soldier, he will not hurt you. Come on, to't.
SIR ANDREW Pray God he keep his oath!
VIOLA I do assure you, 'tis against my will.
                 [*They draw*]

            Enter ANTONIO

ANTONIO [*Drawing*] Put up your sword! If this young gentleman
    Have done offence, I take the fault on me;   265
    If you offend him, I for him defy you.
SIR TOBY You, sir? Why, what are you?
ANTONIO One, sir, that for his love dares yet do more
    Than you have heard him brag to you he will.
SIR TOBY Nay, if you be an undertaker, I am for you. [*Draws*]   270

            Enter OFFICERS

FABIAN O good Sir Toby, hold! Here comes the officers.
SIR TOBY [*To Antonio*] I'll be with you anon.
VIOLA [*To Sir Andrew*] Pray, sir, put your sword up, if you please.
SIR ANDREW Marry, will I, sir; and for that I promised you, I'll be
    as good as my word. He will bear you easily and reins well.   275
1 OFFICER This is the man; do thy office.
2 OFFICER Antonio, I arrest thee at the suit

---

255 SD *Aside*] *Malone; not in* F   263 SD.1 *They draw*] *Rowe; not in* F   263 SD.2 *Enter* ANTONIO] *Dyce, Cam.; after*
262 *in* F   264 SD *Drawing*] *Rowe (after 266); not in* F   270 SD.1 *Draws*] *Rowe; not in* F   272 SD *To Antonio*] *Capell;*
not in F   273 SD *To Sir Andrew*] *Rowe; not in* F

259 one bout one thrust and parry.
259–60 by the duello by the code and conduct proper to duelling.
263 SD The earlier directive to Sir Andrew to be on the lookout for Cesario at the 'corner of the orchard' (148) and the information that he is waiting for his opponent at the 'orchard-end' (189) presumably mean that Antonio and the Officers come on to the duelling scene as if from the street.
270 undertaker (1) one who takes on responsibility for something (as in *Oth.* 4.1.211); (2) one who takes on a fight (as in *Cym.* 2.1.26–7); and,

particularly here, (3) one who meddles in another's business.
270 I am for you I am ready for you. Compare *Shr.* 4.3.151: 'I am for thee straight.'
272 I'll...anon I'll have a bout with you soon. In the presence of the Officers, Sir Toby must sheathe his sword and probably stands out of the way.
274–5 be as...word i.e. surrender Grey Capilet, about which Viola knows nothing. Dent (w773.1) gives other Shakespearean examples of this idiom from the plays written around this date and earlier.

Of Count Orsino.

ANTONIO   You do mistake me, sir.

1 OFFICER No, sir, no jot. I know your favour well,
Though now you have no sea-cap on your head.   280
Take him away; he knows I know him well.

ANTONIO I must obey. [*To Viola*] This comes with seeking you.
But there's no remedy; I shall answer it.
What will you do, now my necessity
Makes me to ask you for my purse? It grieves me   285
Much more for what I cannot do for you
Than what befalls myself. You stand amazed,
But be of comfort.

2 OFFICER Come, sir, away.

ANTONIO I must entreat of you some of that money.   290

VIOLA What money, sir?
For the fair kindness you have showed me here,
And part being prompted by your present trouble,
Out of my lean and low ability
I'll lend you something. My having is not much;   295
I'll make division of my present with you.
Hold, there's half my coffer.

ANTONIO Will you deny me now?
Is't possible that my deserts to you
Can lack persuasion? Do not tempt my misery,   300
Lest that it make me so unsound a man
As to upbraid you with those kindnesses
That I have done for you.

VIOLA   I know of none,
Nor know I you by voice or any feature.
I hate ingratitude more in a man   305

---

282 SD *To Viola*] *Collier; not in* F

279 **favour** features. As again at 332.
283 **answer** Either (1) atone for it by repaying
(as at 3.3.28, 33), or (2) attempt a defence.
287 **amazed** bewildered. (A strong word.)
293 **part** partly.
295 **My having** What I have.
296 **present** present store of money.
297 **coffer** money-chest. Such hyperbole in
referring to the purse or small money-bag Cesario
carries is a comic touch.
300 **lack persuasion** fail to move you.
300 **tempt** try too sorely.
301 **unsound** unorthodox (in not conforming

to the doctrine of manliness). Compare *H8*
5.2.115–16: 'Do not I know you for a favorer / Of
this new sect? Ye are not sound.' Note the religious
diction in 312–14.
304 **feature** shape or form. As again at 317. The
sense 'lineaments of the face' is not in Shakespeare
(Onions).
305 **ingratitude** The idea that ingratitude is an
inhuman quality is frequent in Shakespeare; it is
characterised as 'monstrous' in *Cor.* 2.3.9 and
a 'monster' in *Lear* 1.5.39–40; in *Tro.* 3.3.145–7
Time is called 'A great-siz'd monster of ingrati-
tudes'.

Than lying, vainness, babbling drunkenness,
Or any taint of vice whose strong corruption
Inhabits our frail blood.

ANTONIO   O heavens themselves!

2 OFFICER Come, sir, I pray you go.

ANTONIO Let me speak a little. This youth that you see here,   310
I snatched one-half out of the jaws of death,
Relieved him with such sanctity of love;
And to his image, which methought did promise
Most venerable worth, did I devotion.

1 OFFICER What's that to us? The time goes by. Away!   315

ANTONIO But O how vile an idol proves this god!
Thou hast, Sebastian, done good feature shame.
In nature there's no blemish but the mind:
None can be called deformed but the unkind.
Virtue is beauty, but the beauteous-evil   320
Are empty trunks, o'er-flourished by the devil.

1 OFFICER The man grows mad. Away with him! Come, come, sir.

ANTONIO Lead me on.

                                   Exit [with Officers]

---

320 beauteous-evil] *Malone; not hyphenated in* F   **322**] *As Dyce; two lines in* F (him: / ...sir)   **323** SD *with Officers*] *Theobald; not in* F

306 vainness boasting. Compare 1 Tim. 6.20: 'avoide profane & vaine bablings' (repeated 2 Tim. 2.16). Editors frequently alter the punctuation in F (which is followed here) to make two units with their modifiers or to make a series of four sorts of 'vice' though 'babbling' (without a modifier) scarcely seems to qualify as one.

308 blood nature.

311 one-half...death i.e. half-dead.

312 such sanctity of love such holiness of love (as is directed to a religious object). The religious diction continues with 'image' (= (1) appearance, (2) statue), 'venerable worth' (= worthy of veneration), 'devotion' and in Antonio's next speech with 'idol', 'god' (316) and 'devil' (321). In F the first letter of 'love' looks like a damaged capital 'I' (Iove), though the later Folios read 'love' (Ard.).

317 done...shame disgraced your goodly exterior by the nature of your response. For earlier and later allusions to this motif, see 1.2.50–1 and 5.1.120; 'feature' is used here in the same sense as at 304.

318–21 Antonio's shift to sententious rhyming couplets elicits Sir Toby's mocking reference at 328–9. Dramatically, the verse (as a 'higher' medium than prose) serves to dignify Antonio's philosophic reflections (though they seem only 'sage saws' to Sir Toby).

319 unkind (1) cruel, (2) unnatural. In *AYLI* (2.7.174–6) man's ingratitude is said to be more 'unkind' than the cruel winter wind.

320–1 beauteous-evil...devil i.e. individuals who are beautiful but morally bad are only vacant bodies that have been lavishly, perhaps over, embellished or, perhaps, embellished 'all over' by the hand of Satan. As *OED* points out, the force of 'over' in combination with verbs is extremely difficult to pin down (*OED* Over-*prep* and *adv* 25, 8 and 27). In spite of the consistency of idea and image in these lines many editors take 'trunks' to refer to carved chests holding household furnishings, but for the same use of 'trunk', see 4.2.40 n.; for Shakespeare's frequent contrast between an inner beauty and the outward show, see 317 n.

VIOLA Methinks his words do from such passion fly
       That he believes himself; so do not I.   325
       Prove true, imagination, O prove true,
       That I, dear brother, be now tane for you!
SIR TOBY Come hither, knight, come hither, Fabian. We'll whisper o'er
       a couplet or two of most sage saws.
VIOLA He named Sebastian. I my brother know   330
       Yet living in my glass; even such and so
       In favour was my brother, and he went
       Still in this fashion, colour, ornament,
       For him I imitate. O if it prove,
       Tempests are kind, and salt waves fresh in love.   [*Exit*] 335
SIR TOBY A very dishonest paltry boy, and more a coward than a hare;
       his dishonesty appears in leaving his friend here in necessity, and
       denying him; and for his cowardship, ask Fabian.
FABIAN A coward, a most devout coward, religious in it.
SIR ANDREW 'Slid, I'll after him again and beat him.   340
SIR TOBY Do, cuff him soundly, but never draw thy sword.
SIR ANDREW And I do not –   [*Exit*]
FABIAN Come, let's see the event.
SIR TOBY I dare lay any money, 'twill be nothing yet.

                                               Exeunt

4.1 *Enter* SEBASTIAN *and* CLOWN [FESTE]

FESTE Will you make me believe that I am not sent for you?
SEBASTIAN Go to, go to, thou art a foolish fellow.
       Let me be clear of thee.

---

335 SD *Exit*] F2; *not in* F   342 not –] *Theobald*; not. F   342 SD *Exit*] *Theobald*; *not in* F   344 SD *Exeunt*] *Rowe*; *Exit* F
Act 4, Scene 1   4.1] *Actus Quartus, Scæna prima.* F

324 passion vehement feeling.
325 That he believes himself That he himself
believes (that I am Sebastian).
330–1 I my brother...glass Whenever I look
in my mirror, I see my brother's image to the life
(Kittredge).
332 favour features. As before, 279.
334 if it prove if my hope prove true.
336 dishonest dishonourable.
336 more a coward...hare A proverbial
instance of cowardice, as the Bastard in *John*
(2.1.137–8) notes: 'You are the hare of whom the
proverb goes, / Where valor plucks dead lions by
the beard.' See Tilley H165.

338 denying disavowing.
339 religious in it devoted to it (i.e. to the
concept of 'cowardship').
340 'Slid By God's eyelid.
343 event outcome.
344 yet after all.

Act 4, Scene 1
  Location Before Olivia's house (Capell subst.).
  1 Feste's opening words indicate that this
exchange about Sebastian's identity has been going
on for some time, as does his 'Well held out' – i.e.
well kept up (4).

FESTE Well held out, i'faith! No, I do not know you, nor I am not sent
to you by my lady to bid you come speak with her; nor your name   5
is not Master Cesario; nor this is not my nose neither. Nothing that
is so is so.

SEBASTIAN I prithee, vent thy folly somewhere else.
Thou know'st not me.

FESTE Vent my folly! He has heard that word of some great man and   10
now applies it to a fool. Vent my folly! I am afraid this great lubber
the world will prove a cockney. I prithee now, ungird thy
strangeness and tell me what I shall vent to my lady. Shall I vent
to her that thou art coming?

SEBASTIAN I prithee, foolish Greek, depart from me.   15
There's money for thee. If you tarry longer,
I shall give worse payment.

FESTE By my troth, thou hast an open hand. These wise men that give
fools money get themselves a good report – after fourteen years'
purchase.   20

Enter [SIR] ANDREW, [SIR] TOBY, *and* FABIAN

SIR ANDREW Now, sir, have I met you again? There's for you!
[*Strikes Sebastian*]

8–9] *As verse, Capell; as prose* F   15–17] *As verse, Capell; as prose* F   20 SD SIR...SIR] *Capell; not in* F   21 SD *Strikes
Sebastian*] *Douai MS., Rowe subst.; not in* F

6 nor this...neither For a similar ironic use
of this comparison, see *TGV* 2.1.135–6: 'O jest
unseen, inscrutable; invisible, / As a nose on a
man's face, or a weathercock on a steeple'; for the
triple negative, see 3.1.144 n.

8–20 This exchange, with its emphasis on (1) a
matter of diction and (2) a gift of money, 'twins'
with Feste's encounter with Viola at 3.1.1–49.

8 vent get rid of. As in *Cor.* 1.1.225–6: 'then we
shall ha'means to vent / Our musty superfluity'.
Feste then goes on to pick up (13) the more common
Shakespearean meaning 'utter' (as also in *Cor.*
1.1.209: 'They vented their complainings.').

10–11 He...fool i.e. he has appropriated
'vent' – diction proper to some great man – and
makes use of it in addressing a fool. Feste's
'damnable iteration' then travesties the term.

11 lubber booby.

12 cockney i.e. one guilty of affectations.

12–13 ungird thy strangeness i.e. stop being
outlandish. Literally, 'divest yourself of acting (1)

like a foreigner, (2) aloof and (3) unfamiliar' (the
several senses of 'strange').

15 foolish Greek (1) talker of nonsense or (2)
merrygreek. (1) = 'unintelligible', as in the proverbial phrase (Tilley G439), 'It is Greek to me.'
(2) is a term for a buffoon derived from a character
of that name in Nicholas Udall's *Ralph Roister
Doister* (*SR*, 1566); in *Tro.* 1.2.109, it is used of
Helen both literally and metaphorically.

18 open liberal. This, following the two rewards
earlier received (3.1.36–7, 45), confirms Feste's
identification of Sebastian with Viola.

19 report reputation.

19–20 after...purchase Either 'after a long
time' or 'for a price'. The market value of land was
the sum of the yearly rent for a fixed number of
years, as twelve, fourteen, etc.

21 There's for you Sir Andrew's actions should
accord with Sir Toby's instructions (3.4.341), 'cuff
him soundly but never draw thy sword'.

SEBASTIAN Why, there's for thee, and there, and there!

[Beats Sir Andrew]

    Are all the people mad?

SIR TOBY Hold, sir, or I'll throw your dagger o'er the house.

FESTE This will I tell my lady straight; I would not be in some of your   25
    coats for twopence.   *[Exit]*

SIR TOBY Come on, sir, hold!

SIR ANDREW Nay, let him alone. I'll go another way to work with him;
    I'll have an action of battery against him, if there be any law in
    Illyria. Though I struck him first, yet it's no matter for that.   30

SEBASTIAN Let go thy hand!

SIR TOBY Come, sir, I will not let you go. Come, my young soldier,
    put up your iron. You are well fleshed. Come on!

SEBASTIAN I will be free from thee. *[Draws his sword]* What wouldst
    thou now?

    If thou dar'st tempt me further, draw thy sword.   35

SIR TOBY What, what! Nay, then, I must have an ounce or two of this
    malapert blood from you. *[Draws]*

Enter OLIVIA

OLIVIA Hold, Toby! On thy life I charge thee hold!

SIR TOBY Madam –

OLIVIA Will it be ever thus? Ungracious wretch,   40
    Fit for the mountains and the barbarous caves,
    Where manners ne'er were preached! Out of my sight!
    Be not offended, dear Cesario.
    Rudesby, be gone!

[Exeunt Sir Toby, Sir Andrew, and Fabian]
    I prithee, gentle friend,

---

22 SD *Beats Sir Andrew*] Rowe subst.; not in F   26 SD *Exit*] Rowe; not in F   30 struck] F4; stroke F   34 SD *Draws his sword*] Capell subst.; not in F   37 SD *Draws*] Capell subst.; not in F   39 Madam –] Collier; Madam. F   44 SD *Exeunt...Fabian*] Capell; not in F

---

22 Why...there Sebastian's words (followed by those of Sir Toby) indicate that he has drawn his dagger and uses the hilt to beat Sir Andrew; Kittredge cites *Rom.* 4.5.117–18 for this use of a dagger: 'Then will I lay the serving-creature's dagger on your pate.'

24 I'll...house Sir Toby's threatening hyperbole, as Ard. notes, establishes the location of the scene.

25 straight at once.

28 I'll go...to work Proverbial for adopting a different tactic (Tilley W150).

29 action of battery lawsuit for assault and battery.

33 well fleshed eager for combat. Used originally of a hawk or hound that has been fed only on flesh (Onions). Following earlier commentators, NS takes this speech as ironically directed to Sir Andrew.

35 tempt me try me. There is a double sense: (1) make trial of me and (2) provoke.

37 malapert impudent.

44 Rudesby Ruffian. Used only here and in *Shr.* 3.2.10: 'a mad-brain rudesby full of spleen'.

Let thy fair wisdom, not thy passion, sway   45
In this uncivil and unjust extent
Against thy peace. Go with me to my house
And hear thou there how many fruitless pranks
This ruffian hath botched up, that thou thereby
Mayst smile at this. Thou shalt not choose but go.   50
Do not deny. Beshrew his soul for me,
He started one poor heart of mine, in thee.
SEBASTIAN What relish is in this? How runs the stream?
Or I am mad, or else this is a dream.
Let fancy still my sense in Lethe steep;   55
If it be thus to dream, still let me sleep!
OLIVIA Nay, come, I prithee; would thou'dst be ruled by me!
SEBASTIAN Madam, I will.
OLIVIA   O say so, and so be!

Exeunt

4.2 *Enter* MARIA *and* CLOWN [FESTE]

MARIA Nay, I prithee put on this gown and this beard; make him
believe thou art Sir Topas the curate. Do it quickly. I'll call Sir
Toby the whilst.   [*Exit*]

Act 4, Scene 2   4.2] *Scæna Secunda.* F   o SD FESTE] *This edn; not in* F   3 *Exit*] *Theobald; not in* F

45 **fair** equitable.
46 **uncivil** Here (and perhaps at 5.1.101) 'uncivil' means 'uncivilised' and thus fit for dwellers in 'barbarous caves' (41). Elsewhere (2.3.104, 3.4.215) it is somewhat less emphatic.
46 **unjust extent** unjustified assault.
48 **pranks** mischiefs.
49 **botched up** patched up. For Feste's use of 'botcher', see 1.5.38.
51 **deny** refuse.
51 **Beshrew his soul** Literally, 'curse his soul', a stronger use than at 2.3.70.
52 **started** (1) roused and (2) startled. The first sense (which is used of a hare in *1H4* 1.3.198) initiates a pun on 'hart' and 'heart' (as at 1.1.17–18). For the second sense, compare *AWW* 5.3.232: 'every feather starts you'.
52 **in thee** In accord with the doctrine that lovers exchange hearts.
53 **relish** taste. Used figuratively: 'What is the meaning of this?'
54 **Or...or** Either...or.

55 **fancy** imagination. Many editors take it to mean 'love', which is one meaning of 'fancy' but surely not a relevant one here.
55 **still** ever.
55 **Lethe** The river of forgetfulness in the classical underworld.

Act 4, Scene 2
Location Olivia's house (Rowe).
2 **Sir Topas the curate** See 3.4.230 n. for the complimentary use of 'sir'. Though Shakespeare probably derives the name from the burlesque knight in Chaucer's 'Tale of Sir Topas', the topaz, according to Reginald Scot, 'healeth the lunatic person of his passion of lunacie' (quoted by Furness); Batman upon Bartholome (*De Proprietatibus Rerum* (1582), sig. 2Z4) also records that since the topaz follows the course of the moon, it helps against the 'Lunatik' passion, and he cites Dioscorides as saying it aids against 'evill thoughts and phrensie'.
3 **the whilst** in the meantime.

FESTE Well, I'll put it on, and I will dissemble myself in't, and I would
I were the first that ever dissembled in such a gown. I am not tall   5
enough to become the function well, nor lean enough to be thought
a good student; but to be said an honest man and a good
housekeeper goes as fairly as to say a careful man and a great
scholar. The competitors enter.

Enter [SIR] TOBY [*and* MARIA]

SIR TOBY Jove bless thee, Master Parson.   10
FESTE *Bonos dies,* Sir Toby. For as the old hermit of Prague, that never
saw pen and ink, very wittily said to a niece of King Gorboduc,
'That that is, is', so I, being Master Parson, am Master Parson;
for what is 'that' but 'that' and 'is' but 'is'?
SIR TOBY To him, Sir Topas.   15
FESTE What ho, I say! Peace in this prison!
SIR TOBY The knave counterfeits well. A good knave.

9 SD SIR...*and* MARIA] *Theobald; not in* F   12 Gorboduc] Gorbodacke F, *Capell*

4 **dissemble** (1) disguise and (2) conceal one's
true nature. This is the only example of (1) in
Shakespeare (Onions). Both meanings permit a
satiric glance in the next line to 'dissembling'
puritan members of the clergy who concealed the
Genevan black gown under the traditional white
surplice. See Roger Warren, *N&Q* 218 (1973),
136–8.
5 **tall** Probably 'stout' or 'sturdy' to contrast
with 'lean' in the next line.
6 **function** office.
6–7 **nor lean...student** Like Chaucer's Clerk of
Oxenford; 'student' here means 'scholar'. Though
F's form 'student' is (like 'dexteriously' (1.5.49) and
'jealious' (4.3.27 n.)) an Elizabethan variant, both
forms (with and without the *i*) appear in the early
texts. NS notes, somewhat questionably, that it may
reflect Shakespeare's own practice, since the same
form appears in *Ham.* 1.2.177 (Q1 but not F) and
Wiv. 3.1.38 (F but not Q1).
7 **said** called.
7 **honest** honourable. (The primary meaning in
OED.)
7–8 **good housekeeper** one keeping open
hospitality (and therefore prosperous). In calling up
a jury by which to be tried, Sir John Harington in
his mock-encomium *The Metamorphosis of Ajax,*
ed. E. S. Donno, 1962, pp. 223 ff., specifies that he
will have none but those who are great and good
housekeepers, i.e. wealthy owners of great houses.
Given the fact that Feste has been warned about

being turned away (1.5.14–15), it is fitting he should
commend the dispensing of hospitality in great
houses.
8 **goes as fairly** sounds as honourable. Compare
MV 1.1.127–30: 'my chief care / Is to come fairly
off from the great debts / Wherein my time
something too prodigal / Hath left me gag'd'.
8 **careful** careworn from studies (Onions). In
view of the antitheses posed (an honourable as
against a careworn man, a prosperous householder
as against a poor scholar), this sense of the word
seems altogether right. Onions prints it with a
query.
9 **The competitors** My partners.
11 *Bonos dies* Good day. Correctly *bonus dies.* It
is fitting that Feste as clown (and curate) should use
bad Latin.
11–12 **old hermit...Gorboduc** Like Quinapalus (1.5.29) and Pigrogromitus and the Vapians
(2.3.20), this is an example of Feste's mock learning;
Gorboduc, from the name of a legendary British
king, is the title of the first English tragedy in
blank verse, written by Thomas Norton and
Thomas Sackville and published in 1565.
13 **That...is** Compare Feste's ironic observation
at 4.1.6–7. Both statements can be true, at least in
Illyria.
17 **knave** Literally, 'boy', but often a term of
affection, as with Lear addressing the Fool (1.4.96):
'How now, my pretty knave, how dost thou?'

MALVOLIO (*Within*) Who calls there?

FESTE Sir Topas the curate, who comes to visit Malvolio the lunatic.

MALVOLIO Sir Topas, Sir Topas, good Sir Topas, go to my lady.   20

FESTE Out, hyperbolical fiend! How vexest thou this man! Talk'st thou nothing but of ladies?

SIR TOBY Well said, Master Parson.

MALVOLIO Sir Topas, never was man thus wronged. Good Sir Topas, do not think I am mad. They have laid me here in hideous darkness.   25

FESTE Fie, thou dishonest Satan! I call thee by the most modest terms, for I am one of those gentle ones that will use the devil himself with courtesy. Say'st thou that the house is dark?

MALVOLIO As hell, Sir Topas.

FESTE Why, it hath bay windows transparent as barricadoes, and the   30
clerestories toward the south-north are as lustrous as ebony; and yet complain'st thou of obstruction?

MALVOLIO I am not mad, Sir Topas; I say to you this house is dark.

FESTE Madman, thou errest. I say there is no darkness but ignorance, in which thou art more puzzled than the Egyptians in their fog.   35

MALVOLIO I say this house is as dark as ignorance, though ignorance were as dark as hell; and I say there was never man thus abused. I am no more mad than you are. Make the trial of it in any constant question.

FESTE What is the opinion of Pythagoras concerning wildfowl?   40

MALVOLIO That the soul of our grandam might haply inhabit a bird.

FESTE What think'st thou of his opinion?

---

18 SH, SD] SD *precedes* SH *in* F   28 the] *Anon. conj., Cam.; not in* F   31 clerestories] *Conj. Blakeway (in Var. 1821);*
cleere stores F

21 hyperbolical overreaching, raging. Hyperbole is the rhetorical technique of using exaggerated or extravagant language; as an English name for the Greek term, George Puttenham (*The Arte of English Poesie*, ed. G. D. Willcock and A. Walker, 1936, p. 191) gives 'over-reacher' or 'lowd lyar'.

26 modest moderate. As in 1.3.6.

29 as hell A proverbial comparison (Tilley H397).

30 barricadoes fortifications. From the fact that the first barricades in Paris in the sixteenth century were made of casks (from French *barrique* or Spanish *barrica*) filled with earth and stones.

31 clerestories Windows in the upper part of a wall, particularly in large churches or cathedrals.

32 of obstruction of the light being shut out.

35 puzzled bewildered.

35 Egyptians...fog From Exod. 10.21–3, recounting the 'blacke darkenesse' which the Egyptians endured for three days.

38–9 constant question formally conducted discussion (Onions).

40 Pythagoras The Greek philosopher who held, as Gratiano puts it (*MV* 4.1.132–3), 'That souls of animals infuse themselves / Into the trunks of men'.

41 haply perchance. Onions notes that in Shakespeare's early printed texts, the spelling 'haply' occurs about twice as frequently as 'happily', the form that appears here in F.

MALVOLIO I think nobly of the soul, and no way approve his opinion.

FESTE Fare thee well. Remain thou still in darkness. Thou shalt hold
th'opinion of Pythagoras ere I will allow of thy wits, and fear to   45
kill a woodcock lest thou dispossess the soul of thy grandam. Fare
thee well.

MALVOLIO Sir Topas, Sir Topas!

SIR TOBY My most exquisite Sir Topas!

FESTE Nay, I am for all waters.   50

MARIA Thou mightst have done this without thy beard and gown; he
sees thee not.

SIR TOBY To him in thine own voice, and bring me word how thou
find'st him. I would we were well rid of this knavery. If he may
be conveniently delivered, I would he were, for I am now so far   55
in offence with my niece that I cannot pursue with any safety this
sport to the upshot. [*To Maria*] Come by and by to my chamber.

Exit [*with Maria*]

FESTE [*Sings*]   Hey Robin, jolly Robin,
Tell me how thy lady does.

MALVOLIO Fool!   60

---

57 sport to the] *Rowe;* sport the F   57 SD *To Maria*] *This edn; not in* F   57 SD *with Maria*] *Theobald; not in* F
58, 61, 63, 65 SD *Sings*] *Rowe subst.; not in* F   58–9] *As verse, Capell; as prose* F

---

45 allow...wits certify your sanity.

46 woodcock The proverbially stupid bird. Used of Malvolio earlier (2.5.69).

50 Indeed, I can turn my hand to anything (Malone). The literal meaning is much debated; Furness gives several interpretations, and Dent adds examples to Tilley C421 ('To have a cloak for all waters').

51–2 Thou mightst...not Maria's speech serves as a cue to staging, indicating that Sir Topas has spoken to Malvolio from outside a curtain or some kind of enclosure representing the 'dark room'. Such staging also allows the actor (originally, it seems, Robert Armin) to reveal his skill in impersonating by quick shifts of voice at 80–2 and 84–6, where he speaks as Feste and Sir Topas by turns.

55 conveniently delivered without inconvenience set free.

57 to the upshot to its conclusion. A term from archery, indicating the final shot; the term appears again only in *Ham.* F 3879 (5.2.384).

57 SD* At 5.1 we learn that 'in recompense' for Maria's device, Sir Toby 'hath married her'; his

words here would thus seem most appropriately addressed to her. Also, having no further lines to speak, she would naturally exit at this point.

58–65 Hey Robin...another Feste makes himself known to Malvolio by singing part of a dialogue song (thus representing two voices), attributed to Sir Thomas Wyatt but perhaps developed from an earlier version. The following two stanzas are from Wyatt's *Collected Poems*, ed. Kenneth Muir and Patricia Thomson, 1969, pp. 41–2: (1) 'A Robyn / Joly Robyn / Tell me how thy leman [sweetheart] doeth / And thou shall knowe of myn.' (2) 'My lady is unkynd, perde!' / 'Alack, whi is she so?' / 'She loveth an othre better than me, / And yet she will say no.' The music is by Wyatt's courtly contemporary William Cornyshe, and there are scholarly editions of it by Gustave Reese (*Music in the Renaissance*, 1954, p. 770) and John Stevens (*Music at the Court of Henry VIII*, 1962, pp. 38 ff.). For a full account, including manuscript sources, see Seng, pp. 116–19; he notes that the song of a forsaken lover is a further means to gull Malvolio.

FESTE [*Sings*]   My lady is unkind, perdy.

MALVOLIO Fool!

FESTE [*Sings*]   Alas, why is she so?

MALVOLIO Fool, I say!

FESTE [*Sings*]   She loves another –   65
Who calls, ha?

MALVOLIO Good fool, as ever thou wilt deserve well at my hand, help
me to a candle and pen, ink, and paper. As I am a gentleman, I
will live to be thankful to thee for't.

FESTE Master Malvolio?   70

MALVOLIO Ay, good fool.

FESTE Alas, sir, how fell you besides your five wits?

MALVOLIO Fool, there was never man so notoriously abused. I am as
well in my wits, fool, as thou art.

FESTE But as well? Then you are mad indeed, if you be no better in   75
your wits than a fool.

MALVOLIO They have here propertied me: keep me in darkness, send
ministers to me, asses, and do all they can to face me out of my
wits.

FESTE Advise you what you say. The minister is here. [*As Sir Topas*]   80
Malvolio, Malvolio, thy wits the heavens restore. Endeavour thyself
to sleep and leave thy vain bibble babble.

MALVOLIO Sir Topas!

FESTE [*As Sir Topas*] Maintain no words with him, good fellow. [*As
himself*] Who, I, sir? Not I, sir. God b'w'you, good Sir Topas.   85
[*As Sir Topas*] Marry, amen. [*As himself*] I will, sir, I will.

80, 84, 84–5, 86 SD *As Sir Topas…As Sir Topas…As himself…As Sir Topas…As himself*] *Hanmer subst.; not in* F
85 God b'w'] *Pope;* God buy F

61 **perdy** A corruption of the oath *par Dieu*.

72 **besides** out of. As in *Sonnets* 23.1–2: 'As an
unperfect actor on the stage, / Who with his fear
is put besides his part'.

72 **five wits** i.e. mental faculties. Specifically, the
common wit, imagination, fantasy, estimation and
memory.

73 **notoriously abused** egregiously maltreated;
'notoriously' is apparently another of Malvolio's
special words. The only two adverbial instances in
Shakespeare occur here and at 5.1.356; taken
together with the two adjectival uses (5.1.308,
322), the word nicely conveys Malvolio's own sense
of wounded dignity.

75 **But** Only.

77 **propertied** made a movable object. Perhaps
with the suggestion of a piece of stage property in
the comic interlude that is being performed; at

5.1.350 Feste refers to the deception practised on
Malvolio as an 'interlude'.

78–9 **face me…wits** i.e. brazenly (and falsely)
insisting that I am mad. For a similar usage of 'face
me out', see 5.1.77.

80 **Advise you** Consider.

82 **bibble babble** idle talk. The only instance in
Shakespeare, apart from Fluellen's Welsh version,
'pibble babble' (*H5* 4.1.71).

85 **God b'w'you** God be with you. Equivalent
to modern 'good-bye'. F contracts the form to 'God
buy you', perhaps more difficult for a modern
reader to grasp than Pope's form adopted here.

86 **Marry, amen** Though used elsewhere as a
mild expletive (e.g. 1.3.56, 1.5.104, 3.4.90, 3.4.274),
perhaps here it is intended to carry something of the
original sense of invoking the Virgin.

MALVOLIO Fool, fool, fool, I say!

FESTE Alas, sir, be patient. What say you, sir? I am shent for speaking
to you.

MALVOLIO Good fool, help me to some light and some paper; I tell   90
thee, I am as well in my wits as any man in Illyria.

FESTE Well-a-day, that you were, sir!

MALVOLIO By this hand, I am! Good fool, some ink, paper and light,
and convey what I will set down to my lady. It shall advantage thee
more than ever the bearing of letter did.   95

FESTE I will help you to't. But tell me true, are you not mad indeed
or do you but counterfeit?

MALVOLIO Believe me, I am not. I tell thee true.

FESTE Nay, I'll ne'er believe a madman till I see his brains. I will fetch
you light and paper and ink.   100

MALVOLIO Fool, I'll requite it in the highest degree. I prithee be gone.

FESTE [*Sings*]   I am gone, sir,
                        And anon, sir,
                          I'll be with you again,
                        In a trice   105
                        Like to the old Vice,
                          Your need to sustain;
                        Who, with dagger of lath,
                        In his rage and his wrath,
                          Cries, 'Ah ha' to the devil,   110
                        Like a mad lad,
                        'Pare thy nails, dad?'
                        Adieu, goodman devil.   *Exit*

---

102 SD *Sings*] Rowe *subst.; not in* F   102–13] *As* Capell; *lines end* …sir, / …againe: / …vice, / …sustaine. / …wrath,
/ …diuell: / …dad, / …diuell. / F   113 goodman] Capell; good man F

88 shent scolded.

92 Well-a-day Alas. An exclamation, aptly
picking up Malvolio's 'well' of the previous line.

93 By this hand A conventional oath. On the
Elizabethan stage Malvolio perhaps thrusts forth
his hand from behind an arras or 'within' (18 SD) a
curtained area.

94 advantage profit.

97 counterfeit pretend. Compare the passage
in *AYLI* (4.3.165–82) where Rosalind/Ganymede
insists that her swooning was but 'counterfeit'.

102–13 I am gone…devil No music has been
found for these lines, but, given Feste's vocal skills,
it seems likely they were intended to be sung.
F. W. Sternfeld (*Music in Shakespearean Tragedy*,

1963, p. 113) describes the situation here as that of
a 'musical jester goading an anti-musical puritan'.

106 old Vice A character in the morality plays
who carried a harmless dagger of lath; a predecessor
of the Elizabethan fool.

112 Pare thy nails, dad Tilley (N12) dates its
earliest appearance as 1548, and Ard. notes that in
the undated play *Lusty Juventus* (?1565) the Vice is
the devil's son. Slightly earlier than *TN*, Shakespeare
combined several of the elements of the song to
characterise Pistol as 'this roaring devil i'th'old
play, that everyone may pare his nails with a wooden
dagger' (*H5* 4.4.71–2).

113 Adieu…devil Serving as Feste's (perhaps
dancing) exit line, this is probably addressed to

4.3 *Enter* SEBASTIAN

SEBASTIAN This is the air, that is the glorious sun,
            This pearl she gave me, I do feel't and see't,
            And though 'tis wonder that enwraps me thus,
            Yet 'tis not madness. Where's Antonio then?
            I could not find him at the Elephant,   5
            Yet there he was, and there I found this credit,
            That he did range the town to seek me out.
            His counsel now might do me golden service,
            For though my soul disputes well with my sense
            That this may be some error, but no madness,   10
            Yet doth this accident and flood of fortune
            So far exceed all instance, all discourse,
            That I am ready to distrust mine eyes,
            And wrangle with my reason that persuades me
            To any other trust but that I am mad,   15
            Or else the lady's mad; yet if 'twere so,
            She could not sway her house, command her followers,
            Take and give back affairs and them dispatch,
            With such a smooth, discreet, and stable bearing
            As I perceive she does. There's something in't   20
            That is deceivable. But here the lady comes.

Act 4, Scene 3 4.3] *Scæna Tertia.* F   18 them] *Conj. Dyce²;* their F

Malvolio, although it could be conceived as part of the Vice's speech to the devil. Shakespeare uses the term 'goodman' in several ways, of which two are particularly apt here: (1) prefixed to a designation of occupation, as the address to the grave-digger, 'goodman delver', *Ham.* F 3203 (5.1.14), and (2) jocularly and ironically (Onions) as here and in Prince Hal's speech (*1H4* 2.4.92–4): 'I am now of all humors that have show'd themselves humors since the old days of goodman Adam.' The latter also picks up Adam's occupation as a farmer, as in the well-known medieval rhyme 'When Adam delved and Eve span / Who was then the gentleman?'

Act 4, Scene 3
   Location Olivia's garden (Capell).
   6 was had been.
   6 credit report. This meaning of the word is peculiar to Shakespeare (Onions).
   9 my soul...sense i.e. my reason argues soundly in accord with the evidence of my senses.
   11 this accident...fortune this unexpected event and (this) abundant (good) fortune. The

literal 'accident and flood' is now, appropriately, used metaphorically.
   12 instance example, precedent.
   12 discourse reason. As in Hamlet's well-known soliloquy (Q2): 'Sure He that made us with such large discourse,...gave us not / That capability and godlike reason / To fust in us unus'd' (4.4.36–9).
   15 trust conviction.
   17 sway rule or manage.
   18 *Take...dispatch i.e. take in hand her (household) affairs and promptly settle them; 'dispatch' carries the sense of (1) finishing a business and (2) doing it with speed. F's reading 'their', emended here to 'them' following Dyce's suggestion, represents an easy graphic error. Commentators who retain 'their' explain that 'take' governs 'affairs' and 'give back' governs 'dispatch', but even so the line remains an anacoluthon, lacking in grammatical sequence. Sebastian's observation on Olivia's household management, suggesting a passage of time, serves to make the succeeding action seem somewhat less precipitate,
   19 stable steady.
   21 deceivable misleading.

Enter OLIVIA *and* PRIEST

OLIVIA Blame not this haste of mine. If you mean well,
    Now go with me, and with this holy man
    Into the chantry by; there before him,
    And underneath that consecrated roof,   25
    Plight me the full assurance of your faith,
    That my most jealous and too doubtful soul
    May live at peace. He shall conceal it
    Whiles you are willing it shall come to note;
    What time we will our celebration keep   30
    According to my birth. What do you say?
SEBASTIAN I'll follow this good man, and go with you,
    And having sworn truth, ever will be true.
OLIVIA Then lead the way, good father, and heavens so shine,
    That they may fairly note this act of mine!   35

                          Exeunt

5.1 *Enter* CLOWN [FESTE] *and* FABIAN

FABIAN Now, as thou lov'st me, let me see his letter.
FESTE Good Master Fabian, grant me another request.
FABIAN Anything.
FESTE Do not desire to see this letter.
FABIAN This is to give a dog and in recompense desire my dog again.   5

35 SD *Exeunt*] *Exeunt. / Finis Actus Quartus.* F   Act 5, Scene 1   5.1] *Actus Quintus. Scena Prima.* F

24 **chantry** A private endowed chapel where a priest (or priests) sang masses for the souls of specified individuals.
24 **by** near by.
26 i.e. pledge that you accept me as your spouse. Such a pledge or contract (known as *sponsalia per verbi de praesenti*) was legally binding; the priest describes the ceremony at 5.1.145–52.
27 **jealous** F reads 'jealious', which is an Elizabethan variant, but the modern spelling is the more frequent in Shakespeare's texts.
27 **doubtful** apprehensive.
29 **Whiles** Until.
29 **come to note** become known.
30 **What time** At which time.
31 **According...birth** In a fashion that accords with my social rank.
32–5 The couplets here (in contrast with those at

3.4.318–21) accord with Shakespeare's general practice of giving verse to highborn and romantic characters and using rhyme to signal the end of an act.
35 **fairly note** look with favour on.

Act 5, Scene 1
Location Before Olivia's house (Capell).
5 **This...again** Apparently an allusion to the clever response of the queen's kinsman Dr Bullein when she asked him for a dog on which he doted, assuring him that he could have whatever he desired in recompense; having surrendered it, he followed up with his counter-request, 'I pray you give me my dog againe' (from the *Diary* of John Manningham, who also records a Middle Temple performance of *TN*; see p. 1 above).

Enter DUKE [ORSINO], VIOLA, CURIO, *and Lords*

ORSINO Belong you to the Lady Olivia, friends?
FESTE Ay, sir, we are some of her trappings.
ORSINO I know thee well. How dost thou, my good fellow?
FESTE Truly, sir, the better for my foes, and the worse for my friends.
ORSINO Just the contrary: the better for thy friends.   10
FESTE No, sir, the worse.
ORSINO How can that be?
FESTE Marry, sir, they praise me, and make an ass of me. Now my foes
    tell me plainly I am an ass, so that by my foes, sir, I profit in the
    knowledge of myself, and by my friends I am abused; so that,   15
    conclusions to be as kisses, if your four negatives make your two
    affirmatives, why then, the worse for my friends and the better for
    my foes.
ORSINO Why, this is excellent.
FESTE By my troth, sir, no, though it please you to be one of my friends.   20
ORSINO Thou shalt not be the worse for me; there's gold.
FESTE But that it would be double-dealing, sir, I would you could make
    it another.
ORSINO O you give me ill counsel.

7 **trappings** Figuratively, 'superficial decoration'; literally a caparison for a horse, usually gaily ornamented.

13 **Marry…foes** Feste's paradoxical argument derives from his applying the Latin grammatical rule that two negatives make an affirmative to an English construction, and from the multiple senses his words convey. The Latin rule was well known from the authorised *Grammar* of William Lily, which was frequently alluded to in popular writing.

13 **make…of me** thus I become an ass.

14 **plainly** (1) openly and (2) honestly.

14–15 **profit…myself** (1) benefit in the knowledge of myself (i.e. the knowledge that I am an ass), and (2) improve. The first meaning accords with the Socratic doctrine 'Know thyself' (proverbial from 1481 on, Tilley K175). For the second, compare *MM* 3.2.32–3: 'Correction and instruction must both work / Ere this rude beast will profit.'

15 **abused** (1) deceived, (2) disgraced, (3) insulted, (4) maltreated. This fourth meaning appears also at 4.2.73.

15–17 **so…affirmatives** provided that propositions be like kisses, where 'no, no, no, no' may mean 'yes, yes'. Richard Farmer pointed out a parallel in *Lust's Dominion*, now generally assigned to Dekker, Haughton and Day (written *c.* 1600, printed 1657): '"No, no", says "aye", and twice "away" says "stay"' as well as with a Sidney sonnet which is keyed to the grammatical rule 'That in one speech, two negatives affirm' (*Astrophil and Stella*, 63.14, cited in Furness).

16 **your** Used indefinitely to mean 'that you know of' (*OED* Your 5b). Compare *Ant.* 2.7.26–7.

17–18 **the worse…foes** i.e. with respect to my friends, I am (1) worse off and (2) the less (as in *Lear* 1.4.40–1: 'If I like thee no worse after dinner'); with respect to my foes, I am (1) better off and (2) the greater (as in *AYLI* 3.1.2: 'But were I not the better part made mercy').

20 **By…no** For Feste's oath, see 1.3.3 and n., and for a similar self-disparagement with Viola, see 3.1.46.

20 **though** even though.

22 **But…double-dealing** Except that it would be (1) duplicity and (2) double-giving.

FESTE Put your grace in your pocket, sir, for this once, and let your   25
flesh and blood obey it.

ORSINO Well, I will be so much a sinner to be a double-dealer; there's
another.

FESTE *Primo, secundo, tertio* is a good play, and the old saying is 'The
third pays for all'; the triplex, sir, is a good tripping measure; or   30
the bells of St Bennet, sir, may put you in mind – one, two, three.

ORSINO You can fool no more money out of me at this throw. If you
will let your lady know I am here to speak with her, and bring her
along with you, it may awake my bounty further.

FESTE Marry, sir, lullaby to your bounty till I come again. I go, sir,   35
but I would not have you to think that my desire of having is the
sin of covetousness; but, as you say, sir, let your bounty take a nap.
I will awake it anon.   *Exit*

Enter ANTONIO *and* OFFICERS

VIOLA Here comes the man, sir, that did rescue me.

ORSINO That face of his I do remember well;   40
Yet when I saw it last, it was besmeared
As black as Vulcan, in the smoke of war.

---

25 Put...pocket Pay no attention to your honour. This is intended both literally and metaphorically, with a play on 'grace' as (1) favour and (2) the address proper to a duke. (The second meaning could support the idea that Shakespeare originally intended Orsino to be a duke; see 1.1.0 SD n.) Compare the same verbal play in *MM* 4.3.134–5: 'and you shall have.../ Grace of the Duke...'

25–6 let...it i.e. let your human frailty (as opposed to your assumed honour) follow that 'ill counsel'.

27 so much...to be See 2.2.7 for a similar omission of 'as'.

29 *Primo*...play In his request for a third favour, Feste ingeniously resorts to Latin ordinals, with perhaps an allusion to an intricate mathematical game, purportedly invented by Pythagoras, called the 'Philosopher's Game' or the 'battell of numbers'. Played on a double chessboard, odd and even numbers, each under a king, attempt to capture opponents by various mathematical schemes; one form of capture occurs when two numbers find one of their 'enemies' equalling the addition of the two, as 1 and 2 capturing 3. A manual by Ralph Lever and William Fulwood, published in 1563 and dedicated to the Earl of Leicester, refers to French and Latin versions; utilising elaborate mathematical diagrams, the game was surely not for children as Reginald Scot, cited in NS, implies in likening it to 'children's plaie'.

29–30 the old saying...all Tilley T319 ('The third time pays for all'), with variations. Referring to this idea, Falstaff (*Wiv.* 5.1.3–4) notes that 'They say there is divinity in odd numbers, either in nativity, chance, or death.'

30 triplex Triple time in music.

31 St Bennet St Benedict. Of the several churches in London dedicated to the saint, Halliwell suggests that Feste is referring to St Bennet's at Paul's Wharf, located across from the Globe Theatre (cited in Furness).

32 can fool (1) by jesting and (2) by making a fool of me.

32 at this throw on this occasion. With a quibble on 'a cast of the dice', continuing the diction of gambling from 'good play' (29). In place of a wished-for 'tray-trip', a three, Feste has 'thrown' only an 'ames-ace', two aces, the lowest possible throw (Onions).

35 lullaby farewell. Diction prompted by Orsino's use of 'awake' and carried on in the speech with 'take a nap' and 'will awake'. The only other instance in Shakespeare is in *The Passionate Pilgrim* 15.15.

42 Vulcan Blacksmith in the Roman pantheon.

A baubling vessel was he captain of,
For shallow draught and bulk unprizable,
With which, such scathful grapple did he make   45
With the most noble bottom of our fleet,
That very envy, and the tongue of loss,
Cried fame and honour on him. What's the matter?

1 OFFICER Orsino, this is that Antonio
That took the Phoenix and her fraught from Candy,   50
And this is he that did the Tiger board,
When your young nephew Titus lost his leg.
Here in the streets, desp'rate of shame and state,
In private brabble did we apprehend him.

VIOLA He did me kindness, sir, drew on my side,   55
But in conclusion put strange speech upon me,
I know not what 'twas, but distraction.

ORSINO Notable pirate! Thou salt-water thief!
What foolish boldness brought thee to their mercies,
Whom thou, in terms so bloody and so dear,   60
Hast made thine enemies?

ANTONIO   Orsino, noble sir,
Be pleased that I shake off these names you give me.
Antonio never yet was thief or pirate,
Though I confess, on base and ground enough,
Orsino's enemy. A witchcraft drew me hither.   65
That most ungrateful boy there by your side,
From the rude sea's enraged and foamy mouth
Did I redeem; a wrack past hope he was.

43 **baubling** contemptible. In *Tro.* 1.3.35, Nestor refers disparagingly to 'shallow bauble boats'.

44 **unprizable** i.e. not worth being captured as booty ('prize').

45 **scathful grapple** destructive close fighting.

46 **bottom** ship.

47 **very...loss** even (our) mortification and (our) voices as losers.

48 **Cried** Called out. As in *2H4* 4.1.134–5: 'For all the country in a general voice / Cried hate upon him.'

50 **fraught** cargo.

50 **Candy** Used here, correctly, for the capital of Crete, though the Elizabethans frequently used it in reference to the island itself (E. H. Sugden, *A Topographical Dictionary*, 1925, p. 96).

53 **desp'rate...state** regardless of disgrace and danger (to himself).

54 **private brabble** personal quarrel.

55 **on my side** in my defence.

56 **put...upon me** spoke to me in a singular fashion.

57 **but distraction** unless (it were) madness.

58 **Notable** Notorious.

60 **in terms...dear** in a manner so bloodthirsty and so grievous.

62 **shake off** deny.

64 **on base...enough** on sufficient foundation.

65 **witchcraft** A twin effect: as Viola/Cesario has enchanted Olivia (3.1.97), so Sebastian here is said to have bewitched Antonio.

68 **a wrack** wreckage. See *OED* Wrack *sb*² 1b. In Shakespeare's period 'wrack' was not orthographically distinguished from 'wreck'.

His life I gave him, and did thereto add
My love without retention, or restraint,   70
All his in dedication. For his sake,
Did I expose myself, pure for his love,
Into the danger of this adverse town,
Drew to defend him when he was beset;
Where being apprehended, his false cunning   75
(Not meaning to partake with me in danger)
Taught him to face me out of his acquaintance,
And grew a twenty-years' removèd thing
While one would wink; denied me mine own purse,
Which I had recommended to his use   80
Not half an hour before.

VIOLA   How can this be?

ORSINO When came he to this town?

ANTONIO Today, my lord, and for three months before,
No int'rim, not a minute's vacancy,
Both day and night did we keep company.   85

Enter OLIVIA *and Attendants*

ORSINO Here comes the countess; now heaven walks on earth.
But for thee, fellow – Fellow, thy words are madness.
Three months this youth hath tended upon me,
But more of that anon. Take him aside.

OLIVIA What would my lord, but that he may not have,   90
Wherein Olivia may seem serviceable?
Cesario, you do not keep promise with me.

VIOLA Madam!

ORSINO Gracious Olivia –

OLIVIA What do you say, Cesario? Good my lord –   95

87 fellow – Fellow] *Dyce subst.;* fellow, fellow F   94 Olivia –] *Theobald subst.;* Olivia. F   95 lord –] *Rowe subst.;* Lord. F

69 **thereto** besides.
70 **retention** reservation.
71 **All…dedication** i.e. dedicated (my love) wholly to him.
72 **pure** only. (An adverbial use.)
73 **adverse** hostile.
77 **to face…acquaintance** brazenly to deny he knew me. (As at 4.2.78–9.)
78 **removèd** distant.
79 **wink** blink (an eye).

80 **recommended** committed.
83 **three months before** For the double-time scheme, see p. 16 above, n. 2.
84 **int'rim** F's elision; NS notes the same spelling for metrical reasons in *Sonnets* 56.9.
87 **for thee** as for thee.
90 **but that…have** except that which he may not have (i.e. Olivia's love).
92 **keep promise** i.e. 'ever' to be true (4.3.33). Cesario is manifestly now in attendance on Orsino.

VIOLA My lord would speak; my duty hushes me.

OLIVIA If it be aught to the old tune, my lord,
It is as fat and fulsome to mine ear
As howling after music.

ORSINO   Still so cruel?

OLIVIA Still so constant, lord.   100

ORSINO What, to perverseness? You uncivil lady,
To whose ingrate and unauspicious altars
My soul the faithfull'st off'rings have breathed out
That e'er devotion tendered! What shall I do?

OLIVIA Even what it please my lord that shall become him.   105

ORSINO Why should I not – had I the heart to do it –
Like to th'Egyptian thief at point of death
Kill what I love – a savage jealousy
That sometimes savours nobly? But hear me this.
Since you to non-regardance cast my faith,   110
And that I partly know the instrument
That screws me from my true place in your favour,
Live you the marble-breasted tyrant still.
But this your minion, whom I know you love,
And whom, by heaven I swear, I tender dearly,   115

---

103 have] F; hath *Capell;* has *Pope*

96 **duty** sense of respect, obedience.
98 **fat and fulsome** distasteful and disgusting.
101 **uncivil** uncivilised. See 4.1.46 n.
102 **ingrate and unauspicious** thankless and unpropitious. The latter form is used only this once in Shakespeare.
103 **off'rings** F's elision; found elsewhere for the sake of the metre, as in *Tro.* 3216 (5.3.17) and *Mac.* 2.1.52.
103 **have breathed** Pope and even recent editors correct the 'faulty' plural auxiliary, which probably results from the immediately preceding plural object.
105 **become** suit. But also with an overtone of 'grace', as in *Cor.* 2.1.123: 'The wounds become him.'
106–9 This (short-lived) vehemence on Orsino's part, suggesting some degree of violence, is to be compared with his posture as the moody lover in the opening scene of the play. It is also to be contrasted with the actual violence of Sir Toby's and Sir Andrew's fray with Sebastian which is reported at 161 ff.
107 **Like to th'Egyptian thief** A reference to an episode in the Greek romance *Ethiopica* by

Heliodorus (translated in 1569 by Thomas Underdowne) where an Egyptian bandit intends, but fails, to slay a beloved captive when he despairs of his own life. NS quotes Heliodorus's comment: 'If the barbarous people be once in despair of their own safety, they have a custom to kill all those by whom they set much, and whose company they desire after death.'
109 **savours nobly** Figuratively, 'exudes or is redolent of nobility'.
110 **to non-regardance** into disregard. Used only by Shakespeare (Onions).
111 **that** since.
111 **instrument** Figuratively, 'agent'; literally, 'tool' – here suggesting torture.
112 **screws** wrests.
113 **marble-breasted** Metonymy. Compare Lear's 'marble-hearted fiend' (1.4.259). Ironically, Olivia has earlier accused Cesario (3.4.168) of being 'a heart of stone'.
114 **minion** favourite. From French *mignon*, pet, darling. Frequently used by Shakespeare in a contemptuous sense.
115 **tender** regard.

Him will I tear out of that cruel eye
Where he sits crownèd in his master's spite.
Come, boy, with me; my thoughts are ripe in mischief.
I'll sacrifice the lamb that I do love,
To spite a raven's heart within a dove. [*Leaving*]   120
VIOLA And I most jocund, apt, and willingly,
To do you rest, a thousand deaths would die. [*Following*]
OLIVIA Where goes Cesario?
VIOLA   After him I love
More than I love these eyes, more than my life,
More, by all mores, than e'er I shall love wife.   125
If I do feign, you witnesses above
Punish my life for tainting of my love!
OLIVIA Ay me, detested! How am I beguiled!
VIOLA Who does beguile you? Who does do you wrong?
OLIVIA Hast thou forgot thyself? Is it so long?   130
Call forth the holy father.
                                    [*Exit an Attendant*]
ORSINO   Come, away!
OLIVIA Whither, my lord? Cesario, husband, stay!
ORSINO Husband?
OLIVIA   Ay, husband. Can he that deny?
ORSINO Her husband, sirrah?
VIOLA   No, my lord, not I.
OLIVIA Alas, it is the baseness of thy fear   135
That makes thee strangle thy propriety.

120 SD *Leaving*] *Theobald subst.; not in* F   122 SD *Following*] *Theobald; not in* F   131 SD *Exit an Attendant*] *Capell; not in* F

117 **crownèd** See 1.1.38–9 for Orsino's earlier projection of himself as the 'one selfsame king' of Olivia's affections.

117 **in…spite** i.e. spiting his master (by thwarting his desires).

120 **a raven's…dove** An analogy Shakespeare uses in contrasting the inward nature of a person with his outward appearance, as in *2H6* 3.1.75: 'Seems he a dove? his feathers are but borrowed', and *Rom.* 3.2.76: 'Dove-feather'd raven!' See also 3.4.317 n.

121 **apt** ready. The adjectival form is frequently used for the adverbial.

122 **do you rest** give you repose.

125 **by all mores** by all comparatives.

127 **tainting of** discrediting.

128 **detested** 'abhorred', but also 'denounced'. The logical corollary to Cesario's oath at 126–7.

130 **thou** Olivia continues to use the familiar second-person singular in spite of Cesario's rejection of her.

134 **sirrah** The usual form of address to an inferior, as again at 267, 281; in Shakespeare, except for one occasion (*Ant.* 5.2.229), it is an address to a male.

135 **baseness** meanness. It has both a moral and a social sense, the latter contrasted with the high rank of 139.

136 **strangle thy propriety** i.e. disavow yourself as my husband; 'propriety' is used again by Shakespeare only in *Oth.* 2.3.176, and in a different sense.

Fear not, Cesario, take thy fortunes up;
Be that thou know'st thou art, and then thou art
As great as that thou fear'st.

Enter PRIEST

                         O welcome, father!
Father, I charge thee by thy reverence   140
Here to unfold – though lately we intended
To keep in darkness what occasion now
Reveals before 'tis ripe – what thou dost know
Hath newly passed between this youth and me.
PRIEST A contract of eternal bond of love,   145
Confirmed by mutual joinder of your hands,
Attested by the holy close of lips,
Strengthened by th'interchangement of your rings,
And all the ceremony of this compact
Sealed in my function, by my testimony;   150
Since when, my watch hath told me, toward my grave
I have travelled but two hours.
ORSINO [*To Viola*] O thou dissembling cub! What wilt thou be
When time hath sowed a grizzle on thy case?
Or will not else thy craft so quickly grow   155
That thine own trip shall be thine overthrow?

---

153 SD *To Viola*] *This edn; not in* F

137 **take…up** i.e. accept your (prosperous) state and (happy) lot as the husband of a countess.
139 **As great as that** Of as high rank as he whom. Again, an illustration of Shakespeare's fluctuating intention of casting Orsino as duke or count.
140 **by thy reverence** in keeping with the regard due to you.
142 **To keep in darkness** As determined at 4.3.28–9.
142 **occasion** necessity.
146 **joinder** joining. Not pre-Shakespearean in the general sense, though its legal meaning was the 'coupling of two, in an action against another' (Onions).
147 **close** union.
149 **compact** Accented on the final syllable.
150 **function** office. As at 4.2.6.
153 **dissembling** Compare Feste's comments at 4.2.4 and n. Dissembling and disguise are, of course, major motifs running throughout the play and make

for effects both comic in the sub-plot and serious in the main plot.
154 **sowed a grizzle** scattered grey hairs.
154 **case** Either (1) 'body', as in *Ant.* 4.15.89: 'This case of that huge spirit now is cold', or (2) 'skin', as in *WT* 4.4.814–15, where the Clown (punningly) says 'though my case be a pitiful one, I hope I shall not be flay'd out of it'. There is the additional suggestion, according to the references cited in Furness, that it alludes particularly to the skin of a fox, thus picking up the vocative 'dissembling cub'.
155 Or, on the contrary, will not your cunning so rapidly increase?
156 The line offers both literal and figurative meanings; 'trip' = 'stumble' in both a physical and moral sense; it is also the name of a technical trick in wrestling which causes an opponent to 'fall', i.e. be thrown over on his back, thus bringing about his defeat. See *Shakespeare's England*, 2 vols., 1916, II, 455–6.

Farewell, and take her, but direct thy feet
Where thou and I henceforth may never meet.

VIOLA My lord, I do protest –

OLIVIA   O do not swear!
Hold little faith, though thou hast too much fear.   160

Enter SIR ANDREW [*his head bleeding*]

SIR ANDREW For the love of God, a surgeon! Send one presently to
Sir Toby.

OLIVIA What's the matter?

SIR ANDREW H'as broke my head across, and has given Sir Toby a
bloody coxcomb, too. For the love of God, your help! I had rather   165
than forty pound I were at home.

OLIVIA Who has done this, Sir Andrew?

SIR ANDREW The count's gentleman, one Cesario. We took him for a
coward, but he's the very devil incardinate.

ORSINO My gentleman Cesario?   170

SIR ANDREW 'Od's lifelings, here he is! You broke my head for nothing,
and that that I did, I was set on to do't by Sir Toby.

VIOLA Why do you speak to me? I never hurt you.
You drew your sword upon me without cause,
But I bespake you fair, and hurt you not.   175

Enter [SIR] TOBY *and* CLOWN [FESTE]

SIR ANDREW If a bloody coxcomb be a hurt, you have hurt me; I think
you set nothing by a bloody coxcomb. Here comes Sir Toby
halting – you shall hear more; but if he had not been in drink, he
would have tickled you othergates than he did.

---

159 protest –] *Rowe;* protest. F   160 SD *his...bleeding*] *Rowe subst.; not in* F   175 SD SIR, FESTE] *This edn; not in* F

160 Hold little faith Keep to *some* part of your plighted word. See Abbott 86 for omission of the indefinite article.

160 SD As NS notes, the appearance of Sir Andrew with his bleeding head points to a second fray which Shakespeare has not bothered to account for; it is not likely that Sir Andrew would return to active brawling after his threat of 'an action at battery' (4.1.29), nor would Sir Toby be likely to act in defiance of Olivia's words in 4.1.40–2.

164 broke...across cut my head open from side to side.

165 coxcomb head. As in *H5* 5.1.54–5: 'the skin [of the leek] is good for your broken coxcomb'.

169 incardinate in the flesh. Sir Andrew's rendering of 'incarnate'.

171 'Od's lifelings By God's little lives. Compare the equally diminutive ''Od's heartlings' (*Wiv.* 3.4.57), which, as NS points out, shows that Sir Andrew and Slender even swear alike. For the suggestion that John Sincler (or Sincklo) may have played both roles, see 2.3.18 n.

175 fair kindly. (Adverbial form.)

175 SD F's somewhat early SD can emphasise Sir Toby's slow 'halting' entrance; otherwise, it should perhaps come at 177–8.

177 set nothing by think nothing of.

178 halting limping.

179 othergates in another way. An expression surviving in the north and in Warwickshire (Onions).

ORSINO How now, gentleman? How is't with you?   180

SIR TOBY That's all one. H'as hurt me, and there's th'end on't. Sot, didst see Dick Surgeon, sot?

FESTE O he's drunk, Sir Toby, an hour agone; his eyes were set at eight i'th'morning.

SIR TOBY Then he's a rogue, and a passy-measures pavin. I hate a   185
drunken rogue.

OLIVIA Away with him! Who hath made this havoc with them?

SIR ANDREW I'll help you, Sir Toby, because we'll be dressed together.

SIR TOBY Will you help – an ass-head, and a coxcomb, and a knave,   190
a thin-faced knave, a gull?

OLIVIA Get him to bed, and let his hurt be looked to.

[Exeunt Feste, Fabian, Sir Toby, and Sir Andrew]

Enter SEBASTIAN

SEBASTIAN I am sorry, madam, I have hurt your kinsman.
But had it been the brother of my blood,
I must have done no less with wit and safety.   195
You throw a strange regard upon me, and by that

---

181 H'as] *Rowe;* has F   185 pavin] F2, *Rann;* panyn F   192 SD *Exeunt…Andrew]* *Dyce; not in* F

---

181 **That's all one** No matter. See p. 1, n. 4 above, and compare 351 and 384 below.

181 **there's th'end** that's that. Dent (E113.1) gives it as proverbial and occurring frequently in the early plays.

181 **Sot** Sir Toby earlier (1.5.100) had addressed Feste in the same fashion when he was also 'half drunk', so its double meaning applies here as well.

183 **set** Variously explained; Shakespeare's other instances permit of three possible interpretations: (1) 'sunk out of sight', as in *Temp.* 3.2.8–9: 'Drink, servant-monster, when I bid thee. / Thy eyes are almost set in thy head'; (2) 'fixed', as in *The Rape of Lucrece* 1662: 'with sad set eyes', and *Temp.* 2.1.229: 'The setting [fixed look] of thine eye'; and (3) 'closed', as in *John* 5.7.51: 'O cousin, thou art come to set [close] mine eye.' Ard. suggests an image of the setting sun to contrast with 'eight i'th'morning'; the numerical figure, in any case, seems to prompt Sir Toby's response; see next note.

185 **passy-measures pavin** A 'passing measure pavin' (Italian *passamezzo antico*), a slow stately dance in duple time, in contrast with the more animated galliard in triple time, which is what Sir Toby prefers at 1.3.97, 108. The strains of a pavin or pavan were organised in eights and fours

(F. W. Sternfeld, *Music in Shakespearean Tragedy*, 1963, pp. 250–2). The emendation of F's 'panyn' is readily accounted for by foul case – n for u.

187 **made…them** brought them so low. As in *Ado* 4.1.195: 'Nor fortune made such havoc of my means'. The second, much stronger meaning of 'havoc' in Shakespeare (adding a comical overtone here) is 'indiscriminate slaughter', as in *1H4* 5.1.81–2: 'Nor moody beggars, starving for a time / Of pell-mell havoc and confusion'.

188 **be dressed** have our wounds attended to.

190–1 **an ass-head…gull** Compare a similar run of epithets in *H5* 4.1.77–9 (Fluellen to Gower): 'If the enemy is an ass and a fool, and a prating coxcomb, is it meet, think you, that we should also, look you, be an ass and a fool, and a prating coxcomb…?' For Sir Toby's emphasis on Sir Andrew's thinness, see 1.3.35 and 2.3.18 nn.; for his gulling him, see 2.3.156, and 2.5.154 and 3.2.42 nn.

194 **brother of my blood** my own brother.

195 **with…safety** with sensible regard for (my own) safety.

196 **throw…regard** look (upon me) strangely.

I do perceive it hath offended you.
Pardon me, sweet one, even for the vows
We made each other but so late ago.

ORSINO One face, one voice, one habit, and two persons –   200
A natural perspective, that is and is not!

SEBASTIAN Antonio! O my dear Antonio,
How have the hours racked and tortured me,
Since I have lost thee!

ANTONIO Sebastian are you?

SEBASTIAN   Fear'st thou that, Antonio?   205

ANTONIO How have you made division of yourself?
An apple cleft in two is not more twin
Than these two creatures. Which is Sebastian?

OLIVIA Most wonderful!

SEBASTIAN Do I stand there? I never had a brother;   210
Nor can there be that deity in my nature
Of here and everywhere. I had a sister,
Whom the blind waves and surges have devoured.
Of charity, what kin are you to me?
What countryman? What name? What parentage?   215

VIOLA Of Messaline. Sebastian was my father;
Such a Sebastian was my brother, too;
So went he suited to his wat'ry tomb.
If spirits can assume both form and suit,
You come to fright us.

SEBASTIAN   A spirit I am indeed,   220
But am in that dimension grossly clad

---

200 persons –] *This edn;* persons, F

200 One The same.
200 habit costume. At 3.4.332–4, Viola remarked that she imitated Sebastian in 'fashion, colour, ornament'.
201 A natural perspective A deception or illusion produced by nature, in contrast to that produced by an optical device called a 'perspective glass' (referred to in 249 below). There were many kinds; Reginald Scot, for example, names sixteen, the intent of each being to deceive the eye (*The Discovery of Witchcraft*, ed. Montague Summers, 1930, p. 179). 'Perspective' is invariably accented on the antepenultimate syllable in Shakespeare.
205 Fear'st thou that? Do you doubt that?
211 deity godhead.
212 Of here and everywhere Of being

omnipresent. Compare Hamlet's question to the ghost (*Ham.* F 853 (1.5.156)): '*Hic et ubique?*'
213 blind Figuratively, 'undiscerning'.
214 Of charity Out of the goodness of your heart (tell me).
215 What countryman? A man of what country? The same generalised form of query is used in *Shr.* 1.2.189.
218 So...suited Dressed...like you (and like herself).
219 spirits ghosts.
219 form and suit physical appearance and dress.
220 spirit soul. The 'better part' of an individual as *Sonnets* 74.8 has it.
221 am in that...clad (I) am wearing that corporeal form.

Which from the womb I did participate.
Were you a woman – as the rest goes even –
I should my tears let fall upon your cheek,
And say, 'Thrice welcome, drownèd Viola.'   225
VIOLA My father had a mole upon his brow.
SEBASTIAN And so had mine.
VIOLA And died that day when Viola from her birth
      Had numberèd thirteen years.
SEBASTIAN O that record is lively in my soul!   230
      He finishèd indeed his mortal act
      That day that made my sister thirteen years.
VIOLA If nothing lets to make us happy both,
      But this my masculine usurped attire,
      Do not embrace me, till each circumstance,   235
      Of place, time, fortune, do cohere and jump
      That I am Viola, which to confirm
      I'll bring you to a captain in this town,
      Where lie my maiden weeds; by whose gentle help
      I was preserved – to serve this noble count.   240
      All the occurrence of my fortune since
      Hath been between this lady and this lord.
SEBASTIAN [*To Olivia*] So comes it, lady, you have been mistook.
      But nature to her bias drew in that.

---

240 preserved] F; preferr'd *Theobald*   243 SD *To Olivia*] *Rowe*; not in F

---

222 participate have in common with others.

223 as...even since all other circumstances accord. See 249 below for another example of this use of 'as'.

228–9 And died...years In this recognition scene, Ard. suggests that Shakespeare seems to have forgotten that Viola and Sebastian are twins! It is further suggested there that Viola's speech is possibly a 'deliberate attempt' on Shakespeare's part to suggest that Sebastian is not younger than Olivia. But neither a reading nor a viewing audience would necessarily conclude that the voyage on which the twins were shipwrecked followed pat upon the death of their father, so that Viola's specifying her age at the time of his death is simply to provide another token of identification.

230 record recollection. As in *Ant.* 5.2.118–20: 'The record of what injuries you did us, / Though written in our flesh, we shall remember / As things but done by chance.' Here the accent falls on the second syllable.

233 lets hinders.

236 cohere and jump concur and agree.

239 weeds garments. As at 257.

240 preserved – to serve An example of repetition of the stem of a word which is then used in a different form (paregmenon or polyptoton, a rhetorical device much favoured in the 1590s and following). Some editors from Theobald on have emended 'preserved' to 'preferred' just because of that repetition of sound. However, the device serves to call attention both to Viola's happy reunion with Sebastian and to her devotion to Orsino. Observing that the use of this figure is to delight the ear by the derived sound and to stir the mind by the concord of the matter, Henry Peacham (*The Garden of Eloquence* (1593), Scholars' Facsimiles & Reprints, 1954, p. 55) gives an example from Isaiah, 'the wisdom of the wise'. For another instance, see 264–5 below.

244 nature...in that nature made you follow your own bent in being attracted to a disguised form of myself. The metaphor is from the game of bowls.

You would have been contracted to a maid;   245
Nor are you therein, by my life, deceived;
You are betrothed both to a maid and man.

ORSINO Be not amazed, right noble is his blood.
If this be so – as yet the glass seems true –
I shall have share in this most happy wreck.   250
[*To Viola*] Boy, thou hast said to me a thousand times
Thou never shouldst love woman like to me.

VIOLA And all those sayings will I overswear,
And all those swearings keep as true in soul
As doth that orbèd continent the fire   255
That severs day from night.

ORSINO   Give me thy hand.
And let me see thee in thy woman's weeds.

VIOLA The captain that did bring me first on shore
Hath my maid's garments; he upon some action
Is now in durance, at Malvolio's suit,   260
A gentleman and follower of my lady's.

OLIVIA He shall enlarge him; fetch Malvolio hither.
And yet, alas, now I remember me,
They say, poor gentleman, he's much distract.

Enter CLOWN [FESTE], *with a letter, and* FABIAN

A most extracting frenzy of mine own   265

249 so – as…true –] *This edn;* so, as…true, F   250 wreck] *Rowe;* wracke F   251 SD *To Viola*] *Rowe; not in* F
255 orbèd continent the fire] *Rowe³;* Orbed Continent, the fire, F   265 extracting] F; exacting F2; distracting *Hanmer*

247 a maid and man a virgin youth (Schmidt).

249 as yet…true since now the natural perspective (of 201) appears to be a real (not a deceptive) image.

250 most happy wreck i.e. the shipwreck of 213 with its (now) happy outcome (oxymoron). F's 'wrack' is frequently not distinguished in meaning from 'wreck'.

252 like to me as (you do) me.

253 overswear swear over again.

254 swearings oaths. The only other instance in Shakespeare is in *Wiv.* 5.5.160.

254 keep…soul cherish and preserve in my soul. As in *R3* 2.2.119: 'Must gently be preserv'd, cherish'd, and kept'.

255 As that spherical container (i.e. the sun) doth (keep, preserve, and cherish) its fire. This is a much debated passage: 'orbèd continent' has been taken to refer to (1) the sun, (2) the Ptolemaic sphere and (3) the firmament; 'fire' has been thought to refer

to (1) the element of the sun and (2) the sun itself. F's punctuation puts 'fire' in apposition with 'orbèd continent', making for a difficult but possible reading, particularly since Shakespeare frequently identifies the sun with fire: *Cor.* 5.4.45: 'As certain as I know the sun is fire'; *Lear* 2.2.107: 'like the wreath of radiant fire / On [flick'ring] Phoebus' front'; *Ant.* 1.3.68–9: 'By the fire / That quickens Nilus' slime'; *Tim.* 4.3.184: 'Hyperion's quick'ning fire doth shine' and again 437–8: 'the moon's an errant thief / And her pale fire she snatches from the sun'.

256 Give me thy hand i.e. in a symbolic gesture of marriage.

259 action legal charge.

260 in durance imprisoned.

262 enlarge free.

264 much distract mad.

265 most…own my own most mind-withdrawing madness. For the rhetorical trick of

From my remembrance clearly banished his.

How does he, sirrah?

FESTE Truly, madam, he holds Belzebub at the stave's end as well as
a man in his case may do; h'as here writ a letter to you; I should
have given't you today morning. But as a madman's epistles are no   270
gospels, so it skills not much when they are delivered.

OLIVIA Open't and read it.

FESTE Look then to be well edified when the fool delivers the madman.

[*Reads madly*] 'By the Lord, madam –'

OLIVIA How now, art thou mad?   275

FESTE No, madam, I do but read madness; and your ladyship will have
it as it ought to be, you must allow *vox*.

OLIVIA Prithee read i'thy right wits.

FESTE So I do, madonna; but to read his right wits is to read thus.
Therefore, perpend, my princess, and give ear.   280

OLIVIA [*To Fabian*] Read it you. sirrah.

FABIAN [*Reads*] 'By the Lord, madam, you wrong me, and the world
shall know it. Though you have put me into darkness, and given
your drunken cousin rule over me, yet have I the benefit of my
senses as well as your ladyship. I have your own letter that induced   285
me to the semblance I put on; with the which I doubt not but to
do myself much right, or you much shame. Think of me as you
please. I leave my duty a little unthought of and speak out of my
injury.

The madly used Malvolio.'   290

269 h'as] *Rowe*; has F   274 SD *Reads madly*] *Alexander*; not in F   281 SD *To Fabian*] *Rowe*; not in F

repeating the verb stem in 'distract' and 'extracting', see 240 n. above. Older editors frequently
followed the later Folios and read 'exacting'. In
3.4.14, Olivia acknowledged she was as 'mad' as
Malvolio.

266 remembrance memory.

268 holds...end keeps the devil at a distance.
('Belzebub' is F's spelling in its three instances, as
opposed to 'Beelzebub'.) B. J. and H. W. Whiting
(*Proverbs, Sentences, and Proverbial Phrases*, 1968,
s653) date the expression from *c.* 1375. See Tilley
s807.

270–1 epistles...gospels Feste plays on
'epistles' (specified as 'epistles of love' at 2.3.131)
as (1) letters and (2) New Testament Epistles, and
on 'gospels' as (1) the first four books of the New
Testament and (2) unquestionable truths, with a
glance at the proverb 'All is not gospel that cometh
out of his mouth' (Tilley A147).

271 skills not much does not much matter.

271 delivered (1) transferred to the recipient, (2)
related. The latter meaning is frequent in

Shakespeare, as in *Err.* 2.2.163–4: 'for even her very
words / Didst thou deliver to me on the mart'.

273 delivers speaks (for). Still another meaning
of the verb, as when Menenius wishes to tell the
fable of the belly and the members, the First Citizen
says, 'But and't please you, deliver' (*Cor.* 1.1.94–5).

276 and if.

277 vox voice (Latin). Used here for the tone and
volume appropriate to the impersonation.

278 read...wits read according to your true
faculties.

279 to read...thus 'to read his *wits right* is
to read thus' (Dr Johnson, Var. 1785, quoted in
Furness). An example of hyperbaton (improper
word order) for the sake of the jest.

280 perpend consider. As Schmidt notes, it is a
word used only by Pistol, Polonius and the clowns.

286 with the which i.e. with the letter.

288 leave...unthought of i.e. ignore somewhat my respect (for) and submission (to you)
– decorum proper to a steward.

OLIVIA Did he write this?

FESTE Ay, madam.

ORSINO This savours not much of distraction.

OLIVIA See him delivered, Fabian; bring him hither.

                                                        [Exit Fabian]

    My lord, so please you, these things further thought on,   295

    To think me as well a sister as a wife,

    One day shall crown th'alliance on't, so please you,

    Here at my house, and at my proper cost.

ORSINO Madam, I am most apt t'embrace your offer.

    [To Viola] Your master quits you; and for your service

        done him,   300

    So much against the mettle of your sex,

    So far beneath your soft and tender breeding,

    And since you called me master for so long,

    Here is my hand; you shall from this time be

    Your master's mistress.

OLIVIA   Ah, sister, you are she!   305

Enter [FABIAN *with*] MALVOLIO

ORSINO Is this the madman?

OLIVIA   Ay, my lord, this same.

    How now, Malvolio?

MALVOLIO   Madam, you have done me wrong,

    Notorious wrong.

OLIVIA   Have I, Malvolio? No.

MALVOLIO Lady, you have. Pray you, peruse that letter.

    You must not now deny it is your hand;   310

    Write from it, if you can, in hand, or phrase,

---

294 SD *Exit Fabian*] *Capell; not in* F   300 SD *To Viola*] *Rowe; not in* F   305 Ah] *Sugg. NS;* A F   305 SD *Fabian with*] *Capell; not in* F   306–7 Ay...Malvolio] *As Capell; one line in* F

294 delivered released. A fourth sense of the word in this scene.

295–6 so please...wife if it please you, these matters having been further considered, to have as much regard for me as a sister as you would have had as a wife. Orsino, accordingly, addresses Olivia at 361 as 'sweet sister'.

297 One day...on't The same (wedding) day shall perfect (this) joining of relationship; 'one' = 'same', as in 200 above;

    297 on't of it. A frequent sense.

    298 proper own.

299 apt ready.

300 quits releases.

301 mettle nature.

305 *Ah NS suggests that 'A' (the reading in F) is a common spelling for 'Ah' and refers to the ballad from which Feste sings (quoted in 4.2.58–65 n.). Viola is already Olivia's sister by virtue of the contract with Sebastian (as Ard. points out). The emphasis in the line would thus be on 'she', looking back to Orsino's 'master's mistress'.

308 Notorious wrong See 4.2.73 n.

311 from it differently.

Or say 'tis not your seal, not your invention.
You can say none of this. Well, grant it then,
And tell me, in the modesty of honour,
Why you have given me such clear lights of favour,   315
Bade me come smiling and cross-gartered to you,
To put on yellow stockings, and to frown
Upon Sir Toby, and the lighter people;
And acting this in an obedient hope,
Why have you suffered me to be imprisoned,   320
Kept in a dark house, visited by the priest,
And made the most notorious geck and gull,
That e'er invention played on? Tell me, why?

OLIVIA Alas, Malvolio, this is not my writing,
Though I confess much like the character.   325
But, out of question, 'tis Maria's hand.
And now I do bethink me, it was she
First told me thou wast mad; then cam'st in smiling,
And in such forms which here were presupposed
Upon thee in the letter. Prithee, be content;   330
This practice hath most shrewdly passed upon thee;
But when we know the grounds, and authors of it,
Thou shalt be both the plaintiff and the judge
Of thine own cause.

FABIAN   Good madam, hear me speak,
And let no quarrel, nor no brawl to come,   335
Taint the condition of this present hour,
Which I have wondered at. In hope it shall not,
Most freely I confess, myself and Toby
Set this device against Malvolio here,

312 invention device. This sense of the word is used also at 323, and is so specified at 339.

314 in...honour in the name of decency and propriety (Ard.).

315 clear lights manifest notice.

318 Sir Toby...people i.e. your inferiors, specified in Maria's letter, 2.5.124.

319 an obedient hope a dutiful expectancy.

321 the priest Referring to the impersonating Sir Topas (not to the Priest who was summoned at 131); a curate is an assistant to a parish priest.

322 geck dupe. The only other instance in Shakespeare is in *Cym.* 5.4.67–8: 'And to become the geck and scorn / O'th'other's villainy'; according to Onions, the term survives in midland dialect.

323 played on sported with.

325 the character my handwriting.

326 out of beyond.

328 then cam'st With the second-person singular, the nominative (here 'thou') is readily understood (Abbott 401).

329 forms ways.

329 presupposed earlier enjoined. Used only here in Shakespeare.

331 This...passed This trick has been most mischievously perpetrated.

335 nor no brawl to come nor any squabble in the future. For the use of double negatives, see 3.1.144 n.

336 condition (happy) situation.

337 wondered marvelled.

Upon some stubborn and uncourteous parts   340
We had conceived against him. Maria writ
The letter, at Sir Toby's great importance,
In recompense whereof he hath married her.
How with a sportful malice it was followed
May rather pluck on laughter than revenge,   345
If that the injuries be justly weighed,
That have on both sides passed.

OLIVIA Alas, poor fool, how have they baffled thee!

FESTE Why, 'Some are born great, some achieve greatness, and some
have greatness thrown upon them.' I was one, sir, in this interlude, 350
one Sir Topas, sir – but that's all one. 'By the Lord, fool, I am not
mad.' But do you remember – 'Madam, why laugh you at such a
barren rascal, and you smile not, he's gagged'? And thus the
whirligig of time brings in his revenges.

MALVOLIO I'll be revenged on the whole pack of you!   [*Exit*] 355

OLIVIA He hath been most notoriously abused.

341 against] F; in *Rann, conj. Tyrwhitt*   355 SD *Exit*] *Rowe; not in* F

340–1 Upon...him As a consequence of some rude and uncivil characteristics, and perhaps actions, we had attributed to him in our minds. Compare *AWW* 4.5.74–6: 'His Highness hath promis'd me to do it, and to stop up the displeasure he hath conceiv'd against your son...' For 'upon' meaning 'as a consequence', see Abbott 191; rather oddly, he suggests (244) that there is a confusion in the speech between 'conceiving enmity' and 'disliking parts', but in explaining the motivation for their actions, Fabian is also tactfully implying that *their* conception of Malvolio may not quite square with the actuality. Some editors, following Rann, needlessly emend 'against' to 'in' but only to produce the same interpretation as above.

341–2 Maria...importance It was Maria, of course, who determined 'to gull him into an ayword' and contrived the means to do so (2.3.114 ff. and 139 ff.). Fabian is again being tactful.

342 importance importunity.

343 In recompense...her As projected at 2.5.150.

344 sportful malice merry displeasure (oxymoron); 'malice' is used as in *AYLI* 1.2.277–83, and again in *Cor.* 2.2.21–3: 'Now, to seem to affect the malice and displeasure of the people is as bad as that which he dislikes, to flatter them for their love.' In other contexts it has a stronger force.

344 followed carried out.

345 pluck on induce.
348 fool victim.
348 baffled contemptuously treated. It is the term Malvolio himself had earlier used in considering how he would behave towards Sir Toby (2.5.134).
349–50 'Some...them' Here again (and at 351–2 and 352–3) Feste has a chance to impersonate Malvolio's manner of speaking.
351 that's all one no matter. As at 181 above and again at 384.
352–3 But do you...gagged Specifically recalling Malvolio's putting down of Feste at 1.5.67–72.
354 whirligig of time i.e. a 'whirling gig' (as Mulcaster calls a child's top in *Positions* (1581), ed. R. H. Quick, 1888, p. 80) which time spins. Compare *LLL* 5.1.66–7 where Holofernes exasperatedly says to Moth, 'Thou disputes like an infant; go whip thy gig.' For Sir Toby's earlier reference to the 'parish top' which was used by adults, see 1.3.34.
355 pack gang (of conspirators). As in *Wiv.* 4.2.117–18: 'O you panderly rascals, there's a knot, a ging [= gang], a pack, a conspiracy against me.'
356 notoriously Given Malvolio's repetition of the adjective 'notorious' at 308 and 322, and his earlier use of it in complaining to Feste, Olivia's use of the term here suggests a more lighthearted mood than some critics tend to acknowledge. See 4.2.73 n.

ORSINO Pursue him, and entreat him to a peace.
He hath not told us of the captain yet.

[Exit Fabian]

When that is known, and golden time convents,
A solemn combination shall be made   360
Of our dear souls. Meantime, sweet sister,
We will not part from hence. Cesario, come –
For so you shall be while you are a man,
But when in other habits you are seen,
Orsino's mistress, and his fancy's queen.   365

Exeunt [all but Feste]

(*Clown sings*)

When that I was and-a little tiny boy,
    With hey, ho, the wind and the rain,
A foolish thing was but a toy,
    For the rain it raineth every day.

But when I came to man's estate,   370
    With hey, ho, the wind and the rain,
'Gainst knaves and thieves men shut their gate,
    For the rain it raineth every day.

358 SD *Exit Fabian] Ard.; not in* F   365 SD.1 *all but Feste] Dyce subst.; not in* F

358 the captain i.e. who holds Viola's last token – her maiden weeds (239) – and who is imprisoned at Malvolio's suit (259–60).

359 golden time golden = (1) auspicious and (2) precious (as in *Sonnets* 3.12: 'thy golden time'); time = (1) occasion and (2) season. These multiple significances serve to evoke earlier motifs – the transitory nature of youth and beauty, the reliance on time to resolve situations – and also to evoke the antique 'golden world' (*AYLI* 1.1.118–19) of idyllic contentment.

359 convents calls (us).

360 combination union.

365 fancy's love's. As at 1.1.14 and 2.4.31.

365 SD The exiting of all the cast except Feste, whose song is in place of the usual spoken epilogue, parallels the endings, for example, of *MND* and *AYLI* where Puck and Rosalind, respectively, remain alone on stage to ask for the plaudit. *TN* is the only play of Shakespeare that begins and ends in music.

366–85 The surviving music of Feste's song is a 'traditional tune' with a number of related versions; the earliest is in Joseph Vernon's *The New Songs in the Pantomime of the Witches: the Celebrated Epilogue in the Comedy of Twelfth Night....Sung by*

Mr. Vernon at Vaux Hall, composed by *J. Vernon* [1772]. It was also later attributed to [?Henry] Fielding in a version which was printed by William Chappell in *A Collection of National English Airs*, 2 vols., 1840. Sternfeld (*Music in Shakespearean Tragedy*, 1963, pp. 189–91, and *Songs from Shakespeare's Tragedies*, 1964, pp. 22–5) gives transcriptions of both. For details, see Seng, pp. 123–30.

366–9 When that...day For a related stanza, see the Fool's song in *Lear* 3.2.74–7.

366 and-a The same musical adjustment appears (as NS notes) in *Oth.* 2.3.89 (in the ballad of King Stephen) where F hyphenates 'and-a', though in *Lear* (in another stanza of the Fool's song – see previous note) F hyphenates 'and a little-tyne wit'. Compare the line in Silence's song (*2H4* 5.3.48): 'And a merry heart lives long-a', and the rhymes in Autolycus's ballads (*WT* 4.3.124–6, 4.4.317, 320, 323): 'stile-a', 'mile-a', 'dear-a', 'wear-a', 'ware-a' (these also from F).

368 A foolish...toy A childish prank was accepted as something trivial.

372 i.e. in an adult, such pranks were considered proper only to knaves and thieves.

But when I came, alas, to wive,
　With hey, ho, the wind and the rain,   375
By swaggering could I never thrive,
　For the rain it raineth every day.

But when I came unto my beds,
　With hey, ho, the wind and the rain,
With tosspots still 'had drunken heads,   380
　For the rain it raineth every day.

A great while ago the world begun,
　With hey, ho, the wind and the rain,
But that's all one, our play is done,
　And we'll strive to please you every day.   [*Exit*]   385

378, 380 beds...heads] F; *bed...head* / *Hanmer*   380 'had] *This edn; had* F; *I had* / *Hanmer; still I had* / *Collier*²
382 begun] *Rowe; begon* F   383 With hey] F2; *hey* F   385 SD *Exit*] *Rowe;* FINIS. F

376 swaggering blustering. Compare Sir Toby's advice to Sir Andrew before the mock duel with Cesario, where he acknowledges that a 'terrible oath, with a swaggering accent sharply twanged off' can better attest to an individual's manliness than an actual fight (3.4.150–2).
376 thrive prosper. The rhyme thrive / wive is commonplace, as with Petruchio in *Shr.* 1.2.55–6: 'And I have thrust myself into this maze, / Happily to wive and thrive as best I may.'
378–80 But when...heads This stanza has been variously interpreted (as well as rejected by some as non-Shakespearean). The first interpretation is Kittredge's: 'beds' means 'being drunk on various occasions'; ''had' (380) means 'I had', with an elision of the pronoun (as with F's 'ha's' for 'he has' at 1.5.122 and F's 'has' at 181 and 269 above). A paraphrase would be: 'But on whatever occasion I fell into bed / ... / Like other topers I was always drunk.' (Compare 'drunken heads' with 'drunken

brain' (*Venus and Adonis* 910).) The second interpretation is suggested by Halliwell who (after Hanmer) emended 'beds/heads' to singular forms and quotes a passage from Overbury's *Characters* (1615) which, like the chronological progression in the song, equates 'bed' with death or old age. Thus if a man dies in his infancy, it is said, he has only broken his fast in this world; if he dies in his youth, he has left us at dinner; but at three score and ten 'it is bedde time' (cited in Furness). Accordingly, a paraphrase would be: 'But at the time I reached three score and ten, the normal span of one's life according to the psalmist, Ps. 90.10] like other topers I was always drunk.'
384–5 But...every day These lines have a parallel in the epilogue to *AWW*, where the title of the play is echoed in the request for the plaudit: 'now the play is done; / All is well ended, if this suit be won, / That you express content'. For the aptness of the phrase 'that's all one', see p. 1, n. 4 above.

TEXTUAL ANALYSIS

As Charlton Hinman has determined from his bibliographical investigation of the First Folio, the first 21 quires, allocated to the section of the Comedies (from the beginning of quire A to the end of quire X, pp. 1–252, *The Tempest* to the first 23 pages of *All's Well That Ends Well*), were produced in regular alphabetical sequence.[1] Then because of some 'short-lived' trouble, the normal sequence was interrupted: quire X, which included 12 pages of *All's Well*, was not followed by Y and Z but rather by quires a and b in the section allocated to the Histories (pp. 1–24, *King John* and 2 pages of *Richard II*). Then came a return to the Comedies with quires Y and Z (pp. 253–75, the ending of *All's Well*, 1¼ pages, and *Twelfth Night*). There was another short delay occasioning another shift to the Histories with quire c (pp. 25–36, 12 pages of *Richard II*) and, finally, a return to the Comedies with the last 3 quires given over to *The Winter's Tale* (Aa–Cc, pp. 277–303). Thus the sequence of printing that was followed in bringing the section of the Comedies to completion was as follows:

A–X, a–b (*King John* and 2 pages of *Richard II*), Y–Z (1¼ pages of *All's Well* and *Twelfth Night*), c (12 pages of *Richard II*), Aa–Cc (*Winter's Tale*).

Twelfth Night occupies signatures Y2–z6, with the verso blank (pp. 255–75, with 265 mispaged as 273). In itself, this blank verso suggests some irregularity in the sequence of printing, since it is the only instance of a blank page coming between plays in the section of the Comedies, though there are two such in the section allocated to the Tragedies with *Timon* and – the originally cancelled – *Troilus and Cressida*, both of which caused difficulties in the sequence of printing, the latter probably because of problems of copyright. Having determined, by several sorts of bibliographical analysis, the order of the printing of the plays in the Folio, Hinman concluded that the copy for both *Twelfth Night* and *The Winter's Tale*, which would complete the section of the Comedies, was not readily available, though, since neither had been printed before, it would not have been in their case a question of copyright, and he concluded that it was probably the result of some 'short-lived' trouble (II, 521). What that short-lived trouble might have been is discussed below.

By tracing the compositor's preferred spellings – *do, go, heere* – Hinman established that it was Compositor B who set all of *Twelfth Night*;[2] he also established that only 3 pages of the text were proofread and that this proofing removed only 3 inked space quads, leaving the text untouched (I, 263–4). Though Compositor B, in fact, set more

[1] This survey of the textual history of *Twelfth Night* is based on Hinman's invaluable two-volume study (*The Printing and Proof-reading of the First Folio of Shakespeare*, 1963; the pagination is that of the original numbering in the Folio not of the modern pagination in the Hinman facsimile cited at p. 152, n. 1).

[2] Hinman, I, 422. For other preferred characteristics of Compositor B, see Alan E. Craven, 'Justification of prose and Jaggard Compositor B', *ELN* 3 (1965), 15–17, and T. H. Howard-Hill, 'The compositors of Shakespeare's Folio Comedies', *SB* 26 (1973), 61–106.

than half of the Folio, Hinman characterises him as taking all manner of liberties with the text and exhibiting a careless disregard for the authority of the copy.[1] Such evaluation can, of course, be made most readily when there is an earlier printed exemplar extant for comparison. Since *Twelfth Night* was set from manuscript, there is no certainty as to whether Compositor B did or did not take any undue liberties; and, all editors agree, the text is remarkably free of verbal cruxes though there are some misprints or, perhaps, misreadings, some probable misassignment of speeches, and some missing stage directions.[2] The division into acts and scenes is adequate except perhaps for 3.4.231, where the exiting of Cesario with Fabian clears the stage as if a new (but unmarked) scene was to begin. One peculiarity of the text is the use of Latin to indicate the end of four of its five acts. Though it is the normal practice in the Comedies to have *Finis* at the end of Act 5, a notation of it at the end of the other acts is not.

Act 1 reads *Finis, Actus primus* (the comma saving it from 'gross' grammatical fault, though it is changed to the correct *primi* in F2+).
Act 2 reads *Finis Actus secundus* (changed to *secundi* in F2+).
Act 4 reads *Finis Actus Quartus* (changed to *Quarti* in F2+).

The same ungrammatical *Finis Actus Primus* appears at the end of Act 1 of *Love's Labour's Lost* while a simple *Finis*, apparently standing for the full phrase, appears at the end of Act 1 of *The Two Gentlemen of Verona*. Neither of these plays was set by Compositor B. The text of *Love's Labour's Lost* derives from the first quarto (1598), which like most quartos lacks act and scene division, and it is generally accepted as having derived from Shakespeare's (very) foul papers. In this case the ungrammatical Latin ending *may* have been used to fill up the bottom of the b column in the Folio where otherwise there would have been a good bit of 'white' space. *Two Gentlemen of Verona* is also generally accepted as deriving from foul papers but this time from a transcript of them made by the scribe Ralph Crane, and its use of the Latin form at the end of Act 1, together with the similar instances in *Twelfth Night* at the ends of Acts 1, 2 and 4, cannot be accounted for on the basis of the typographic appearance of the page. E. E. Willoughby, who first pointed out the five instances, concluded, somewhat diffidently, that all of them were provided by the same person, while W. W. Greg concluded that in the case of *Two Gentlemen of Verona* and *Twelfth Night* they were non-editorial and probably in the copy which the compositors used from the start.[3] As pointed out above, *Two Gentlemen* probably derives from a transcript of Shakespeare's foul papers prepared by Ralph Crane. Could the source of copy for *Twelfth Night* also have been a transcript of Shakespeare's foul papers?

This is, in fact, what Robert K. Turner suggested in 1975 in his careful analysis

[1] *The First Folio of Shakespeare* (The Norton Facsimile), 1968, pp. xviii–xix.
[2] An anomaly appears at 1.5.138 SD where the name *Violenta* is given in place of Viola; the same name, curiously, is also wrongly substituted in *All's Well That Ends Well* (3.4.0 SD) for Diana. Since the quire in which this appears was also set by Compositor B, Robert K. Turner ('The text of *Twelfth Night*', *SQ* 26 (1975), 130 n.) suggests that on seeing the abbreviation *Vio.* he merely expanded it to the name he had set, a good bit earlier, in *All's Well*.
[3] Willoughby, 'Phrases marking the termination of acts in the First Folio', *MLN* 45 (1930), 463–4, and Greg, *The Editorial Problem in Shakespeare*, 1942, 3rd edn, 1954, pp. 128 n., 141, 145 and n.

of the text (cited at p. 164, n. 2), and his suggestion was endorsed in the Arden edition which appeared in 1975. Up until then the generally accepted view was that the copy for *Twelfth Night* was a prompt copy (or a transcript of it), though, as G. Blakemore Evans observed in 1974 (Riverside edn, p. 440), the evidence for its theatre provenance is comparatively slight. Turner not only presents evidence to counter this prompt-copy theory, but he also presents cogent reasons for acknowledging that the copy-text was a scribal transcription of Shakespeare's foul papers.

Defined as the author's last complete draft before its being transcribed in a fair copy, foul papers exhibit the following characteristics: (1) loose ends, false starts and unresolved confusions in the text; (2) inconsistencies in designating characters in speech headings and in stage directions, particularly exits, which would have to be straightened out in the prompt-book; (3) the appearance of indefinite and permissive stage directions; and (4) a vague number of supernumeraries.[1]

As Turner points out, *Twelfth Night* exhibits a good many of these characteristics. There is the confusion about the rank of Orsino, whether duke or count; there are some inconsistencies and loose ends; some exits are not provided for (1.5.26, 88, 114, 179, 266; 2.2.38; 2.3.100; 2.4.12; 3.1.78; 3.4.14, 54, 57 (incomplete), 167, 184, 323 (incomplete), 335, 342; 4.1.26, 44; 4.2.3, 57 (incomplete); 5.1.131, 192, 294, 355, 358) just as some entrances are missing or incomplete (1.5.26 SD omits the attendants whom Feste addresses at 32 and 43; 5.1.305 SD (incomplete)). The number of supernumeraries is not specified (*other Lords*, 1.1.0 SD.2; *sailors*, 1.2.0 SD; *Attendants*, 1.4.8 SD; *others*, 2.4.0 SD; *Lords*, 5.1.5 SD; *Attendants*, 5.1.85 SD). Curio is specified as entering with 'LORDS' in Act 5 but has nothing to say or do. Asides are not marked, though this lapse is common in printed dramatic texts. Some of the stage directions, moreover, could as easily be authorial as theatrical, for example 'Enter Valentine *and* Viola *in man's attire*', 1.4.0 SD; 'Enter Viola *and* Malvolio *at several doors*', 2.2.0 SD. At 3.1.115, Olivia says, 'The clock upbraids me with the waste of time'; an experienced dramatist, envisioning the scene, might well have inserted the earlier '*Clock strikes*'. Finally, the scant evidence that any oaths or profanities were expurgated argues for copy based on foul papers since they, of course, antedated the Act of Abuses (1606).

Given, then, the degree to which the text of *Twelfth Night* exhibits the characteristics of foul papers as well as the characteristics of a scribal copy – for example, the regularisation of Orsino's title in stage directions but not within the text – when could such a copy have been made? It could, of course, have been before the preparation of the prompt copy, but since there was an interruption of the sequence of the printing of the Comedies, Jaggard (the head of the printing-house and a member of the syndicate that undertook to publish the Folio) may have decided that it was preferable to halt production of that section until good copies were available before setting both *Twelfth Night* and *The Winter's Tale* and thus completing the section of the Comedies. It should be recognised that *The Winter's Tale* is generally accepted as having been

[1] See Fredson Bowers, *On Editing Shakespeare and the Elizabethan Dramatists*, 1955, pp. 13–14; W. W. Greg, *The Shakespeare First Folio*, 1955, p. 142; David Bevington, *Complete Works of Shakespeare*, 1980, p. 81.

set from a transcript made by Ralph Crane especially for inclusion in the Folio, the prompt-book having, it seems, been lost.[1] If a transcript of *Twelfth Night* had also been prepared at this time, the 'short-lived' trouble delaying the printing of both plays that Hinman referred to (see p. 163 above) would thus be accounted for by the time required to prepare scribal copies for both plays.

It may be recalled that the first four Comedies in the Folio were also set from transcriptions especially prepared for the press, which led Greg to conclude that at the outset transcription appears to have been the editorial policy for the printing of the Folio (*First Folio*, pp. 217, 336). These four comedies (*Tempest, Two Gentlemen, Merry Wives* and *Measure for Measure*), together with *Winter's Tale*, are generally accepted as set from scribal copies prepared by Ralph Crane. Of the Folio's fourteen comedies, these five plus *As You Like It* and *Twelfth Night* are the only ones which are regularly divided into acts and scenes.[2] Copy for *As You Like It* is also accepted as a transcript but of exactly what is debated: Evans (1974) suggested a transcript of 'some form of Shakespeare's manuscript (perhaps "fair copy")'; Agnes Latham (1975), a transcript of 'good prompt copy' made either when the play was new or later for the Folio; and Richard Knowles (1977), a form of Shakespeare's manuscript but now, specifically, 'foul papers'.[3]

Thus it appears that half of the Comedies, and these characterised (like *Twelfth Night*) by division into acts and scenes, were set from scribal transcriptions. That it was standard practice to employ scribes within printing-houses was, most interestingly, substantiated in 1977 by James Binns. In a survey of about 550 Latin books printed in England between *c.* 1550 and 1640, he noted that it was standard for a printer to employ a scribe to make a fair copy of an author's work. In one of the instances he cites, the printer accounts for compositorial errors in the printed text on two grounds: (1) the scribe's 'hasty copying' of the manuscript and (2) the 'maladroit hands' of the workmen.[4] Although his references are to works in Latin, the practice of printers in Latin and English must have been much the same; such a conclusion would certainly be indicated by one instance Binns cites dating from 1584 where there is a rare reference to printing by formes; the practice of casting off copy for books printed in England, it may be remembered, was first posited in 1948.[5]

Was, then, the scribe responsible for the transcription of *Twelfth Night* a nameless employee of the Jaggard firm or was he Ralph Crane, who, possessing 'one blest Gift,

[1] G. B. Evans, *The Riverside Shakespeare*, 1974, p. 1604, citing the *Office Book* of the Master of the Revels from Malone's *Shakespeare*, 1790, I, Pt. ii, p. 226, since the *Office Book* was also subsequently lost.
[2] *The Taming of the Shrew* is imperfectly divided and the rest of the plays have act division only.
[3] Evans, p. 400; Agnes Latham (ed.), *AYLI*, 1975, p. xi; Richard Knowles (ed.), *AYLI*, 1977, p. 334.
[4] 'STC Latin books: evidence for printing-house practice', *The Library*, 5th ser., 32 (1977), 1–27. Also of great editorial interest are the comments relating to the necessity of correct punctuation for clarity of meaning.
[5] William H. Bond, 'Casting off copy by Elizabethan printers: a theory', *PBSA* 42 (1948), 281–91. A check of *STC* books published by the Jaggard firm up to 1623 (on the basis of Paul G. Morrison, *Index of Printers, Publishers and Booksellers*, 1950) reveals that the firm was in the main oriented to publishing books in English; in 1608, however, it published Robert Glover's *Nobilitas et civilis* and in 1620 a now untraced *Lexico-Graeco-Latinum*.

A ready Writers Pen', is accepted as having transcribed at least five of the Comedies?[1]
Some of the general characteristics of Crane's manuscripts appear in the text of
Twelfth Night: the division into acts and scenes; the heavy use of colons and
semi-colons (see p. 53 above); the use of apostrophes to mark shortened forms (like
ha's), along with a preference for *o'th* (the only form in *Twelfth Night*) over *a'th*, and,
most conspicuously, to mark the elision of *-ed* forms even in prose passages; the heavy
use of parentheses for parenthetical remarks and single words of address; and, lastly,
hyphenated forms.[2]

According to the specialist on Crane's scribal characteristics, T. H. Howard-Hill,
it is his orthography, however, that is the most decisive factor in providing evidence
of his practice.[3] He concludes, in accord with what has long been believed, that Crane
transcribed the first four Comedies and *The Winter's Tale* for the Folio, but he also
concludes that he worked from foul papers, which in the case of *The Winter's Tale*
underwent two transcriptions, once to replace the missing prompt-book (relicensed
on 19 August 1623) and a second time from his own transcription to provide the copy
that was used for setting up the Folio text.[4]

In his attempt to establish the characteristics of Crane's transcripts that might be
reflected in the Folio Comedies, Howard-Hill examined the ones set by Compositor
B, including *Twelfth Night*. After excluding possibly justified spellings in long lines
and those for which there were no alternatives, he considered for this play 47 examples
of what he believed represented B's 'preferred' spellings (*Ralph Crane*, Appendix 4).
These examples were taken from a study by W. S. Kable who based his investigation
on the assumption that B had set all the Pavier quartos,[5] a collection of 10
Shakespearean and non-Shakespearean items published in 1619 by Thomas Pavier
and printed by the Jaggard firm, 5 of which carried false dates. Subsequently Kable's
findings were questioned on two grounds: (1) that B as sole compositor of the Pavier
quartos has not been established and (2) that the study showed statistical error.[6]

For his investigation of *Twelfth Night*, Howard-Hill correlated these 'preferred'
spellings of B (as set forth by Kable) with the 'preferred' spellings of Crane (as
determined by his own studies), along with other possible spellings of these words,
and concluded that Crane did not prepare the copy for *Twelfth Night*. But since the

---

[1] See F. P. Wilson's informative account, 'Ralph Crane, scrivener to the king's players', *The Library*, 4th ser., 7 (1926–7), 194–215. The quotation comes from one of Crane's biographical prefaces, cited *ibid.*, p. 196.
[2] See Evans's textual note to *The Tempest* (p. 1636) for a fuller listing of Crane's characteristics. He notes that the combined appearance in the text of four or five of the seven he lists may be taken as strong evidence of Crane's hand in the manuscript copy.
[3] *Ralph Crane and Some Shakespeare First Folio Comedies*, 1972, p. 91.
[4] *Ralph Crane*, pp. 130–1, and 'Knight, Crane and the copy for the Folio *Winter's Tale*', *N&Q* 211 (1966), 139–40.
[5] 'Compositor B, the Pavier quartos, and copy spellings', *SB* 21 (1968), 131–61, and *The Pavier Quartos and the First Folio of Shakespeare* (Shakespeare Studies Monograph Series), 1970.
[6] See Peter W. M. Blayney, '"Compositor B" and the Pavier quartos: problems of identification and their implications', *The Library*, 5th ser., 27 (1972), 179–206; the correspondence between Blayney and S. W. Reid, *The Library*, 5th ser., 31 (1976), 143–5, 392–4; and also Howard-Hill, *Ralph Crane*, p. 154, n. 101.

evidence of B's preferred spellings as established by the Pavier quartos has been challenged – that is, since the 47 control words Howard-Hill uses for *Twelfth Night* may *not*, in fact, represent B's preferences – it follows that the result of his findings is also open to question. Moreover, by noting (thanks to Howard-Hill's Oxford Concordances) the frequency of the 47 spellings Compositor B actually set in *Twelfth Night*, one finds that Crane-spellings (some of which may have concurred with B's preferences) appear more than 50 per cent of the time. Specifically 56 per cent of the total frequency reflects Crane's spellings; if those appearing in *possibly* justified lines are excluded, the percentage rises to 59.[1] Twelve of Crane's 47 preferred spellings (such as *beutie*, *breif*, *togeather*) are not represented in the text at all.[2] On the face of it, these frequencies do not seem to eliminate the possibility that he could have been the scribe. Still, until we know more of his preferred spellings, together with those of Compositor B (as Howard-Hill recognises, *Ralph Crane*, p. 99), we shall not know with any degree of certainty whether the transcript of *Twelfth Night* (and perhaps that of other texts in the Folio) was his work or that of an anonymous scribe with similar habits.

Though the identity of the scribe is uncertain, the argument that the copy from which Compositor B set the generally excellent text of *Twelfth Night* was scribal rests on three bases. It rests on the nature of the text, which exhibits characteristics of foul papers as well as characteristics of a scribal copy. It rests on the delay in setting and machining the last two of the Comedies, which resulted in the interruption of an orderly printing sequence for the section allocated to the Comedies. And it rests, finally, on the evidence that printers commonly employed scribes to prepare copies for their compositors, at least in the case of books printed in Latin, and that the Jaggard firm also did so in preparing certain of the Folio Comedies. On these several bases, it seems most likely that the Folio copy for *Twelfth Night* falls into the same category as those other Comedies set from scribal copies – that is, it derives from a transcript, and specifically, in this case, a transcript of Shakespeare's foul papers.

[1] Whether or not a spelling *may* have been affected by the compositor's need to justify is not easily determined, since the point in the line when a compositor adopted a particular spelling may have been before the end of the measure was reached, in what S. W. Reid calls 'anticipatory justification' ('Justification and spelling in Jaggard's Compositor B', *SB* 27 (1974), 91–111). To take an example from Howard-Hill's list: *breefe* appears twice, once in a possibly justified line; *briefe*, with the same number of characters, appears once but this, too, in a possibly justified line; neither of these represents Crane's preference. It should be noted that I have included the plurals for *heart*, *jest* and *hour* in my frequency count; these plurals do not appear in Howard-Hill's list though *master/s* does.

[2] Though only 47 words are used in the analysis of *Twelfth Night*, Howard-Hill compiled a list of some 2,200 Crane-preferred spellings ranging in date from 1618 to 1632 (*Ralph Crane*, p. 61). Allowance, of course, should be made for changes in habits over the years. In 1631 Crane presented a 'manuscript' of a theological tract ('The Faultie Fauorite') to the Earl of Bridgewater as a New Year's gift; now in the Huntington Library, this shows, for example, that while he invariably used his preferred spelling *deuill* (21 instances), he also, invariably, opted for *heart* (15 instances) though his preferred spelling as given by Howard-Hill is *hart*. Crane's own variability within the manuscript is illustrated by the spelling *powre/full* (7 times) as against *power/full* (18 times) – this in a small manuscript consisting of $52\frac{1}{2}$ pages of 14–15 lines each.

READING LIST

This list includes details of books and articles referred to in the Commentary and may also serve as a guide to those who wish to undertake further study of the play.

Belsey, Catherine. 'Disrupting sexual difference: meaning and gender in the comedies', in John Drakakis (ed.), *Alternative Shakespeares*, 1985, pp. 166–90

Berry, Ralph. *Shakespeare and the Awareness of the Audience*, 1985, ch. 5

Billington, Michael. *Directors' Shakespeare: Approaches to 'Twelfth Night'*, 1990

Bloom, Harold (ed.). *William Shakespeare's 'Twelfth Night': Modern Critical Interpretations*, 1987

Callaghan, Dympna. '"And all is semblative a woman's part": body politics and *Twelfth Night*', in R. S. White (ed.), *New Casebooks: 'Twelfth Night'*, 1996, pp. 129–59

Charles, Casey. 'Gender trouble in *Twelfth Night*', *Theatre Journal* 49 (1997), 121–41

Davies, Stevie. Penguin Critical Studies: *William Shakespeare: 'Twelfth Night'*, 1993

Dawson, Anthony. *Watching Shakespeare: A Playgoers' Guide*, 1988, ch. 4

Elam, Keir. '"In what chapter of his bosom?": reading Shakespeare's bodies', in Terence Hawkes (ed.), *Alternative Shakespeares 2*, 1996, pp. 140–63

Fielding, Emma. *Actors on Shakespeare: 'Twelfth Night'*, 2002

Gay, Penny. *As She Likes It: Shakespeare's Unruly Women*, 1994, ch. 1
   '*Twelfth Night*: "the babbling gossip of the air"', in Richard Dutton and Jean Howard (eds.), *The Blackwell Companion to Shakespeare: The Comedies*, 2003, pp. 429–46

Gurr, Andrew. *Playgoing in Shakespeare's London*, 1987; 2nd edn, 1996

Hamburger, Maik. 'A spate of *Twelfth Night*s: Illyria rediscovered?', in Werner Habicht, D. J. Palmer, Roger Pringle (eds.), *Images of Shakespeare: Proceedings of the Third Congress of the International Shakespeare Association*, 1988, pp. 236–44

Howard, Jean E. *Shakespeare's Art of Orchestration*, 1984
   The Stage and Social Struggle in Early Modern England, 1994, pp. 112–16

Jardine, Lisa. 'Twins and travesties', in *Reading Shakespeare Historically*, 1996, pp. 65–77

King, Walter N. (ed.). *Twentieth Century Interpretations of 'Twelfth Night': A Collection of Critical Essays*, 1968

Leggatt, Alexander (ed.). *The Cambridge Companion to Shakespearean Comedy*, 2002
   Shakespeare's Comedy of Love, 1974

Neely, Carol Thomas. 'Lovesickness, gender, and subjectivity: *Twelfth Night* and *As You Like It*', in Dympna Callaghan (ed.), *A Feminist Companion to Shakespeare* , 2000, pp. 121–43

Osborne, Laurie E. *The Trick of Singularity: 'Twelfth Night' and the Performance Editions*, 1996

Palmer, D. J. (ed.). *'Twelfth Night': A Casebook* , 1972

Pennington, Michael. *'Twelfth Night': A User's Guide*, 2000

Potter, Lois. *'Twelfth Night': Text and Performance*, 1985

Shapiro, Michael. *Gender in Play on the Shakespearean Stage: Boy Heroines and Female Pages*, 1996, pp. 151–65

Sinden, Donald. 'Malvolio in *Twelfth Night*', in Philip Brockbank (ed.), *Players of Shakespeare 1*, 1985, pp. 41–66

Smith, Bruce J. (ed.). *'Twelfth Night or What You Will': Texts and Contexts*, 2001

Smith, Peter J. 'M.O.A.I. "What should that alphabetical position portend?" An answer to the metamorphic Malvolio', *Renaissance Quarterly* 51 (1998), 1199–224

Summers, Joseph 'The masks of *Twelfth Night*', in D. J. Palmer (ed.), *Casebook*, 1972, pp. 86–97

Taylor, Gary. 'Who is Viola? What is she?', *To Analyze Delight*, 1985, ch. 3

Thomson, Peter. '*Twelfth Night* and playhouse practice', *Shakespeare's Theatre*, 2nd edn, 1992, pp. 91–113

Traub, Valerie. *Desire and Anxiety: Circulations of Sexuality in Shakespearean Drama*, 1992, ch. 5

Wanamaker, Zoë. 'Viola in *Twelfth Night*', Russell Jackson and Robert Smallwood (eds.), *Players of Shakespeare 2*, 1988, pp. 81–92

Wardle, Janice. '*Twelfth Night*: "One face, one voice, one habit, and two persons!"', Deborah Cartmell and Michael Scott (eds.). *Talking Shakespeare: Shakespeare into the Millennium*, 2001, pp. 105–22

Wells, Stanley. *Royal Shakespeare: Four Major Productions at Stratford-upon-Avon*, 1976, pp. 43–63

(ed.). *'Twelfth Night': Critical Essays*, 1986

White, R. S. (ed.). *New Casebooks: 'Twelfth Night'*, 1996